The Concise Guide to
EUROPEAN
PORCELAIN

D1136299

The Concise Guide to
EUROPEAN
PORCELAIN

Geoffrey Godden

BARRIE & JENKINS
LONDON

First published in 1996 by Barrie & Jenkins Ltd

Barrie & Jenkins Ltd
Random House, 20 Vauxhall Bridge Road,
London SW1V 2SA

Random House Australia (Pty) Limited
20 Alfred Street, Milsons Point, Sydney
New South Wales 2061, Australia

Random House New Zealand Limited
18 Poland Road, Glenfield
Auckland 10, New Zealand

Random House UK Limited Reg. No. 954009

A CIP catalogue record for this book
is available from the British Library

1 3 5 7 9 10 8 6 4 2

ISBN 0 71 264582 9

Designed by Behram Kapadia

Printed and bound in Great Britain by
B P C Hazells Ltd, Aylesbury, Bucks

Contents

Acknowledgements

As I have been gathering information on the types of Continental porcelain featured in this book for very many years, it is probable that I have neglected to record the help received from many persons. I regret any omissions and beg those involved to excuse my lack of professionalism in this regard. I can therefore now only acknowledge in a very general way those persons who assisted me to learn something of the mystery of European porcelains after I belatedly began to write this book in the early 1990s, some forty-five years after my initial interest.

I must initially acknowledge my debt to my local friend, Peter Norman, who has so neatly drawn the majority of the marks reproduced in this book. His practised sure hand has added materially to the appearance of the book and his clear drawings will surely prove helpful to all readers. Thank you Peter, for your patience.

My other helpers and sources of information include: Miss J. Abbey; the late Len (and Yvonne) Adams; Victoria Bergesen; The British Museum, London; Mr and Mrs D. Chitty; Messrs. Christie's; Howard Coutts, Ceramic Officer, The Bowes Museum; Mrs Aileen Dawson, of the British Museum; Gerald Dupernex; Roger and Shirley Edmundson; Anton Gabszewicz; Jonathan Gray; Guildhall Library staff; the late Reginald G. Haggar; Mrs Pat Halfpenny, former Director Ceramics Dept., Stoke-on-Trent City Museum; Christopher Halton of Phillips; J. C. (Tim) Holdaway; International Trade Publications Ltd, publishers of *Tableware International*; Keele University Library staff; Dan Klein; Barry Lamb; Terence A. Lockett; Stafford Lorie; Mrs Patricia McColl; Mr and Mrs H. W. Melling; Nicholas Merchant; Philip Miller; Patrick Molho of Porcelaine de Paris; Jennifer Opie; Messrs. Phillips, Son & Neale; Tamara Tréaud, Archivist, Manufacture Nationale de Sèvres; Public Record Office, Kew; Jeremy Rex-Parkes, Christie's; Miss Gaye Blake Roberts; Letitia Roberts, Sotheby's New York; Rachel Russell, Ceramic Dept., Christie's; Bill Saks; John Sandon of Phillips; Henry Sandon; Rosalind Savill, of the Wallace Collection; Messrs. Sotheby's London, New York and Billingshurst; Stoke-on-Trent City Museum & Art Gallery; Victoria & Albert Museum, London; Josiah Wedgwood & Sons Ltd; Christopher Weston of Phillips; West Sussex Library Service; West Sussex Reference Library and staff at Worthing.

Additionally I am indebted to the institutions, firms or individuals acknowledged in the Plate captions for photographs or for the opportunity to borrow articles to be photographed for inclusion in this book. The majority of these objects have not previously been illustrated and are therefore all the more interesting. My local firm of very professional photographers Messrs. Walter Gardiner is responsible for all the illustrations credited to my own firm of Godden of Worthing Ltd, and for many other photographs.

Lastly, but most importantly, I must acknowledge my long serving secretary Miss Janet Belton for typing my near-illegible longhand notes and numerous corrected and messy drafts. Thank you Janet.

Preface

This concise guide is concerned with the identification of Continental porcelains. It may be regarded as the companion to my popular 1990 book The Concise Guide to British Pottery and Porcelain, or as a handy, inexpensive version of my 1993 major work, Godden's Guide to European Porcelain.

Since I joined my father's antique business over fifty years ago, I have viewed and attended thousands of auction sales and visited, by invitation, tens of thousands of private homes. I have received a vast number of letters from owners of old porcelains seeking information on the age and origin of their treasures. And I have, over the years, discovered that a surprisingly large proportion of decorative and useful porcelains found in Britain originated across the Channel on the Continent of Europe mainly in South Germany or in or around Limoges in France. Inexpensive little porcelain trinkets made for the South Coast tourist market in the early 1900s bearing, for example, views of my own local Worthing Pier, were made not in the Staffordshire Potteries but in Germany!

While there is a wealth of information available on the classic and costly porcelain of the type to be seen in national museums or in the galleries and shops of leading dealers, there is a serious lack in our knowledge of that vast range of relatively inexpensive Continental pottery and porcelain that exists in our homes the 'popular' wares. Such ceramics were popular because they were decorative and inexpensive – in fact, 'cheap and cheerful' – a sure-fire path to commercial success. The German manufacturers in particular supplied such pieces to the world's markets in the 19th century and early years of the 20th century.

In general these low-priced goods were made by the smaller firms, not by the state concerns such as Meissen in Germany or the French national factory at Sèvres. These and other leading manufacturers had very high standards and of necessity their products were costly and enjoyed a restricted, high-class market. In the same way, in the 1920s, there were many more Austin Sevens on the road than Rolls-Royces! The owner of the little Austin, however, may well have gained more pride and enjoyment from his purchase than the owner of the Rolls. Much the same is surely true of the popular porcelains which were widely purchased, treasured and handed down from generation to generation – just as if these fancy wares were rare, original Dresden (that is Meissen), Sèvres or Chelsea specimens.

The small Meissen figure (or Dresden, to use the term favoured in England) shown in Plate 1 was produced at the true Meissen factory in the middle of the 18th century. It is a valuable museum or collector's piece which could realistically be valued in four figures. Yet in the much larger general market, where buyers are seeking decoration or ornaments to enhance their home, the non-Meissen, so-called Dresden, late 19th-century centrepiece shown in Plate 2 will almost certainly be preferred. It is larger, more showy and more useful than

Plate 1. An early Meissen porcelain figure of Doctor Boloardo, modelled by J. J. Kaendler. Well-modelled but simple, without ornate base or floral backing. c.1740–50. 7½ ins high. (Sotheby's)

Plate 2. A Dresden-style late 19th-century centrepiece or comport, over-elaborate and fussy to suit the later market wanting showy wares at moderate prices. c.1880. 16½ ins high. (H. A. Grant)

the true Meissen figure, yet it should be more readily available at about a tenth of the price of the old figure.

This handbook will not attempt to rival the excellent specialist books on the leading Continental porcelains but instead emphasis will be placed on the less costly but more readily available decorative objects made by the smaller firms for the mass market. In the main I am concerned with those examples priced in the range £20 to £500, with occasional progressions into a few more costly types.

However, to understand the copies and reproductions of Meissen, Sèvres or Vienna porcelains, some knowledge of the originals is essential. The book opens therefore with a chapter on these market leaders, whose styles have been widely copied and whose influence can be seen in many examples of 18th-century English porcelain. In the 19th and 20th centuries, those important styles spawned a rash of blatant fakes and forgeries, and Chapter 2 deals with this troublesome question. Chapter 3 describes the large 19th-century market for low-priced porcelains and the type of articles imported from France and Germany to satisfy it. The main section, in Chapter 4, comprises a list of the ceramic centres arranged in alphabetical

Plate 3. An inexpensive pair of small German porcelain figures made for the mass-tourist market. Impressed Conta & Boehme shield-mark and model number 4141. c.1800–1900. 5½ ins high. (E. H. Chandler)

order. A host of Continental firms and various types of object or body are included. The standard marks and cyphers as used by the major producers are illustrated. General advice and guides to dating are given in Chapter 5.

Just as the Staffordshire potters produced over many years thousands of unmarked earthenware figures and groups (the cottage ornaments, the chimney figures and animals) so on the Continent a host of small-scale porcelain manufacturers produced cheap figures and ornaments which were exported to the British Isles and other countries in great quantity. A typical pair of German figures of the period 1880 to 1900 is shown in Plate 3. These are obviously not works of art nor will they be found in museum collections but they were quite inexpensive and they probably gave great pleasure to the original buyers and their descendants. Figures of this general type were mass-produced and are still not rare, nor should they be costly.

When comparing the porcelain of the major makers with the cheaper, more popular pieces, it is not a matter of who is right or wrong. These pieces and thousands of similar examples of both types are catering for different markets or tastes. I am certainly not falling into the trap of writing on taste; I only wish to be one of the few who seek to discuss or even mention such relatively late showy ceramics that have been neglected for far too long.

GEOFFREY GODDEN
Sunny Worthing

The Market Leaders: Meissen, Sèvres and Vienna

The three great and very well-known Continental state or royal porcelain factories at Meissen in Germany, Sèvres in France and Vienna in Austria were undoubtedly market leaders. They are household names known to many people who have no real knowledge of antique porcelain.

They have always enjoyed this high reputation and consequently their best productions have always been in demand and costly. Consequently, their styles have been very widely copied, at first legitimately by contemporary firms seeking to keep up with fashion and show off their own skills. In 18th-century English porcelain we can therefore find many examples of Chelsea, Derby, Worcester or Bristol which shown the strong Continental influence of Meissen (then called 'Dresden' in Great Britain) and Sèvres. Sometimes the marks of these Continental factories were employed on these English porcelains which could be charitably referred to as being in the style of Meissen or Sèvres.

When we come to the later copies, the examples were made mainly on the Continent in the 19th and 20th centuries. We find very many small manufacturers making blatant fakes or forgeries of the 18th-century wares, often purely to dupe the collector. Such dangerous copies are the subject of Chapter 2.

Here, I wish to give a brief résumé of the history of the three large and important factories and to make a few basic points regarding the products and the marks. Obviously, in a handbook such as this, it is not possible to give the full story, but in the case of Meissen and Sèvres there are very good specialist books available to study listed in the Bibliography.

MEISSEN OR DRESDEN

Meissen is situated some twelve miles from Dresden in the German state of Saxony. In the early 18th century it was an independent state ruled by Augustus the Strong. His interest in founding a porcelain factory, the first in Europe to produce true (Oriental-type), hard-paste porcelain was perhaps fuelled by his love of Chinese and Japanese porcelains. It was also thought, erroneously, that the production of porcelain was as profitable as producing gold from base metals – the age-long dream.

The German alchemists entrusted with the task of producing

white, semi-translucent porcelain were Ehrenfried Walter von Tschirnhaus and Johann Friedrich Böttger. Their early experiments were carried out at Dresden and by the end of March 1709 some success had been achieved.

In January 1710 the relatively small factory was established at Meissen, some thirty-five years before the British were able to produce any type of porcelain body. The early Meissen porcelain of the approximate period 1710–25 is smoky-white in colour, sometimes tinged brown. This does not mean that any off-white porcelain will be early Meissen! These original pieces are excessively rare and are hardly likely to be found outside museums or grand collections.

Probably more noteworthy or successful were the Böttger coloured bodies, the refined (often dark chocolate-coloured) stonewares which were sometimes neatly engraved, cut and partly polished – as one would a gem-stone. These very hard stonewares, like the white-bodied porcelains, also emulated some Oriental imports but they were usually of European form. These Böttger stonewares are likewise rare and costly and they will not bear any mark.

From quite early in the factory's history, human and animal models were produced, again sometimes emulating Oriental prototypes. The large European animal and bird models are exceptions and show well how the German modellers and workmen had mastered the great difficulties of producing and firing successfully large-size porcelain objects. They are *tours de force*, even if they do show open stress cracks or tears in the body. No expense was spared in producing such prestigious articles. This was a state factory, which had to show its superiority.

Specialist books will be unrealistically illustrated with the early pre-1750 Meissen porcelains. However, newish collectors or students of ceramics are most unlikely to find such delights. They are and have always been rare and costly. More common are the crossed-swords-marked porcelains that may be 19th- or even 20th-century Meissen, or wares made by other firms to emulate these Meissen porcelains. True Meissen porcelains of whatever period will be of very good quality and extremely decorative. Even some of the later mock-Dresden is most attractive and has the advantage of being more modestly priced than the true Meissen would have been.

As I have explained in my larger 1993 work, *Godden's Guide to European Porcelain*, the old 19th-century writers tended to regard any post-1760 Meissen porcelain as late and uninteresting. Today we can be more practical and suggest that the pieces likely to be available will be of a later period, for even examples made in 1800 are nearly 200 years old.

Although the Meissen factory mark has remained remarkably constant (much too constant for ease of dating) over the years, some changes were made and these can be helpful. Between

1763 and 1774 a dot was placed between the hilts of the swords, as shown here. This period is variously known as the 'Academic', 'Dot' or 'Kings' period or, to use the French term, 'Saxe au Point'. Note that all Meissen marks are painted in blue, under the glaze.

From 1774 to 1814 a small star or cross-like device appears between the hilts, replacing the earlier dot. This cross relates to the Marcolini period, when Count Camillo Marcolini was Director. Not so long ago this period was treated with disdain. At the time, however, the Meissen porcelains were still market leaders. The porcelain and the decoration was of high quality, and the shapes and figure models were still being widely emulated, as were the marks.

Plate 4. Representative pieces from a Meissen porcelain dinner and dessert service, well-painted in traditional style but without expensive moulded designs. Crossed-swords with Marcolini period star. c.1774–85. Tureen 9¾ ins high. (Messrs. Christie's)

Plate 5. An attractive well-modelled and neatly-potted pair of small Meissen ornamental figures of traditional type. Crossed-swords mark and incised model number F99. c.1820–40. 4¾ ins high. (Mrs P. Mead)

Plate 6. An attractive and typical Meissen group of the type much copied by British and Continental manufacturers. Crossed-swords mark and incised model number C75. c.1820–40. 6¼ ins high. (Mrs P. Mead)

Plate 7. A typically attractive and well-modelled Meissen group, being part of a set. Crossed-swords and incised model number G91. c.1820–40. 6¾ ins high. (Messrs. Godden of Worthing Ltd)

One should bear in mind that the factory was smaller than one might believe, the output was relatively low, considering the large market available, and the cost was relatively high. Until about the 1830s there was a rarity value which, coupled with the high esteem of the Meissen (or Dresden) name, made these pieces highly desirable and well worth copying even by large, important factories.

Very many of the attractive Meissen figures, groups, ornamental centrepieces, etc., were produced in or after the

Plate 8. An imposing well-modelled Meissen group of heavy weight, with high quality enamelling. Crossed-swords mark. 10 ins high. (Messrs. Godden of Worthing Ltd)

Marcolini period, indeed most post-date the 1820s. These were made over a very long period because they were decorative, well-modelled and popular. I show a small selection of such traditional Meissen pieces in Plates 5–8.

The approximate period of introduction of these and other Meissen models can be ascertained by reference to the incised model numbers which appear under the base. Note that these numbers are incised by hand, as if drawn into butter with a matchstick or nail. Old, genuine Meissen examples should not have neatly impressed numbers as if formed from a printer's die.

In 1763 and 1764 all existing figure models were numbered for reference; these ranged up to 3051. After this, letter prefixes were added and new models bore the following reference numbers. I have added in brackets the *approximate* date of the introduction of each series.

A.1	to	A.100	(1765)
B.1	to	B.100	(*c.*1766–7)
C.1	to	C.100	(*c.*1768–70)
D.1	to	D.100	(*c.*1770–1)
E.1	to	E.60	(*c.*1772–4)
E.61	to	E.100	(*c.*1774–6)
F.1	to	F.100	(*c.*1776–8)
G.1	to	G.100	(*c.*1779–81)
H.1	to	H.100	(*c.*1782–5)
I.1	to	I.100	(*c.*1786–7)
J.1	to	J.100	(*c.*1787–9)
K.1	to	K.100	(*c.*1789–95)
L.1	to	L.100	(*c.*1795–1805)
M.1	to	M.100	(*c.*1805–13)
N.1	to	N.100	(*c.*1814–18)
O.1	to	O.100	(*c.*1818–21)
P.1	to	P.100	(*c.*1822–5)
Q.1	to	Q.100	(*c.*1825–7)
R.1	to	R.100	(*c.*1827–9)
S.1	to	S.100	(*c.*1829–31)
T.1	to	T.183	(*c.*1831–3)
U.1	to	U.100	(*c.*1833–4)
V.1	to	V.100	(*c.*1834–5)
W.1	to	W.100	(*c.*1836–42)
X.1	to	X.100	(*c.*1843–7)
Y.1	to	Y.100	(*c.*1847–9)
Z.1	to	Z.100	(*c.*1849–50)

After 1850 a new series was commenced, the numbers now ranging from 101 to 200 with various letter prefixes. These are listed with the *approximate* period that each series was *first* employed.

A.101	to	A.200	(*c.*1850–3)
B.101	to	B.200	(*c.*1853–5)
C.101	to	C.200	(*c.*1855–7)
D.101	to	D.200	(*c.*1858–60)
E.101	to	E.200	(*c.*1860–2)
F.101	to	F.200	(*c.*1862–4)
G.101	to	G.200	(*c.*1865–8)
H.101	to	H.200	(*c.*1869–70)
I.101	to	I.200	(*c.*1870–2)
J.101	to	J.200	(*c.*1873–5)

K.101	to	K.200	(c.1876–8)
L.101	to	L.200	(c.1879–81)
M.101	to	M.200	(c.1882–3)
N.101	to	N.200	(c.1883–4)
O.101	to	O.200	(c.1885–90)
P.101	to	P.200	(c.1891–4)
Q.101	to	Q.200	(c.1895–7)
R.101	to	R.200	(c.1898–9)
S.101	to	S.200	(c.1899–1902)
T.184	to	T.200	(c.1900)
U.101	to	U.200	(c.1904)
V.101	to	V.200	(c.1904–5)
W.101	to	W.200	(c.1905–6)
X.101	to	X.200	(c.1906–8)
Y.101	to	Y.200	(c.1908–9)
Z.101	to	Z.200	(c.1909–10)

Plate 9. A Meissen floral-encrusted bottle vase in typical decoration. Much favoured and copied by other makers. Crossed-swords mark. c.1860–80. 13 ins high. (Messrs. Sotheby's)

From 1910 a new series was started at A.201 proceeding to A.300, then B.201 to B.300, and so on. From early on in this series the numbers were impressed with standard dies.

The existence of these reference, or model numbers, incised into the base of the figure or group, can be helpful in dating the piece. For example, a figure with the number U.75 cannot have been produced before 1830, but it does not follow that a figure with an early number, perhaps one without the letter prefix, is of the period when the figure was first used, because the popular models were produced into the present century with the *original* model number. However a post-1763 Dresden-type figure or group without incised or impressed model numbers is open to grave doubt, unless purchased from a reliable source. The Meissen figure and group models of the 1800–20 period remained popular and in production for a surprisingly long time and in the middle of the 19th century the management seemed content to a very large extent to trade on past glories.

There exist in the British Museum three printed German-language price lists of Meissen porcelain which contain very small engravings of popular lines; these are reproduced in *Godden's Guide to European Porcelain*. They are unfortunately undated but they are believed to link approximately in period with various Meissen and Berlin bills dated October 1839 which are preserved in the same collection. These sheets show an assortment of figures, groups, clock cases, candelabras, vases and fancy articles, many of which are embellished with raised porcelain flowers.

This very popular type of Meissen porcelain was introduced in the 18th century but rose to the fore in the 19th. Plate 9 shows a typical Dresden vase in this style, which in German was called *Schneeballen* (or snowballs). Such floral display, usually with added birds, occurs on many objects. Such wares were made for ornament rather than for use, and was widely copied both on the Continent and in England. The English manufacturers often acknowledge the source of this inspiration, the shapes in the factory pattern or shape books being termed, for example, 'Dresden scroll vase' or 'Dresden match pot'. These English examples might also bear a copy of the Dresden crossed-swords mark!

About or soon after 1851, the two swords were painted with slight pommels or handles. These pommelled swords continued to about 1924 although, being individually hand-painted, this feature is more pronounced on some specimens than on others.

From 1924 the old, simple, unhandled swords returned but a dot was added between the tip of the blades. This mark was discontinued in about 1934.

Plate 10. A Meissen onion pattern plate painted with traditional formal pattern in underglaze-blue. Note factory mark incorporated in base of main stem, a post-1893 feature. Crossed-swords mark and B4 impressed. c.1900. Diameter 7¾ ins. (D. White)

From the 1930s the swords tended to be drawn with a slight curve, so that if you continue each blade the tips join each other. The older versions had straight blades which if continued merely progress further apart. In the post-war period additional year marks, variously placed dashes, have been added. From about 1960 the word 'Meissen' was added to wares made for export.

Apart from the ornate fancy and highly coloured Meissen porcelains the factory also produced more staid, useful wares including some formal patterns painted in underglaze blue. The best known of these is variously called the Onion pattern or Flowering Onion pattern (Plate 10), a design based on an Oriental original and having little or no connection with its later name. This so-called Onion pattern has proved exceedingly popular over a long period, and several variations occur. It was introduced in the 1730s but 18th-century examples are uncommon. The popularity of this blue design, devoid of gilding, was slow to take hold and it was probably not until the middle of the 19th century that demand really took off. By the 1870s this pattern or aspects of it were being adapted to fit nearly every shape produced by the Dresden factory. Even figures were decorated in underglaze blue to complement the large blue Onion pattern dinner, dessert and tea services.

In the second half of the 19th century blue porcelains of various types were extremely popular. One of the advantages was the relatively low price of such simple repetitive blue designs. No great skill was required by the painters, no extra firings were needed (as was the case with overglaze enamel patterns) and no gilding was added to the standard version. It would have represented one of the cheapest patterns made at the prestigious German state factory but, when applied to their forms – openwork bordered dessert plates, well-modelled baskets and centrepieces – it took on a new aspect. Some obviously more costly examples do have added gold trim but basically the true so-called Dresden Onion pattern is painted only in cobalt-blue under the glaze.

The Dresden blue Onion pattern porcelains are still very popular with collectors, some of whom specialize in this one design. Obviously, the more decorative and the rare shapes command far more than the standard objects such as plates or cups and saucers which were produced in their tens of thousands over a very long period – up to the present day, in fact. The design has a timeless quality, enhanced perhaps in the case of the Dresden factory by the fact that the famous crossed-swords device occurs as part of the design on some versions, painted in at the base of the main branch (see Plate 10). Its presence may not increase the value of the piece but it makes it a little more interesting, although this additional mark is said only to have been introduced in 1893.

The universal popularity of the pattern led to it being copied (some more closely than others) at many other smaller factories. It can even occur on English earthenwares but most copies will be of German porcelain. With this pattern as well as with other types, marks comprising or including the words 'Meissen' or 'Dresden' will not appear on articles made at the state factory.

The Connoisseur magazine of December 1907 illustrated several then current Dresden productions, most of which were in the retail establishment of Ernst Wahliss in 88 Oxford Street,

London. The very large stocks of 'Royal Dresden' porcelain stocked at 'The Wahliss Galleries' in London were featured in several advertisements and articles early in the 20th century. Some of these advertisements, such as that in *The Connoisseur* of November 1908, reflected on the very high value of old examples and the low price of the same model available in the gallery. Illustrating a traditional Dresden three-figure group of a crinolined lady taking tea and entitled 'The Countess Kossel' the advertisement states: 'At a recent sale of Royal Dresden China the group was said to have realised 1,150 guineas … our price £9.' The advertisement also featured the much copied 'Royal Dresden Monkey Band'. The term 'Royal Dresden' was used to add prestige to the porcelains and perhaps to lift the genuine pieces above the level of the less costly 'Crown Dresden' wares, decorated within the city of Dresden.

Most specimens of Meissen porcelain found today in the British Isles comprises traditional types – that is in the main reissues of old figure models, groups, old designs on tea, dessert or more rarely dinner services. However, this is merely because the buying public favoured such popular, proven lines. Those British buyers who favoured new styles, perhaps in the *Art Nouveau* manner, tended to purchase their native Royal Worcester, Doulton or Minton porcelains.

This does not mean that the Meissen factory did not produce such wares, novel in form and decoration. The examples illustrated in *The Magazine of Art* of April 1899 in an article titled 'The Art Movement' are far divorced from traditional Dresden articles. Indeed, it is claimed that some of the Copenhagen designs inspired the German designers. Such Meissen 'Art' or 'Modern' styles are very rarely found in England and one can only assume that they did not catch on. Perhaps they were too expensive for the market. Most people still required the traditional decorative figures, as they do today. However, the Meissen factory did produce some wonderful new models and designs in the post-1890 period. Some good examples are in the Victoria & Albert Museum and others are featured in some of the more recent reference books.

The Meissen firm now trades under the name Staatliche Porzellanmanufaktur Meissen. It is no longer a state-owned factory. In post-war years it has been – in modern international terms – a relatively small concern, employing about 150 persons. It and the original moulds, etc., have survived changing times remarkably well. As well as modern designs, the wealthy at least can order reissues of 18th-century Meissen classics. The modern factory has a museum collection as well as demonstration rooms.

It would be wise to bear in mind that not every porcelain object bearing a crossed-swords mark will be genuine Meissen although in most cases such pieces will have decorative merit.

Even with genuine examples, the chances that the piece is 18th-century are remote.

In Chapter 2 I will discuss some of the later fakes and forgeries of Meissen porcelain which bear a reasonable copy of one of the original marks. There are, however, a vast number of decorative porcelains made very much in the old Meissen (or Dresden) style and which do not bear a direct copy of the crossed-swords mark, although such porcelains have been known to have been described as 'Dresden'. Some mention of these originally medium- or low-priced 'essays' in the Dresden style is made in Chapter 3 but see also the entries in Chapter 4 relating to Hill-Ouston, Plaue, Sitzendorf, Volkstedt and Wolfsohn.

SÈVRES

The next Continental porcelain factory to consider in this important class is undoubtedly the French royal (later national) factory of Sèvres, near Paris. The name is now almost a household word and is, like its mark – crossed Ls – very widely known. Yet purists will correctly term the earliest Sèvres porcelains 'Vincennes', for the factory was established at the Château de Vincennes in the early 1740s, assisted by workmen from the Chantilly manufactory. Early experiments, as always, met with great difficulties but by July 1745 the Vincennes products, under Charles Adams, had reached an acceptable commercial standard for the venture to receive royal acknowledgement in the form of an official privilege to produce wares after the style of Saxon porcelain – that is, the Meissen wares which were often referred to in France as 'Saxe'.

In the period 1745 to 1750, the small French works was showing a loss rather than a profit, but firm foundations were being laid. In 1753 the King, Louis XV, a large shareholder in the concern and entitled to a quarter share of the profits, gave the company permission to use the title 'Manufacture Royale de Porcelaine' and to use as a factory mark the royal cypher, the crossed, cursive double 'L'. This mark had been used unofficially for some years previously.

The enterprise moved to Sèvres (to the south-west of Paris near St Cloud) in 1756. Sèvres was an outstanding success artistically, but not commercially. However, Louis XV came to the rescue in 1759 when he purchased the Sèvres factory. It remained a royal factory until 1793 when it was taken over by the new French Republic. Happily, in an era when all things royal were being destroyed in France, the Sèvres factory was regarded as a national asset so that the works, the personnel and the records were preserved.

The typical early Sèvres body and glaze was of the soft-paste type. It has a beautiful warm feel with a rather generously applied thick glossy glaze. Many factories, in England and on the Continent, attempted to attain this excellence but lacking royal backing and a rich clientele, few succeeded. Nevertheless, it would not be true to say that no other factory produced attractive soft-paste porcelains.

Today, especially in England, Sèvres soft-paste porcelain is regarded as the ultimate in visual ceramic perfection with the enamel colours sinking slightly into the glaze to give gentle, warm-looking, semi-translucent tints. Seemingly, however, at the time the chemists were still trying to produce hard-paste porcelain, similar to Meissen and the Chinese imports. This was the technical goal. Nevertheless, the very valuable richer types of 18th-century Sèvres porcelain made for palaces, royal commissions and gifts was of the soft-paste type.

The well-known and much copied mark was, in the 18th century, always hand-painted overglaze, usually in blue enamel, so that very many slight variations can occur, and certain points should be borne in mind. First, remember always that a mark is easily forged. In the case of the Sèvres mark it occurs more often on non-Sèvres porcelain than on the genuine article! Second, from 1753 a series of year-letters was added to the centre of the standard mark – rather like the changing year-marks on British silver. These centrally placed initials commenced with 'A' in 1753 and continued to 'Z' in 1777, omitting the W, not used in France. A double series was then started in 1778 with AA. This progressed until PP was used in 1793 but from July in that fateful year the royal mark was discontinued.

Apart from the standard factory mark and the year-letter or letters, various other initials or signs were added to denote the work of individual artists, ground-layers or gilders. Tables of these personal signs as they relate to at least the leading Sèvres decorators are given with their working periods in most specialist books on Sèvres porcelain and in some general works. However it must be remembered that many redecorated or later reproductions will bear copies of such personal signs or other initials or devices.

The later fakists of Sèvres porcelain tended to place an early year-letter in their copies of the Sèvres mark. An 'A' for 1753, or a 'B' for 1754, often occur. However, their forgeries tended to be of the more flamboyant type, with rich ground colours. Such showy styles are not normally associated with the mid 1750s. The apple green was not introduced until 1756, Rose Pompadour (a pink) until 1757, Bleu de Roi in about 1758. Due regard must, therefore, be paid to the mark. Do the year and the style of the piece equate? Most probably not.

The double L royal cypher mark also serves to differentiate between the soft-paste body and the later hard-paste perfected

Plate 11. Two Sèvres floral-painted plates of a standard type shown with a matching three-piece fruit-cooler. Sèvres crossed 'L' mark, with year letter for 1772 and painter's personal marks. 1772. Cooler 8 ins high. (Messrs. Sotheby's, New York)

Plate 12. A typical Sèvres soup plate, the centre painted in monochrome. Sèvres factory mark with year letter for 1756. Painter's tally mark for Dodin. 1756. Diameter 8½ ins. (Victoria & Albert Museum (Crown Copyright))

Plate 13. An attractive Sèvres biscuit porcelain group. Incised 'F' initial for the modeller Falconet. c.1760–70. 5½ ins high. (Messrs. Phillips)

around 1769. A crown was added to the mark to distinguish the harder body but the soft body and its matching glaze were still used for special pieces until 1804.

It is notable that the two leading 18th-century European factories, Meissen and Sèvres, went their separate ways. Few if any shapes or styles of decoration were copied one from the other. Sèvres is always very French, royal or even feminine. It cannot be mistaken for Meissen.

None of the magnificent Sèvres vases and more elaborately decorated articles which might be termed 'Palace Sèvres' are illustrated here because the non-specialist is unlikely to come across such costly items and should assume that all such decorative wares are 19th-century copies. This is obviously an over-statement but it is a safe belief. Fine and typical 18th-century Sèvres porcelain can be seen in many major British museums, noticeably in the Victoria & Albert Museum (don't miss the Jones collection on the lower floor), the Wallace Collection, the British Museum and, further afield, the Bowes Museum at Barnard Castle. Most of the stately homes and larger houses that are open to the public also contain some Sèvres porcelain.

The Sèvres factory evolved and produced a wonderful array of ceramic forms, sometimes modelled by sculptors. Dinner and dessert services included objects not made elsewhere, objects that reflected the upper-class life enjoyed by the factory's favoured few: grand pairs or garnitures of vases or pot-pourri's were well represented and were often mounted in crisp ormolu or gilded bronze; finely decorated complete tea and coffee services, small sets on trays (the déjeuner services); richly decorated cabinet coffee cans and stands. Most of the Sèvres shapes were eagerly copied in England and elsewhere. Several 18th-century Sèvres shapes were standard forms used elsewhere even 100 or more years later! The forms of 18th-century decoration typically comprise flower sprays, painted on the white porcelain (Plate 11) rather than rich ground colours. The plate shown in Plate 12 is likewise very typical.

Other famous Sèvres products that were copied elsewhere were the white biscuit figures (Plate 13) and groups in unglazed porcelain. These emulate marble statuary and, like the larger marble essays, they were modelled by famous French sculptors such as Falconet. Of course, once the master model had been made, the porcelain examples were produced from a series of working moulds.

The soft-paste white Sèvres biscuit models are especially charming and were always held in high regard. The 18th-century examples do not bear a Sèvres factory mark but those made after 1860 do bear the impressed 'Sèvres' name. The fashion for white, unglazed figures was also taken up by many other Continental factories. The Victorian fashion for British parian, a creamy-white, usually unglazed, fine-grained porcelain, also to some degree owes its introduction to the fame of Sèvres biscuit porcelain and some so-called Victorian examples were first introduced at Sèvres in the previous century! Unlike Meissen, the Sèvres factory produced relatively few glazed and enamelled figures. Some of the more expensive Sèvres dessert services were supplied with biscuit centrepieces and decorative small figures or groups which were displayed on the table.

The royal period of Sèvres porcelain and indeed of France came to a temporary end in 1792–3 with the Revolution and the establishment of the Republic. Fresh marks incorporated the initials 'RF', for République Française, with the name 'Sèvres'. This place name had not been incorporated in earlier marks because all who mattered knew well that the royal monogram, the double 'L' was the mark of that factory.

The days of the Republic must have been difficult for the management of the factory. Its main customers had been lost and during the time of the terror foreigners were not visiting Paris. Also the old protective prohibitions on the rival French factories were lifted and the many Paris porcelain factories were able, with their lower overheads, to take a share of whatever market there was left. Among the very necessary economies was the sale of the large stocks of white porcelain which had accumulated at the factory. These blanks, which were often slightly faulty 'seconds', could not have raised very much cash but they proved of great value to a host of decorators who were able to finish and resell what was genuine soft-paste Sèvres porcelain.

One of the fortunate occurrences which helped to shape the recovery of the Sèvres factory was the appointment of Alexandre Brongniart as director of the factory in 1800. He was a scientist with apparently no prior experience of ceramics yet he was later to write the monumental ceramic textbook *Traité des Arts Céramiques* (1844), which is still referred to. Another fortunate occurrence was that Napoleon took a great interest in the Sèvres factory and, in effect, continued the practice of the former Kings of France of showering expensive porcelain gifts where they would make the most diplomatic impact.

The period of the Revolution and then the first Imperial epoch (1804–14) saw also a revolution in ceramic taste at Sèvres. The shapes became more masculine, more classical in an Empire manner – a taste which in England would be called Regency. Napoleon's exploits in Egypt gave rise both in France and England to a mock Egyptian decorative style. The traditional high quality remains but they are quite different from the porcelains made thirty years earlier.

In the 19th century the Sèvres marks were changed as the fortunes of the country or its rulers swayed. From about 1803 to 1809, variations of the Manufacture Impériale mark were employed. These marks were printed, stencilled or hand-painted and various year cyphers were added below the main device – the one here relates to 1806. From 1810 to 1814 a crowned eagle was used.

During the second Royal epoch (1814–48) various overglaze printed marks were employed. The royal double L device returned in 1814 to mark the reign of Louis XVIII. The last two numerals of the year appear in the centre under the word 'Sèvres'.

In 1824 when Charles X succeeded, the crossed C device was used. Again, the last two numbers of the year appear under the main device. This Charles X mark varies; the main types are reproduced here.

Plate 14. A superb quality early 19th-century Sèvres two-piece jardinière with blue ground and tooled gilding. The panel signed by J. de Gault. Printed mark. c.1820. 8¾ ins high. (Mrs P. Rivers)

The following printed mark was used from August 1830 to the end of that year, as Charles X had abdicated and returned to England.

Sèvres
30.

Plate 15. A graceful Sèvres vase (one of a pair) richly gilt with blue borders. Printed mark and dated 1824. 13 ins high. (Messrs. Godden of Worthing Ltd)

In August 1830 the Duke of Orleans became King Louis-Philippe I. Various printed marks were used in the 1830s and 1840s. These all incorporated the last two numerals of the year or the year in full. Here are some of these Louis-Philippe marks.

Sèvres porcelains of the post-1830 period sometimes bear several marks and perhaps two different dates. One mark will signify when the piece was potted, another will relate to the time of decoration, which could well be three or four years after it was potted.

A surprisingly high number of pieces will also bear printed Château marks – 'Château des Tuileries', 'Château de Fontainebleau' and so on. This does not mean that they are unique pieces personally used by a King of France! These sets seem to have been produced in large quantities. They are attractive and even beautiful but not especially rare. These examples can also be found with the crowned 'N' device of Napoleon III.

It is possible that some of these Château and other pieces were not decorated at the Sèvres factory but that other decorators acquired Sèvres blanks which they painted in an inferior manner. In this connection one must remember that the Sèvres management, like that at Meissen, cut across or cancelled their oblong printed potting mark such as 'S55' when the blank was found to be faulty and it was sold on in its undecorated state. The subsequently painted piece may well be very attractive but it will not be Sèvres decoration.

Louis-Philippe abdicated in February 1848 and fled to England. This gave rise to the Second Republic (1848–51) and once more 'République Française' (R.F.) initial marks were introduced. The two basic types, bearing different year numerals, are shown here. In 1845 it was decided to mark each piece in chrome-green under the glaze. While this underglaze mark guarded against faking, it does mean that any blanks that showed faults after glazing and were subsequently sold as 'seconds' will bear the underglaze green Sèvres mark, although the decoration will most probably have been added elsewhere. The mark should have been cancelled by a ground-out line but this was often overlooked.

In January 1852 the Second Imperial epoch commenced with the election of Louis Napoleon as Prince-President. He was later to be declared Emperor Napoleon III. Again the eagle mark was employed. When a 'T' is found below this device it denotes the use of a new type of soft-paste body. It was not as successful or beautiful as the 18th-century body and glaze.

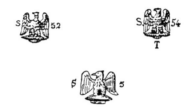

From about 1854 the crowned 'N' mark was employed with the last two numerals of the year appearing at the right. Again, a 'T' below denotes the softer body.

This mark continued in use until 1870 although there were variations relating to the decoration and to the gilding of the piece. These simply have the additional wording 'Décoré à Sèvres' or 'Doré à Sèvres'.

The oval underglaze chrome-green 'S.' year-mark was also placed on the undecorated blanks from about 1848 to 1879 but, if the blank was faulty and discarded as a 'second', a cut was made across this simple green mark.

While the mid 19th-century Sèvres porcelains may not have met with favour in the British Isles, they were of excellent quality and the decorative techniques in particular aroused international interest. The French national factory continued to show an impressive selection of wares – porcelain, and sometimes earthenware and enamels – at the various international exhibitions. Reports on these can still be useful in sign-posting various differences in style or in the types of Sèvres being produced.

The basic form of Sèvres mark changed again in 1871 to mark the Third Republic epoch. The standard printed circular mark comprises the initials 'R.F.' with 'S' and the last two numerals of the year added. Variations with 'Décoré à Sèvres' also occur, printed in red.

In 1880 this circular mark was used and continued until 1889, with year numerals.

From 1890 to 1904 a similar mark but without year numerals was used.

A rare relief-moulded or impressed mark was used from 1888 to 1891.

A new type of triangular mark, printed in green, was introduced in 1900. This simply comprises the initial 'S' with the full year shown below. Other marks were used relating to the decoration and separately to the gilding.

Later 20th-century Sèvres marks are usually self-explanatory and comprise the place-name 'Sèvres' or the initials 'R.F.'. The year of production or decoration is usually included in the mark.

A good account of the 19th-century history of the Sèvres factory will be found in the English edition of E. S. Auscher's *A History and Description of French Porcelain*. Some 20th-century, very smart Sèvres porcelains are featured in Patricia Bayer's general book *Art Deco Source Book* (Phaidon, Oxford, 1988).

VIENNA

The Vienna factory was important but not really in the same league as Meissen or Sèvres. I have chosen to include it as the

Plate 16. A decorative and typical Vienna porcelain plate painted with classical figure subject en grisaille after Kauffman. Blue Vienna shield-mark and impressed numbers for 1798. Diameter 9 ins. (Messrs. Sotheby's, New York)
Plate 17. A typically superb quality Vienna porcelain covered (cabinet) cup and stand, with rich tooled gilding. Blue shield-mark. c.1850–60. Cup 4 ins high. (Messrs. Godden of Worthing Ltd)

traditional very decorative Vienna style was much copied after the factory closed in 1864. In this respect it can be considered to be a leader.

The Vienna porcelains fall into three main periods. The first was when the factory was privately owned; in the middle period, it was a state-run concern; and finally, after the factory was closed, much Vienna-style porcelain continued to be made. Most Vienna-type porcelains, usually bearing the old shield or 'beehive' mark as it is erroneously called, were made well after the main factory had been closed in 1864. This famous and much-copied mark was taken from the armorial bearings of the Habsburg family; the point of the shield is the bottom of the device. The genuine shield mark will be in underglaze-blue (not in overglaze enamel) and it will be hand-painted. Consequently, it should show slight irregularities in the drawing, unlike a later printed copy.

The city of Vienna (Wien) was the site of the second European hard-paste factory. The period from 1718 to 1744 is known as the Du Paquier period, after the first director Claude Innocent Du Paquier. He was greatly helped by workmen and painters poached from the Meissen factory. Du Paquier porcelains are unmarked and are extremely rare, especially outside Austrian and German collections.

By the early 1740s Du Paquier was in great financial difficulties. He was saved by a loan from the state which was in effect a state takeover and in 1749 the enterprise was materially helped by the discovery of large deposits of the all-important kaolin in Hungary. From this period the Austrian shield-shape (Bindenschild) mark with two cross-bars was introduced and used by the factory which can now be called the Imperial and Royal factory. This mark occurs either impressed or painted in blue. It is important to note that when the blue mark is painted in underglaze-blue the outlines will be slightly blurred by the covering glaze. Overglaze enamel renditions, with sharp outlines, normally indicate a late date – after the main factory had closed in 1864. In addition to the standard underglaze-blue shield mark, many examples made from about 1784 bear impressed year numerals, using the last two digits. After 1800 the last three digits appear, 801 for 1801, 802 for 1802, and so on.

In general the Vienna hard-paste porcelains are rather thicker in the potting than the German porcelains. They are consequently heavier in weight. The body can also be a little greyer or sometimes more creamy than Meissen and other major makes. The gilding is usually of very good quality. Most Imperial and Royal Vienna porcelains are tableware shapes although the decoration may well limit them for use today as purely cabinet pieces. However, some figures and groups were made, usually in the general style of popular Dresden products.

The decoration of the tablewares and particularly the plates is usually of good quality and can be extremely fine. However, the all-over, rich (raised) gilt style of decoration which is so often associated with the Vienna porcelains is not typical and is certainly not characteristic of the 18th-century products. Unfortunately, most of the good quality, clean-looking, rather restrained late 18th-century Vienna porcelains do not seem to be in great demand in the British Isles. Most buyers of Vienna porcelain favour the usually more showy figure-panelled porcelains, even if they have nothing to do with the true Vienna factory! The porcelains are basically in demand for their decorative merit – the more decoration the better!

The style of decoration traditionally associated with the Vienna factory is shown in Plate 16, where very finely painted classical figures are surrounded by elaborate borders and much raised gold-work. Obviously, other major factories produced rich objects, but the Vienna factory was undoubtedly the market leader in this style from about the 1780s into the 19th century. In general, the more elaborate the decoration, the later the piece will be.

The Vienna factory continued (but did not prosper) up to 1864. The shapes of the period 1800 to 1820 tended to be simple and Empire in style, rather than florid or rococo. The exhibits at the Great Exhibition in Hyde Park in 1851 included figures and groups but these are rarely found. Most Vienna porcelains are elegant, useful, tablewares. Some richly decorated porcelains combined the use of raised gilding with platinum to give a silver effect.

From about 1820 the Vienna mark tended to be painted rather smaller than before and the outline may be more triangular than shield-shaped. It may also appear in impressed form rather than the normal underglaze-blue version. Some slightly faulty porcelains were sold in the white. On such pieces the original mark was cancelled by the addition of two cut lines across the shield. Another way of distinguishing the faulty pieces was to overpaint the mark with the capital letter 'A', usually in red or green over the glaze. Most, if not all, such slightly faulty pieces were subsequently decorated outside the factory and were then put on the market, but the decoration at least will not have originated at the Vienna factory, good as the later painting may be.

By the time of the 1851 Great Exhibition in London, the Imperial Porcelain Manufactory of Vienna was clearly past its greatest days. The official catalogue entry for this once-important state factory read:

Letter-weights, groups, figures of porcelain. Vases, plates, dishes, sauce tureens and stands, punch bowls, casseroles,

Plate 18. A very decorative Vienna-style plate well painted with figure subject, within rich gilt border. Blue shield-mark. c.1865–75. Diameter 9¼ ins. (Messrs. Sotheby's)

compotiers, wine coolers, large vase and stand, fruit dishes, ice-pail, letter-weights, inkstand, a table, coffee cups, groups, figures, paintings.

At the 1862 London International Exhibition, the *Art Journal*'s 324-page catalogue could spare only a third of a page for the Vienna factory's contribution. It was stated against the two engravings (a jug and a vase): 'The Royal Manufactory of Vienna supplied us with but few objects calculated for engraving.'

By 1864 the situation had declined to such an extent that the state decided to close the 'factory, there having been no buyers when an attempt had been made to sell it as a going concern. Most accounts of the Vienna factory and of Viennese porcelains close at this point. In fact, most so-called typical Vienna porcelain was made or at least decorated after the factory had closed.

When the factory closed, there were large stocks of old white blanks available, and a trained workforce of painters and gilders now out of work. Many of these decorators bought blanks –

some of which might have been quite old and all of which would have the original Imperial shield mark – very cheaply, painted them up in their accustomed styles and sold them in the normal way of business. In 1879 Frederick Litchfield noted in the 'modern' section of *Pottery and Porcelain. A Guide to Collectors*:

> Since the break-up of the State establishment, a number of the workmen and artists, formerly employed there, have set up small ateliers on their own account, and continue to produce specimens similar in character to those of the extinct factory; and some of these modern paintings are very artistic and show great finish, the gilding is also very good.

By 1879, these decorating studios or ateliers would probably have run out of old Vienna blanks but the demand still existed for richly decorated Vienna-style porcelains and the artists would have catered for this demand by purchasing white porcelains from other sources. As the state factory was no longer in existence they felt free to use the old, well known and respected mark to make their own products all the more saleable. However, Frederick Litchfield later noted:

Plate 19. An inexpensive Vienna-style dessert dish. In this case the signed 'Kaufmann' [sic] panel is printed not hand-painted. The gilding is very thin and poor compared with the more costly work. Printed shield-mark. c.1900–10. 9¾ ins. (V. Pilbeam)

These private firms vary very considerably in degrees of merit, and of late years [he was now writing in or slightly before 1912] an over-decorated, cheaper and more tawdry description of Vienna china has been placed on the market. This would seem to have damaged the sale of the better class of modern Vienna, and now only the really old specimens are in any request. Imitations of Vienna china bearing a forged mark have also been made by some Dresden firms.

By the 1880s probably more than twenty Continental firms were producing decorative colourful porcelains in the old Vienna style (Plate 18). Most, if not all, of these would have copied the well-known old Vienna shield-shape mark. Often the later copies bear a reversed mark which looks like a beehive.

When the factory closed in 1864 the archives, designs, records of shapes as well as many of the moulds or master-models for the different forms were sold to a local earthenware manufacturer, Josef de Cente. Any de Cente reissues of old Imperial factory models will bear the de Cente name. However, de Cente seems to have made little use of this material and c.1902 it was sold again, this time to the firm of Ernst Wahliss.

Ernst Wahliss was an enterprising retailer who, by the late 1880s, had opened premises in Vienna, Paris and London and was selling at 'Original Vienna Prices' a wide range of decorative pottery and porcelain. Wahliss's advertisements claimed a 'Gold Medal' at the 1885 exhibition and the 'Highest award at all exhibitions'! Wahliss died in 1900 but his two sons Hans and Erich carried on the business – now almost an empire – under the original name. The very large London retail showrooms, The Porcelain House, at 88 Oxford Street contained five floors packed with pottery, porcelain and glass wares from the leading firms Dresden, Wedgwood, Minton and Royal Crown Derby, and, of course, Vienna-style wares. These Vienna goods were rather more than Vienna-styled, for in about 1895 Ernst Wahliss had purchased a porcelain factory at Turn-Teplitz, in Bohemia, where the original Vienna moulds bought from de Cente were subsequently put to good commercial use.

The Wahliss Galleries received an extraordinarily favourable write-up (or perhaps it was a self-written blurb!) in a supplement to the high-quality collectors' magazine *The Connoisseur* of December 1906. From the illustrations to this, and from other Wahliss advertisements, it is clear that the Wahliss Vienna-style goods were of a very high quality. The prices for Wahliss's 'Vienna school' porcelains were very high for that period, £100 or more for important large vases – but these were superb products.

These Wahliss porcelains in the Vienna style were made in Turn-Teplitz, not in Vienna. Some pieces bore special 'E W' printed marks, which usually incorporate the place-name 'TURN' as well as 'VIENNA' (or 'WIEN', the Austrian name). Other marks feature the personal name 'WAHLISS'.

Basically, there are two very different classes of later Vienna-style porcelain: the good and the bad! The good can be very, very, good and some specimens probably represent the ultimate in quality ceramic decoration, although they may not be to everyone's taste. However, in some of today's markets – in the oil-rich Middle Eastern countries and in Japan, for example – such richly decorated Vienna porcelains are highly valued.

Perhaps in Britain the old-school collectors have too hastily dismissed the wares which were made after the closure of the Imperial and Royal factory in 1864. Yet these later porcelains, in some cases painted by the original factory artists, only lack one dubious attribute – they were not made at a factory whose management had lost its way!

Apart from the Wahliss Vienna School wares, there were many other, mainly German, firms that were producing Vienna-style goods, very often with the Vienna shield-shape mark. The square dish illustrated in Plate 19 probably looks very good to the layman but it is an example of a large class of 20th-century mass-produced goods made to sell at a low price. The centre (bearing the fake signature 'Kauffmann') is printed, not hand-painted, and the reverse carries an overglaze shield mark with the country name 'Germany' – both cannot be correct!

These cheap or relatively inexpensive wares, which can be earthenware rather than porcelain, met a ready market. W. P. Jervis writing from the USA in the 1890s notes, 'There can, of course, be no more Royal Vienna, though it is advertised and offered for sale every day!' Yet it was being made and sold because it was popular. It was colourful in a rather gaudy way and it looked good value for money. This is still the case today.

Listed here in alphabetical order are some of the Continental manufacturers and decorators of Vienna-style porcelain made after the state factory had closed. I have added the dates of establishment. Several of these firms were active well into the 20th century and all are known to have used a version of the original shield-shape mark or, when the device is reversed, the so-called 'beehive' mark. This list of copyists is probably not complete but it really does not matter which of these firms or individuals made any given pieces. What is important is the quality of the article and its decorative merits.

| Ackermann & Fritze | Volkstedt | (*c*.1908+) |
| Philipp Aigner | Vienna | (*c*.1900) |

B. Bloch & Co.	Eichwald	(c.1871+)
Bourdois & Bloch	Paris	(c.1890+)
Franz Dorfl	Vienna	(c.1880+)
Bernard Grossbaum & Sons	Dresden	(c.1891+)
Haas & Czjzek	Schlaggenwald	(c.1867+)
C. M. Hutschenreuther	Hohenberg	(c.1814+)
Joseph Kawan	Vienna	(c.1907+)
Carl Knoll	Fischern	(c.1848)
Oswald Lorenz	Dresden	(c.1880+)
Porcelaine de Paris	Paris	(c.1860+)
Radler & Pilz	Vienna	(c.1864+)
Joseph Riedl	Giesshubel	(c.1890+)
Samson & Co.	Paris	(c.1860+)
Erdmann Schlegelmilch	Suhl	(c.1881+)
Oscar Schlegelmilch	Langewiesen	(c.1892)
Robert Franz Staral	Vienna	(c.1886+)
Carl Thieme	Potschappel	(c.1872+)
Vienna Porcelain Factory	Augarten	(c.1922+)
Joseph Vater	Vienna	(c.1894+)
Ernst Wahliss	Turn-Teplitz	(c.1894+)

Any porcelain bearing the signature 'Kauffman' (correctly spelled with one 'n' but often rendered as 'Kauffmann'), 'A. Kauffman' or 'Angelica Kauffman' is a late copy. The figure-subject decoration will almost certainly be a cheap print and the piece a mass-produced commercial production made down to a price. This famous 18th-century painter never decorated any porcelain but her designs were widely copied.

The rich, so-called 'Vienna' style of decoration at its best is of the finest quality and the figure painting and the intricate raised gilding must have been very costly to produce. Yet at the same time much the same general appearance could be obtained at a fraction of the cost by taking short cuts. Sometimes the figure-subject design may be a touched-in photographic reproduction. Other classical figure subjects were produced from cheap mass-produced litho transfers of the type used by children which slides off its paper backing. The thin cheap gilding could even be applied as a print or litho. It must be remembered, however, that these very cheap mock-Vienna wares gave pleasure to folk who could never afford a quality production.

2

FAKES AND FORGERIES

A great many later copies of fashionable collectable objects exist. Indeed, the later essays outnumber the originals. These later pieces, whatever we may call them, fakes, forgeries, reproductions, reissues, may well be very decorative and some are rightly quite highly valued, but they are not the 18th-century originals. Their value is almost entirely dependent on their decorative value.

Some of these later Continental essays can be of higher quality and more decorative than the articles they seek to emulate. See, for example, the two Toby-like jugs shown in Plates 20 and 21. The first is a rare Staffordshire earthenware example produced in about 1870. The more traditional type shown in Plate 21 is in hard-paste porcelain, well made and neatly decorated. It is, however, a Continental reproduction, or worse, in that it bears an improbable mock Chelsea gold-anchor mark. Yet the owner most probably respected this Continental Toby jug more than the genuine Staffordshire earthenware example of the same period which has not the 'finish' of the 'wrong-un'. In some markets the look of the piece can be very important, even paramount.

Many of these fakes and copies are now legally antique, having been produced over 100 years ago. They have in many cases acquired over the years an imposing pedigree. There is a difference between a fake and a forgery. Forgeries are totally fraudulent pieces, whereas fakes began life as genuine pieces, perhaps purchased in the white or sparsely decorated state, then given new or additional decoration in an effort to increase the value of the now enhanced (or spoilt!) piece. A copy may be a production made with reasonably honest intent but turned into a deceptive forgery by removing a modern mark or adding a new, false, collectable signature or mark. In practice, good quality fakes, forgeries and reproductions relate to expensive, commercially desirable and usually rare articles that can be expected to meet a ready demand and repay the efforts of the forger. It follows that in the field of Continental ceramics there are a great many copies of Dresden (Meissen), Sèvres, Vienna and other well-known makes.

This chapter will consider 19th-century or later copies, fakes, forgeries and reproductions of 18th-century ceramics, usually but not invariably porcelains. Such copies vary greatly in quality and in period but the market for them was vast. The better and/or older copies can be very good and dangerously deceptive, even to the experienced collector or dealer. There are, how-

Plate 20. A 19th-century Staffordshire earthenware Toby-type jug in the style of collectable 18th-century types. Unmarked. 9½ ins. (Messrs. Godden of Worthing Ltd)

Plate 21. A good quality Continental porcelain copy of an English traditional Toby jug. A decorative piece spoilt by the addition of a mock-Chelsea anchor mark in gold. 10 ins high. (Messrs. Godden of Worthing Ltd)

ever, thousands of cheap decorative figures, groups and trinkets which are really only forgeries in that such pieces bear a bold Chelsea-type anchor mark in gold, or some other desirable mark or signature. Most are of hard-paste porcelain bearing a glittery hard glaze quite unlike most of the wares they seek to emulate which, in the case of most English factories, were of a softer body and glaze.

The reader should be quite clear that when a sales catalogue has magic names such as 'Sèvres', 'Meissen', 'Dresden', 'Vienna', 'Chelsea' and so on printed in inverted commas, the piece is not from that factory! The collector who purchases such a piece, believing it to be from the stated factory, will have no redress, for inverted commas are now used in this way by the leading auctioneers when they are aware that the piece so described is a copy. Read the catalogue carefully. The position is much more dangerous when the auctioneer or other agent or seller is not aware of the later origin of the piece and offers it as genuine.

Collectors of 18th-century English wares are concerned especially with the Continental, mainly French, copies. However, there are also very many copies of Continental porcelains such as Meissen, Sèvres, etc., as well as European copies of Chinese porcelains. By the nature of fakes they do not bear the name or mark of the perpetrator!

A candid statement was made by the manager of a 'Fine Art Gallery' in Bond Street, who was brought to court by the Royal Worcester Company in 1898 for selling Paris copies of old square-marked Worcester porcelain as originals. The manager is reported as saying in defence: 'These things are made, and we have to sell them. Other places do the same ... It is no use to keep dummy china, if you tell customers so.'

While she was on her now famous buying trips to Europe, Lady Charlotte Schreiber attempted to trace the source of the flood of reproductions available in Britain from at least the 1850s onwards. For example, in May 1877 the Schreibers visited Tournai. 'The principal object of our present visit to Tournai was to inspect the Porcelain Manufactories, and to see what is really made at them.' After visiting the Peternick works where only earthenware was produced, Lady Schreiber continued:

> We went on to Mr Boch's large establishment ... We asked if they made any figures and were shown into a small room full of groups etc, in biscuit, done from the old models, which they still possess. Also a quantity of pure white vases of the old Sèvres forms, which go to Paris and are there decorated by the dealers, and are sold for fine genuine 'Vieux' Sèvres. We have thus accounted for the deceptions as to old Sèvres and old Tournai biscuit groups, but we have seen no traces of forgeries of Worcester. N.B. The Bochs do not use any mark for their pottery or porcelain. They do not decorate their wares and use no gold on any of them. (*Journals*, 2 vols, London, 1911)

Lady Schreiber likewise discovered another source of mid 19th-century mock-Sèvres porcelain, at the Bettignies works at St Amand:

> [We] proceeded to St Amand, in the neighbourhood of which are M. Bettignies' works. His family were the original proprietors of the Tournai factory in its palmy days, some century since. They have been at St Amand some 60 years … First he took us to see his rooms full of finished pottery and porcelain; the latter consists of white pieces, *pâte tendre* soft paste copied from the old Sèvres, which he told us was bought by dealers in Paris to be there painted and duly sold as old. Some of the forms are very fine indeed, and most of them are exact copies of old Sèvres. Among them were a few figures and groups, and we were especially interested in spying out two hexagonal covers, which could only have been made for imitation of Worcester vases, and many oviform vases etc which are evidently made to imitate Worcester and Chelsea. All he would tell us was that they all went to Paris to be decorated and sold as old.

Apart from new, 19th-century reproductions, many of which were decorated at specialist studios in Paris, there also exists the more dangerous class of Sèvres porcelain that was basically genuine but redecorated in a fashionable and costly style. This trick probably dates back at least to the early days of the 19th century. A writer in the *Art Journal* magazine in 1857 drew his readers' attention to one form of this deception:

> The art of making the soft porcelain of Sèvres of the best period having been lost, and the best specimens of that period fetching enormous prices, the dealers some years ago discovered a method of giving to inferior specimens the outward appearances of the finest. They filed off the old paintings, and employed skilful enamel-painters to copy and otherwise imitate the works of the best Sèvres artists on the ground thus prepared and, on passing these spurious specimens through the fire, it was found that they had in their first manufacture, absorbed so much glaze that enough remained to come up to the surface and combine with the new enamel colours which were being vitrified. This plan was so successful that the market was flooded with specimens of the best period, and the very richness of the harvest led to suspicion and discovery of the fraud. So excellent are some of these specimens that none but the most experienced dealers can detect them, and even these have been at fault, and have had to apply to the museum at Sèvres.

The craft was practised on both sides of the Channel. The difficulty with such repainted specimens is that the shape, the porcelain and to some extent the glaze and the mark are 'right' –

all are genuine. However, they wear a new flamboyant dress, added to enhance the appearance and hoped-for value.

It must be admitted that from a purely decorative point of view these dressed-up Sèvres porcelains, repainted 100 years or so after the porcelain was made, do have a value, are quite desirable and can be costly. There are two different markets for Sèvres porcelain, the purist's demand for original decoration and the market for decorative pieces in a mock 18th-century style. Each has many devotees. Also, of course, the entirely 'wrong', mock-Sèvres 19th-century porcelains are saleable because they are decorative and far less costly than originals might be – if they could be found. Such pieces exist, perhaps happily accepted in old collections.

It is unlikely that sparse simple patterns, floral sprigs, etc., will be redecorated, for the object of the exercise was to enhance such genuine pieces with the then sought-after ornate decoration – figure subjects, for example, set within coloured borders, with gilt enrichments.

A bubbled, discoloured, dull or spotted glaze, or a dark footrim, should sound warning bells. These are almost sure signs of refiring and therefore of redecoration. However, the absence of such refiring faults does not necessarily prove the piece to be genuine. A good forgery made in a soft-paste porcelain will not show refiring pointers because it has not been later repainted and refired. It is entirely 'wrong'. It must be remembered that not all such forgeries, fakes and reproductions of 18th-century porcelain were made on the Continent. The English porcelain essays in this style, particularly those made at the Coalport factory in Shropshire and by Mintons in Stoke, can be extremely good.

Of the Continental manufacturers, the reproductions of Continental and English 18th-century porcelains made by the important firm of Edmé Samson (& Co.), established in the 1840s, must be considered in some detail. The name Samson is certainly the best known of all the Paris manufacturers yet the firm is not included in many standard works and even when Samson is mentioned the name is usually used in a derogatory sense, referring to the firm's well-known activities in reproducing collectable 18th-century ceramics. As one leading British authority wrote early in this century: 'His manufactory is probably responsible for more disappointments on the part of young collectors than any other half-dozen makers of spurious china grouped together.'

Samson's fame has resulted in practically every Continental fake or reproduction being attributed to this firm, irrespective of the quality of the article. In attributing such pieces to Samson the seller is attempting to up-grade the fake, to make it respectable. It is a sad story for, if the Samson firm had concentrated its real expertise in producing fashionable, useful and decorative wares,

Plate 22. A Continental hard-paste copy of an English Plymouth porcelain mug painted with exotic birds in landscapes. Complete with copy of the Plymouth tin mark ♃ . c.1860–80. 4 ins high. (T. H. Prince)

Plate 23. A selection of high-quality Samson copies of Meissen animal models. Formerly part of the Samson Works Collection. c.1850–80. Begging models 12½ ins high. (Messrs. Christie's)

the name of Samson of Paris would rank with the leading international firms because the quality is so superb. Plates 22–6 show typical examples which surely make this point quite clearly.

The Samson works produced a vast number of essays in the style of Dresden, Sèvres, Chantilly, Nymphenburg, Chelsea, Bow, Derby, Chinese and other porcelains as well as earthenwares, enamels and even glass wares. If only they had employed more often their own Samson name-mark, collectors would be collecting these French wares with open arms instead of shying away from them. In recent years some decorative figures, groups

Plate 24. A selection of high-quality Samson copies of old Meissen figures. Formerly part of the Samson Works Collection. c.1850–80. Central group 9¼ ins high. (Messrs. Christie's)

Plate 25. A good quality pair of Samson copies of Nymphenburg porcelain figures. Formerly part of the Samson Works Collection. c.1850–80. 8 ins high. (Messrs. Christie's)

Plate 26. An imposing set of Samson figures representing the Continents. Formerly in the Samson Works Collection. Meissen-style blue cross mark. Models 5842–5845. c.1860–80. 10½ ins high. (Messrs. Christie's)

and vases have rightly been commanding reasonable (even four-figure) sums.

The recorded facts on the Samson firm in Continental reference books are extremely scarce and are often conflicting. Fortunately, one of our most respected English collectors, the late Wallace Elliot, wrote to the firm in or before 1937 seeking information and he received a six-page reply, some of which he quoted in his paper, 'Reproductions and fakes of English eighteenth century ceramics, *Transactions of the English Ceramic Circle*, vol. 2, No. 7 (1939).

The House of Samson was founded in 1845 by Edmé Samson at 7, Rue Beranger. He was a decorator of china only. It was his son, Emile Samson (1837–1913), who first began the reproductions of early porcelains, earthenwares, and enamels. After Emile's death in 1913 the firm was carried on by his son Leon Samson, and at his death in 1923 by his grandson, the great-grandson of the original Edmé.

In 1937 Samson claimed to mark all specimens. It is doubtful, however, whether all Samson reproductions bear a clear Samson mark, perhaps the later pieces do but certainly not the entire, very large, output.

The history of the Samson firm may be divided into two periods. First, we have the period when 'Papa Samson' was producing a relatively small number of good-quality reproductions which were mostly unmarked. These early Samson essays would not have been inexpensive novelties as were some later non-Samson fakes and reproductions. His products were of high quality and must have been comparatively costly. Second, we have the later, post-1885 Samson wares, produced when Emile was running the company. During this time the quality of the pieces deteriorated to some degree as output was increased to cater for a larger and probably less discriminating market.

The London auctioneers Christie's sold in 1971, 1979 and 1980 an interesting and lengthy series of figures, groups, vases and other objects which had originated from the Samson works museum or reference collection. These pieces were consigned by a person who had purchased the Samson Company which no longer continues the old trade. A study of the fine selection of Samson porcelains sold in London is most instructive and is evidence of the wide variety of articles and types produced by this Paris manufacturer. Space precludes further discussion here, but I quote at length from the catalogue in *Godden's Guide to European Porcelain*.

Several of the figures and groups which I attribute to the Samson firm on account of their superior quality bear under the base neatly impressed numerals. This feature is not recorded in the catalogues except in one case where 'incised' numbers are mentioned. However, these neatly impressed model numbers certainly indicate a 19th-century Continental origin when they appear on copies of Chelsea, Bow or Derby specimens.

Another point to observe in these French hard-paste copies of English figure porcelains is that they almost invariably have one or more small neat holes pierced in an unobtrusive spot, usually at the back of the model. This vent hole (to let trapped air out of the hollow centre when the piece is fired) looks as if a hatpin or needle has been inserted. (This Continental method is not exclusive to the Samson works.) In this respect they are quite different from English figures which usually have open bases so that a vent in the body is not required.

The Samson figures from the first period (the 'Papa Samson' examples) are heavy in weight. The body and glaze is hard and in the case of copies of English soft-paste porcelain the modelling is far sharper than it is on the thicker-glazed originals. Sharper is a good word in this context for if the flowers and leaves have been chipped – a common occurrence – you can very easily cut your fingers or hand on the fracture.

Reviewing the Samson products in the 1990s, it is clear that this firm was a market-leader in the 19th-century in its chosen field. I believe that Samson is a name to be respected but we should be very careful in attributing fakes and reproductions to this firm. By no means were all such pieces made by the Samson Company, indeed probably less than 10 per cent of Continental copies of English 18th-century porcelain was made by this leading Paris firm. Alas, all now tend to be described as Samson, perhaps in an endeavour to add value and desirability to inferior tourist-type trinkets.

Another leading and long-established French manufacturer of reproduction 18th-century porcelain was situated on the Rue de la Pierre-Levée. This was established by Jean-Marx Clauss in about 1829 (but claimed links with the earlier Paris La Courtille factory) and he was succeeded by his son Alphonse between 1846 and 1868, and then by Eugène up to 1887. In 1887 Marc Clauss took Achille Bloch and Leon Bourdois into partnership and these ran the factory after Clauss retired in 1890. Bourdois retired in about 1900, leaving Achille Bloch and later his son to continue the firm until the present managing director Paul Molho succeeded. This important firm has reputedly produced over 25,000 models, and still produces good-quality decorative pieces under the trade name 'Porcelaine de Paris'.

In the latter part of the 19th-century and the early years of the 20th this firm produced a wide range of porcelains made in the style of Dresden, Sèvres, Vienna, Capodimonte and other fashionable Continental and British wares. The colourful, large hard-paste copies of English punch bowls were perhaps made by this firm. Examples sometimes bear a copy of the Rockingham Griffin mark. Sometimes the initials, E.C., A.B. or B.B. were added to old-style marks such as the crossed-swords device. This firm seemingly also copied English wares.

Recently I saw in a local shop a very decorative hard-paste figure bearing this red-painted Derby-type mark on the reverse.

The initials 'ABP' added to the Derby-type mark lift this piece above the level of reproductions and fakes which bear only close copies of Chelsea anchors or other collectable marks.

Two weeks later I acquired a post-war colour-illustrated catalogue or publicity brochure which included these Derby-style models among a very decorative array of such reproduction figures and groups. The present firm, Porcelaine de Paris, produced this interesting publicity brochure with colour illustrations of their products in the 1950s or 1960s. Unfortunately, it is not dated but it includes 31 pages showing 357 basic shapes or figure models. The different classes comprise Sèvres-style vases and caskets (some with metal mounts), Paris porcelains in the classical style of the period 1800 to 1830, Chinese export market-type wares, some with armorial bearings (incorrectly called 'Lowestoft'), Chinese *Famille-Rose* styled vases, figures, bird and animal models, and a good range of relief-moulded Capodimonte-styled porcelain in 58 different forms.

The items illustrated in the brochure are not priced but they could not have been cheap and many models, the large vases and intricate groups, must have been made in quite small numbers. The brochure shows a multitude of objects of the type that are usually attributed, erroneously, to the better-known Samson firm. The many figures and groups are mainly in the Dresden style but several are in the manner of Derby originals such as Falstaff, and various pairs of gardeners.

One initial mark used by Achille Bloch and Leon Bourdois has the initials 'BB' placed back to back under a crown. This device was registered by the firm in 1891; it is sometimes found on copies of old Derby porcelain.

This device may be that which I have seen referred to as 'blue crown, orb and butterfly'. This description was used by a provincial auctioneer as if it was a Dresden mark: 'A Dresden group of three male and three female figures playing blind man's bluff … with underglaze blue crown, orb and butterfly mark.' This device was not used at the Dresden factory, it is a French post-1891 Bloch and Bourdois mark which can occur on a wide variety of good-quality, decorative porcelains.

Another rather similar red-painted mark is found on some Continental hard-paste copies of Derby figures and other ornamental wares. This strange version of a Derby mark is drawn below. It occurs on good-quality specimens which could well have been made by the Porcelaine de Paris firm or its predecessors in the 1870–1900 period.

The firm's President Michel Bloit's splendid illustrations in his book *Trois Siècles de Porcelaine de Paris* show the high quality of the porcelains, which have real decorative merit. Much use was made of gilt mounts and the range of models was very wide. The author was able to draw on official records which show this firm to have produced really sumptuous articles. Apart from the initial marks which I have cited, copies of the Sèvres, the Capodimonte, the Vienna and a mock Oriental seal mark was also used.

It would be convenient to use the term 'Porcelaine de Paris' for these essays, although most examples were admittedly produced by earlier related partnerships. These mainly 19th-century 'Porcelaine de Paris' examples are of a very good quality

Plate 27. A Paul Bocquillon of Paris advertisement, reproduced from the British trade publication, The Pottery Gazette Diary for 1914, showing typical reproduction lines.

and are very decorative. The present management does not produce such earlier style wares but concentrates on high-quality modern porcelains.

Information on another French manufacturer of old-styled collectable porcelains is provided by a single illustrated advertisement published in the *Pottery Gazette Diary* of 1914 (Plate 27). The firm of Paul Bocquillon of Faubourg St Denis, Paris, is practically unknown now but seemingly, before the First World War, it specialized in 'reproduction of old china and earthenware'. This advertisement angled at the British trade mentioned Lowestoft, Chelsea, Derby and Worcester porcelains as well as Chinese wares, Saxe (the French name for Dresden) and Sèvres porcelains as well as Moustiers, Rouen and Delft earthenwares.

Although Paul Bocquillon doesn't seem to have advertised his wares in *The Pottery Gazette* after 1914, the firm seemingly carried on at least into the 1930s. Dieter Zühlsdorff's book of marks covering the 1885–1935 period lists printed marks (below) attributed to 1932 onwards. Such clear marks show that the Bocquillon concern was still specialising in this part of the business but such honest marking does not occur on the earlier essays made before about 1914.

Reproduction
P.B.
Paris
Made in France

Plate 28. French porcelains emulating in the added decoration Chinese Export Market porcelains with European armorial bearings. The teaware forms, however, are in the style of Worcester not Chinese shapes! c.1860–80. Diameter of plate 9¼ ins. (Messrs. Godden of Worthing Ltd)

Yet another maker of reproduction antique porcelains were Messrs G. Mansard and J. Houry of 34 Rue de Paradis, Paris. In 1905 the *Pottery Gazette* noted that this partnership 'exhibited a large number of their reproductions of old china. These include Sèvres, Dresden, Capodimonte, Lowestoft, Chelsea and an interesting variety of Persian and Chinese decorations'.

A J. Mansard ran a decorating studio at this Paris address reputedly as early as the 1830s and J. Houry is recorded as having his own decorating establishment from *c*.1863. By at least 1905, seemingly, the two families were working together producing a wide range of reproductions for the British, and one assumes, other markets. The probability is that these goods bore close copies of the old marks – those so much in demand by collectors.

One of the leading 19th-century manufacturers of reproductions of various collectable types was Moritz Fischer, of Hungary, whose work was very well known and highly regarded in his time, and indeed he showed his wares at various 19th-century exhibitions; yet today one hardly hears his name. Probably his essays in the style of antique ceramics are regarded as Samson or perhaps they pass as genuine pieces! Certainly they will not bear a Fischer name-mark. A review of his stand at the 1878 Paris Exhibition did however state that you could have any mark you like added to the Fischer wares. One can therefore expect to find such Hungarian porcelains bearing copies of the Chelsea anchor mark and other devices which were thought to make the products more saleable.

Several contemporary accounts show that Moritz Fischer, and later his son Samuel, specialized in copies of antique Sèvres and Dresden porcelains and also in reproductions of Oriental wares. However, other contemporary reviews also mention copies of Bow and Chelsea porcelain so we may assume that Fischer did not neglect the large and remunerative British market for his reproductions. The fact that I cannot illustrate any Fischer reproductions, points to their superb quality, as these pieces in general have not been identified.

Many manufacturers of mock-Dresden, Sèvres, Vienna or early English porcelains were situated in Germany, for example, Dressel Kister & Co, of Passau in Bavaria. This firm was established in about 1840 and continued to the early 1920s and is known to have copied 18th-century Höchst and Ludwigsburg models using the original moulds and copying the old marks.

Some reproductions of Crown Derby and other porcelains were apparently made by, or decorated in, the Dresden Studios of Greyner (or Greiner) & Son. *The Stationery Trades Journal* of January 1882 carried an announcement for 'Greyner Dresden Wares' stocked by the London firm of Henry Dreydel & Co. These German 'Ceramic Novelties' comprised 'Reproduction of Old Crown Derby, Old Dresden, Lowestoft and Copenhagen, in plates and bowls'. Although this Dresden firm is recorded as employing a G & S initial mark (see Chapter 4), it is most unlikely that these reproductions angled at the British market bore the mark of the true maker. It is thought that the Greyner studio commenced work in the early 1870s.

Many of these reproductions would have been quite inexpensive, showy goods made down to a price not up to a quality. We are not now speaking of top-quality productions such as were made by Samson and some other leading firms. The market for the less expensive tourist-type goods was vast and several London wholesalers specialized in the trade, selling their wares to hundreds of small shops up and down the country. One now forgotten firm was H. Mayer & Co. of 42 Snow Hill, London, selling Continental goods wholesale and for re-export only.

Mayer's advertisement in the 1885 *Pottery Gazette Diary* stated that the buyers 'having lately returned from the Continent are now enabled to show the latest productions … A choice assortment of reproductions of ANTIQUE and rare pieces of CHELSEA, CROWN DERBY, WORCESTER and MARSEILLES wares. These are specially suitable for Bric-a-Brac Dealers and Dealers in Articles de Vertu.' This Victorian wholesaler also advertised Dresden China, Vienna China and Sèvres China but then this was long before the days of the Trades Descriptions Act!

Most of these cheap and cheerful goods should not trouble a present-day collector, who has some basic knowledge of hard and soft paste and the feel and atmosphere of 18th-century English porcelains. They are, however, troublesome to those who regard only the mark. If a piece bears a gold anchor device they refer to any reference book where they are informed that this device was used at the Chelsea factory. This is true as far as it goes but there are many ifs and buts to be considered.

One of the basic almost standard forms of decoration which one might expect on gold anchor marked Chelsea porcelains of the 1760s would be colourful birds in landscapes. Well, the gold anchor marked plate shown in Plates 29 and 30 bears this decoration. Yet this specimen is quite 'wrong' in every aspect and it should not confuse or mislead any but the newest collector; but bearing as it does a gold anchor device it was probably made to deceive. It may be difficult to tell this from the illustration, but the porcelain is very hard, glittery and cold-looking, as is the covering glaze. The original would have been soft paste, much

Plate 29. A pale yellow bordered Continental hard-paste plate, with coloured-in prints of exotic birds. Printed mock-Chelsea gold anchor mark as shown in Plate 30. c.1900–15. Diameter 8½ ins. (J. M. Stanley)

thicker in the potting and therefore heavier. The body and glaze here is too white, too perfect! It does not show any of the small defects that one expects with genuine gold-anchor Chelsea soft-paste porcelain. No small tears, slightly open cracks, spots, pooling of the glaze, no warping, no ground-down footrim, to make it sit squarely on a table. No stilt-marks where the piece was supported in the gloss-firing. All these missing signs of an original piece merely relate to the reverse side before the face or top of the plate are examined.

Turning this plate up we find that the birds are in fact printed (or at least a printed outline has been coloured over), not hand painted. The colours are wishy-washy and flat, not full of spontaneous life and colour. The original birds are usually described as 'exotic' and they appear so. These printed copies seem to have passed their sell-by date!

The border colour is a pale yellow, a highly unlikely colour for Chelsea to have used. The gilding is thin, cheap-looking and was applied as a print or litho. The ribbon-like decoration from

Plate 30. The all too clean back of the Continental hard-paste plate shown in Plate 29. Note the large gold-printed anchor mark and gilt reference number. (J. M. Stanley)

which the main flowers hang has an *Art Nouveau* feeling of the early 1900s. Returning to the illustrated reverse side, the mock-Chelsea gold anchor device is too large and this is also printed, not hand-painted. The number 70 also appears printed in gold. This is probably the manufacturer's catalogue or reference number and is out of keeping with a Chelsea original. I award the maker of this piece nought out of ten for this effort but the original owner was probably quite happy that this plate was a genuine Chelsea specimen.

In this chapter I have perhaps over-emphasized the Continental reproductions of English porcelains but these particularly interest our own collectors more than similar copies of Sèvres, Chantilly or even Dresden porcelains. Obviously the Continental manufacturers tended to export their copies to the best market for such goods. In the case of reproductions of English porcelain the market was in Britain and to some degree in North America. These copies were very widely distributed.

While on the subject of fakes and forgeries, readers should be warned that many reissues occur. These are 19th- or 20th-century examples produced from original 18th-century moulds. In most cases these have been reissued in recent times as the models are still saleable. They have a period charm and appeal that is timeless. These traditional models are fine, as long as they are not sold as antique. The best example of the continued production of 18th-century figure models and groups must be the Meissen factory which has survived two World Wars and still continues to produce figure compositions that were first conceived more than 200 years ago. These Meissen models have been in almost continuous production over this period. They have, however, not been produced as forgeries but are always properly marked with the current symbols. These Meissen essays are by no means the only traditional designs still being produced, either by the original firms or by others who may have acquired the old moulds or master-models.

In my early collecting days I purchased my share of fakes. In so doing I learnt from them and so expanded my fund of knowledge and experience. Needless to say, these bad buys were made in small junk shops where I was hoping to find a hidden bargain. I would not have been duped had I had then the good sense (and funds!) to patronize a knowledgeable dealer, one who would have given me a fully described receipt. We only learn such wisdom later in life!

3

The Vast Middle-class Market

It is impossible to overestimate the vast market for the less expensive types of colourful or novel pottery and porcelain in the second half of the 19th century. This expanding market was certainly not confined to Britain, it covered the world, as populations and their standards of living increased. The British trade annual *The Pottery Gazette Diary* published from 1882 and the related monthly journal *The Pottery Gazette*, are full of interesting advertisements featuring the types of wares made by many manufacturers or sold by various wholesalers.

In general these goods were produced by the smaller Continental firms who were cutting corners, making commercial goods down to the lowest possible price. They were able to undersell the British manufacturers for various reasons but basically their wages were lower and their firing-cycle was more economical.

They supplied the vast trade of novelties that the retailers in seaside resorts and the like could sell for pence rather than pounds. Many of these mainly German manufacturers supplied cheap mugs, plates, teapots, etc. inscribed in cheap gilding 'A Present from Worthing' (or any other town). These were the tourist goods that attracted, at their low prices, similar attention to that later given to the picture postcards available at the same type of outlet. Many of these London wholesalers of Continental porcelain also specialized in selling slightly faulty 'seconds'. The low price was seemingly more important in this market, than the quality of the wares offered.

Although we tend to regard all such Continental 'nick nacks' as being Victorian in period, many are of a traditional resort type produced over a long period. The German open-work edge 'A Present from Worthing' plate shown in Plate 31, has for example a printed named view of Worthing pier and new pavilion. That new pavilion was not opened until June 1926. The brief 1893 Sanderson & Young advertisement is typical. They offered to retailers up and down the country 'Novelties of every description for seaside. View and Motto china. Immense variety.' For a pound this London firm would send a 'carefully selected assortment illustrating our stock'!

The 1884 *Pottery Gazette Diary* contained one of a series of advertisements for the goods supplied by the large London and Paris wholesaling firm of Blumberg & Co. The less expensive goods were listed as:

Plate 31. A 20th-century German porcelain printed plate made for the English south coast tourist market or for the town of Worthing in particular. Similar inexpensive pieces would have been made for all resorts. Printed mark 'Germany'. c.1926–30. Diameter 7 ins. (Geoffrey Godden)

Candlesticks – Pillar and Flat; Flower Pots, painted; Table Toilet Sets, special designs and shapes; Figures, Animals, Birds, &c.; Nick-nacks of every description, from 4s. per doz. upwards; Pottery in all the newest styles and makes; Faience, Vallauris, Sarreguemines, &c. &c.; Reproductions of old Rouen and other Wares; Imitation Dresden Cups and Saucers, cheap and good; Bisque Figures, from 5s. to 320s. pair; Dessert Sets, in large variety; Terra Cotta Figures and Vases; Imitation Bronze Vases in Pottery; Hand-painted Porcelain Plaques, in all qualities; Figure Candelabras, Candlesticks, &c.; A very fine assortment of Raised Floral Goods; Hungarian Goods and Austrian China, very choice.

Hyman A. Abrahams & Sons (Est. 1854), importers of foreign glass ware of Houndsditch boasted a full page advertisement in the 1889 issue. This is of considerable interest as in several cases the contemporary price ranges are quoted. These seem to be the wholesale prices, as in some instances the price is per dozen.

It is amazing how many firms of importers and wholesalers there were in London in the last quarter of the 19th century. These were not only selling their wares to British retailers but they were also, almost certainly, trading with many other countries, for London was one of the main centres of world commerce; the Abrahams advertisement ends with a note intended for overseas customers. This great importation of low- and medium-priced goods had been helped by the fact that in 1860 import duty had been abolished.

The stocks held by these large-scale (often international) wholesalers differed greatly from the porcelains displayed by the established Houses holding Royal Warrants. These included Thomas Goode, Mortlocks, Phillips, Litchfields and such leaders in the London retail trade. Such firms stocked the highest class goods both of British and of Continental origin – Minton, Royal Worcester, Meissen, Sèvres, Berlin and similar costly porcelains.

However, between the two we have a truly vast market for the middle range of pottery and porcelain that would have been purchased to enhance the tens of thousands of small detached or semi-detached homes that were being built in the 1860–1900 period, as our towns and cities encroached on the countryside or took in surrounding small villages.

It is quite difficult to trace source material for the Continental ceramics imported to cater for this very considerable trade. For these wares have not been featured adequately in existing standard reference books.

Some interesting trade catalogues of the 1870s and 1880s serve at least partly to show the basic division between home-produced, useful wares and the more decorative goods that were largely imported from Continental Europe. I refer to the catalogues issued by Albert Marcius Silber (born in Germany in 1833) and his London and Paris based company. This traded under his own name, or from c.1857 as Silber & Fleming, until the late 1890s.

The catalogues in the British National Art Library at the Victoria & Albert Museum were all acquired in December 1898 soon after the company ceased trading after more than forty years. The earlier catalogues of the 1870s are quite small and are only illustrated with a few line engravings. They are interesting however, as in many cases the prices are given against each entry; such information is lacking from the larger catalogues issued in the 1880s. Separate very detailed price lists were issued relating to the later catalogues, but few of these survive. I quote some of these prices below but it must be remembered that they are wholesale, nett prices at which Silber & Fleming sold on the goods to a host of retailers. It may well be realistic to allow at least a 50 per cent mark-up for the final customer.

Silber & Fleming's English catalogue of c.1885 was republished in 1991 as *The Victorian Catalogue of Household Goods*. This is amazing value for anyone interested in late Victorian wares. It includes good engravings of a vast array of silver, silver-plate, glassware, clocks, cooking utensils, sanitary goods, tools, travel goods, carriages, firearms, dolls, etc., apart from the ceramics which are the main interest here.

Before mentioning the imported Continental objects it would be helpful to record that the English wares mainly comprised our specialities – the type of goods which we would have been exporting to the Continent and other major markets. Firstly, we have earthenware and ironstone-type dinner services, in this case mainly comprising printed or printed-base designs. These include Wedgwood and Ashworth (formerly Mason) ware with several other makes which I have not identified as yet. Some china dinner services were also included and these underline the middle or slightly higher class of market catered for in this catalogue; two of the porcelain dinner services were described as being French. It is noteworthy that even with the earthenware dinner sets, matching tea or coffee wares were also featured.

This and other firms also catered for special orders and armorial bearings, crests or initials could be added to the edge or centre of most stock patterns. The Silber wording reads: 'Dinner ware, with crests, Monograms, &c. Monograms, crests and Masonic devices; Regimental, hotel and other badges, printed or painted in one or more colours on every description of china and earthenware to order.'

The many porcelain dessert services included in the Silber & Fleming catalogues included both English bone china examples and French and German hard-paste sets. In general the Continental examples were less expensive than our bone china sets but this may have been because in the case of Silber's stock, the foreign ones were not as finely decorated. The 1872 catalogue, includes the entry: 'Dessert services. French china (our own special designs), coloured bands, gold lines, assorted fruit or flower centres, 18 pieces, viz. 12 plates, 4 low comports, 2 tall comports. 18/6d, 19/6d, 21/-, 25/-, 30/-, 32/6, 35/-, 45/-.' The graduated prices, depending on the quality and extent of the decoration, ascended to £10 for a set of eighteen pieces. In the same list the English services start at £1 10s and rose to £15.

A large section is devoted to tea and coffee services in porcelain and earthenware. This section also includes 'Tête-a-tête sets, Jugs, Teapots, Cheese covers, egg-stands, sardine boxes, china tea services on revolving trays, etc.' Again, most of these goods appear to be of British manufacture and need not be lingered over except to note the make-up of the standard services. These comprised, 28, 35 or 40-piece services and obviously the price would have been related to the size of the set. Even in the 1880s teapots and sugar boxes were not included in the standard sets, although they were available separately, at additional cost. Also

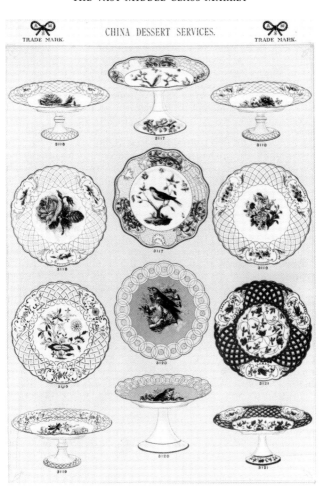

Plate 32. Meissen-styled late Victorian dessert wares reproduced from Silber & Fleming's trade catalogue. The complete services were priced from £3 15s 0d to £11 11s 0d. c.1882.

at this period, only the more costly 40-piece set had the small, individual plates that we now accept as normal and which are often assumed to have been included in all post-1860 services.

Most of the decorative two or four person tea sets on trays were almost certainly of French origin. Since the days of Royal

Sèvres the Continental manufacturers have specialized in such niceties. The style had greatly changed by the 1880s but these sets seem to speak with a French accent and the separate price list describes the first as being of French china. In the 1870s such Silber sets were priced from 5/6d to £2 10s 0d.

Apart from the decorative articles for the cabinet and Sunday table setting, Silber catalogues also include a great many more utilitarian objects. Many of these combine function with grace or decorative merit and reflect a past age. Just as the bedroom toilet sets with their large water jugs and basins remind us that the houses were not as a rule equipped with hot running water in bed or bathrooms, so the popular water filters remind us that the basic water supply may not have been pure or treated. These were not only used in kitchens but were, according to the descriptions, also used in living rooms: 'Table or Dining room Filters highly decorative in appearance, combined with perfect filtration in Doulton ware, silicon or figures glazed wares, made in two sizes, 1 gallon or 5 pints … capable of purifying 25 gallons per day.'

It is also interesting to see that many jugs, in pottery, porcelain or glass, and flare-topped vase forms were sold with a funnel-shaped separate top unit which contained the charcoal or other type of water filter. The top container was filled with water and the purified contents then dripped down into the jug where the resulting clean water was ready to use.

Where do the Continental porcelains come in this London dealer's catalogue? Largely, but not exclusively, in the section, headed: 'FINE ART POTTERY. CHINA, LAVA, AND EARTH-ENWARE, CANDELABRA'. The first page in the Art Pottery section comprises a range of Meissen-style floral-encrusted mirrors, usually described as being in the 'old Dresden style' (Plate 33). These ornate, fancy mirrors which were sold in various sizes and styles, with or without arms or branches for the candle holders, were extremely popular over a long period. The large 'old Dresden-style' mirror frame with candle holders was priced at £3 3s 0d, whilst the popular simple oval mirrors were priced at £1 8s 9d to 9/6d according to size and model.

Another page of ornate Dresden-style German porcelain mainly features pairs of the ever-popular candlelabra or comport. The large mirror shown in the middle of the page was thirty inches high, an imposing example, priced at ten guineas. The point was also made that china-framed mirrors can be made in any size. The Continental manufacturers were certainly striving to satisfy their customers. The prices too were seemingly modest. If we take the three fancy ornaments shown at the bottom of the illustration, the figure-supported candlelabra were four guineas the pair, the centrepiece was £2 12s 6d and it was suggested the three units would make a 'very handsome set'. These types of Dresden-styled porcelains are of the type associated

Plate 33. A selection of ornate floral-encrusted Meissen-style mirrors, reproduced from Silber & Fleming's British trade catalogue. The large, central mirror was priced at £3 3s 0d. c.1882.

with Carl Thieme of Potschappel, Richard Eckert of Volkstedt or Alfred Voigt of Sitzendorf (see Chapter 4).

Several other, mainly German, manufacturers made such goods, which sometimes bear mock-Dresden crossed-swords marks. Silber's certainly would not have been the only whole-saler dealing in such fancy articles. They enjoyed a very wide market and would have been made by one of the lesser firms which successfully sought to undersell the Saxon state manufactory. They did this simply by cutting corners and sacrificing quality. They, however, described their goods as being in the popular, prestigious, 'Dresden-style'!

A selection of 'flower pots' or jardinières are almost certainly of French origin. Most seem to have been made in the Limoges district but they are, in my experience, seldom marked. Of course some English firms made such objects in bone china or in earthenware, but these Silber examples will have been produced in French hard-paste porcelain. Like all objects, the quality of the decoration can vary from very good down to almost slapdash, although those here featured seem to have been of rather better than average quality. Such goods were usually sold in pairs but presumably the final buyer could purchase a single example.

The 1872 Silber catalogue lists 'China flower pots, with coloured grounds, painted birds, flowers, &c., 5/6d, 6/6d, 7/6d, 8/6d, 9/6d, 10/6d, 12/6d' up to £3 per pair. Another of the mid 1870s catalogues includes 'China flower pots, with or without handles', with prices ranging between 5/6d and £2 2s 0d per pair.

Many candlesticks are featured, some of the tall pillar-type (called piano candlesticks), others the low, handled, chamber candlesticks with conical extinguishers, used for lighting the way upstairs to bed. Candlelight was at this period in the 1880s still ruling supreme; most towns did not introduce electricity for nearly twenty years.

Apart from the rather utilitarian pillar and chamber candlesticks many others were rather more fancy, having figure-supported bases. Again it was not stated, but most examples featured in this catalogue were likely to be of French origin. In the mid-1870s the flat-type or chamber candlestick decorated in simple bedroom style 'plain band and flowers' ranged from 16/0d to 22/0d per dozen, whereas the larger but simpler to produce tall, pillar variety were priced at 6/6d to 18/0d per dozen. The wholesale nature of the business is underlined by the price list notations. For example the 'China candlestick, with figure of cupid supporting socket; the base is in the form of a leaf decorated in pink or blue. Height about 6½ inches' was dispatched in 'original case of 25 dozen each, cases free, 8/6d per dozen'.

With candlesticks we can mention 'Trinket sets', a standard, useful set of articles usually on a porcelain tray for use on a lady's dressing table. Most are of French origin and some include a pair of pillar candlesticks, with covered boxes, pintrays and sometimes a ring-stand. The cheaper, eight-piece sets without trays were priced between 4/6d and 7/6d the set. Those with a tray ranged from 6/6d up to 32/6d.

Another favourite Continental line was small, toy tea-sets originally sold in cardboard boxes. These have always been popular and our porcelain manufacturers made such sets from at

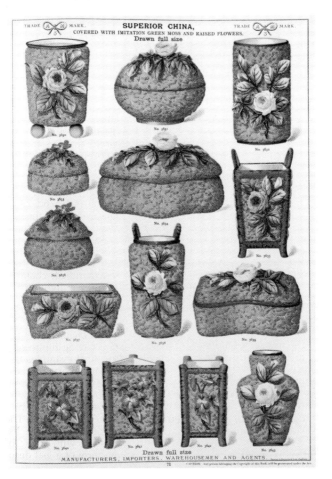

Plate 34. A selection of inexpensive Continental porcelain mock-moss and floral-encrusted trinkets, selling for sale under a shilling apiece. Reproduced from Silber & Fleming's 1882 catalogue.

least the 1760s onwards. The Continental hard-paste porcelain sets of the 1870s and 1880s were quite roughly made and are sparsely decorated to be sold wholesale at various prices from 3/3d to 9/6d per boxed set. Such inexpensive novelties were also included in Silber's 'special selections for Bazaars'.

Small ornamental vases, baskets and pots with a moss-like

ground and raised porcelain flowers were extremely popular at this period, both with British and Continental manufacturers. These are generally unmarked and difficult to attribute. The examples featured in this Silber catalogue and shown in Plate 34 are most probably Continental examples. This belief is strengthened by the fact that the colour-printed page is credited to Pawson & Brailsford of Sheffield rather than to Allbut & Daniel of Hanley who seem to have been responsible for the lithographs of the Staffordshire ceramics. These floral encrusted pieces are rather fun but they are not valuable articles and cannot be considered as collectors' pieces. They were originally very inexpensive – the small vases shown at the top of the Plate were priced at 8/6d per dozen.

The prices for ornamental vases varied greatly; prices given in the unillustrated 1876–7 catalogue show the range of vases then available, ranging wholesale from 7d to £25 per pair.

Another page of decorative objects, helpfully headed 'French China Vases', is shown in the 1885 catalogue. This page is not reproduced in colour, but many of these vases must have been very attractive, most would have been enhanced with gilding; indeed this is made clear in the descriptions – 'rich broad gold lace border', 'heavily gilt handles and gilt lines' or 'heavily gilt border and handles, maroon and gilt foot'. These vases were probably made in or around the French ceramic centre of Limoges but the names of the makers are not given and in my experience these French vases are unlikely to have borne a manufacturer's name or trade mark.

The four vases reproduced at the foot of the 1885 illustration are of earthenware, not porcelain. The two outside examples are described as 'Majolica', that is earthenware decorated with tinted glazes. The Silber catalogue includes several pages of British majolica but these popular wares were also produced widely in Europe and these examples were almost certainly French. They were all priced in pairs, from left to right – £1 18s 6d, £2 5s 0d, £1 12s 6d and £5 5s 0d.

The two central vases are described as 'Barbotine'. This term is usually applied to ceramic decoration in slight or high relief. In these cases the flowers and leaves will have been separately modelled and applied to the body of the vase. In the late Victorian period they were very popular being inexpensive and looking to be very good value. Today when most examples are chipped or otherwise damaged and very dirty, we regard them with less enthusiasm!

Several pages of this Silber catalogue include engravings of small, inexpensive novelties, small figures, animals, baskets, covered boxes, vases, etc. These appear under the general heading 'China Ornaments', with notes such as 'When ordering china ornaments, kindly allow us to add the latest novelties for such an amount as you may order … a nice assortment for any shop.

26 gross fill a good package.' These goods were obviously of a very inexpensive nature. The early 1870s Silber catalogue lists: 'China toys 1d articles in whistles, boxes, figures &c., 30 different kinds, 8/8d per gross'. Seemingly such articles were only sold in groups of 144 mixed articles, at about ¾d (three farthings) per article. The larger cats and dogs were priced at 4/- per dozen.

In the catalogue of the late 1879s such goods were still priced at 8/6d for 144 but were now described as: 'China toy figures, assorted subjects, coloured and gilt 8/6d per gross'. Other small ornaments were at the same period described as: 'A large assortment of china animals, birds, figures, decorated in colours and gold', varying in price from 4/- to 60/- per dozen.

Messrs. Silber were also advertising many pairs of seemingly good quality decorative figures, mainly 'in Dresden style'. These hand-painted and usually gold-enriched figures appear to have been of French manufacture and many were probably in unglazed bisque porcelain. A few sample engravings from the catalogue are shown in Plates 35–6. The examples shown in Plate 36 are described as being bisque suggesting that the others were glazed, although the engravings give the impression that these models were decorated bisque of the type that had earlier been produced by the Gille factory, see Chapter 4.

The Silber catalogue of the mid 1870s features similar Continental figures which were sold with thin blown-glass domes and wood stands. The glass domes must have greatly increased the difficulty of transportation, even if their cost was small. The descriptions give the wholesale price range in general terms:

China figures, large, bisque or glazed, complete with shade and stand, 2/3d, 4/6d, 8/6d, 12/6d (up to) 42/- per pair.
Large very fine China do., 21/-, 25/-, 30/-, 42/-, 50/- per pair.
Ditto do. large and very fine 80/-, 100/-, 120/-, 140/-, 160/-, 180/- per pair.

The English (mainly Copeland) undecorated parian figures were rather less expensive, ranging from 3/6d to 100/- per pair. These also were supplied under glass domes and stands. Most of the wood stands were blacked, but slightly more expensive examples were gilt.

The elegant Silber bisque china 'Dresden-style' figures shown in Plate 36 were priced at 27/6d per pair, other attractive figures of children musicians were priced at 8/6d a pair, for seemingly good quality examples.

Some, usually unmarked, French porcelain groups show a family seated around a table playing chess, cards or taking tea. It would seem that these groups were very popular in the 1860–1900 period and are to be found in various qualities and sizes; a typical example is shown in Plate 37. Groups of this type

Plate 35. A selection of coloured china Continental figures in the Dresden style but probably made in France. Featured in Silber & Fleming's trade catalogue of c.1882.

were sold by Silbers in the mid 1870s. The contemporary pricings illustrate how such popular groups or ornaments were available at different prices, depending on the quality of finish and the size of the model: 'China groups with shades and gilt stands, chess-players, whist-players, coffee-drinkers, 3/6d, 4/6d, 5/6d, 6/6d, 7/6d, 10/6d, 13/6d each.' This quotation also

Plate 36. Two pairs of French biscuit (unglazed) decorated porcelain figures in the Dresden style. Such decorative figures were extremely popular. Reproduced from Silber & Fleming's trade catalogue of c.1882.

shows how simple variations on a basic idea, figures seated around a table, can be marketed, each being extremely popular – as well they might be at these prices!

Apart from the colourful Continental figures this London wholesaling firm also stocked a very wide range of parian figures, busts and groups. A two-page listing gives the titles and

Plate 37. A French glazed porcelain group of a popular but inexpensive type. Very broadly in the Dresden style and originally sold with gilt stands and glass shades from 3/6d upwards. c.1870–80. 5 ins high.

sizes of over 600 models. Most of these seem to have been of Copeland's manufacture. It is of interest to note that some models featured in the 1880s were introduced at the time of the 1851 Exhibition! The nude 'Greek Slave' was listed at 10/6d but this and other uncoloured parian models must have appeared quite drab compared with the colourful Continental figures also on offer.

Although this book is concerned with porcelains, not with glass, I must mention that the Silber catalogue contains over sixty pages of late Victorian glass. Ornamental objects as well as table glass, Silbers claiming that their stock of 'coloured and decorated glass ware is by far the largest held in this country'. Some of the illustrated, coloured and hand-painted glassware is truly magnificent and in quality rivals, if not exceeds, most types of porcelain vases. Many of the glass vases were made and sold in sets of three (as Plate 38), with the larger central vase having a cover. Few such complete sets remain intact today and in practice a pair of vases is easier to use or display, than a set of three!

A very few specimens of glassware have been reproduced as I know from experience that such superb semi-opaque glass ware

COLOURED AND DECORATED GLASS.

Plate 38. A selection of popular and decorative Continental coloured glass vases of the type which vied with porcelain examples. Reproduced from Silber & Fleming's 1882 trade catalogue. Set of three vases on bottom line were priced at £1 10s 0d the set.

can be mistaken for china. Apart from the vases, centrepieces, etc., some toilet sets were produced in decorated coloured glass. These articles in particular emulate similar sets made in porcelain and in the case of the less expensive ceramic examples, the glass sets will be decorated in a superior manner.

Time and again in studying these trade catalogues one is reminded that art is international. Not only were we exporting vast quantities of our own goods but we were importing equally large amounts of ceramics and other ware from most manufacturing countries. On other occasions the cost and trouble of exporting or importing was obviated by simply copying the types of ware or styles of design most in demand. In this way some English firms copied popular French or German types – as these Dresden-styled toilet wares, whilst numerous Continental firms sought to emulate traditional English lines – Wedgwood's jasper-ware, for example.

Certainly by the end of the 1880s the average (!) British home would have been embellished with a very mixed selection of pottery, porcelain and glass wares. English, French, German, Italian, Spanish, Danish, Hungarian ceramics. The colourful good value Chinese and Japanese wares featured in the Silber catalogues, would also have been represented, used and enjoyed. This interesting mix is reflected today in most general antiques dealers' shops, in auctions, antiques fairs and markets.

In general these articles were chosen on their decorative merits and on their keen price. For many reasons the imported goods very often undersold the English bone china productions. If prestige names such as Dresden, Sèvres or Vienna were applied, so much the better, the owners enjoyed their treasures all the more. Profits were made, pleasure was given and no great harm had been done!

4

A–Z OF CONTINENTAL PORCELAIN

This section is admittedly not comprehensive, the selection of entries is indeed very personal. It contains brief comments on many aspects of collecting that are not directly concerned with individual factories or types of ceramic. It also contains reference to some types of pottery where I deem these to be of interest or relating to the main theme of this handbook – the types of Continental ceramics available to the collector.

I have included some personal, candid comments, on such subjects as price guides and repairers, and various items of general advice which I hope will be helpful to the non-expert reader. There are brief comments on subjects that may not be treated in other works, but at the same time this alphabetical section certainly does not seek to rival the larger comprehensive encyclopaedias.

ALEXANDRA PORCELAIN WORKS
The entry relates to the wares usually in the Vienna style produced by the above named firm at Turn-Teplitz in Austria. The two printed marks reproduced appear in the English trade magazine *The Pottery Gazette Diary* of 1910, under the London address, 88 Oxford Street.

This was the English address of the large Wahliss showrooms. Ernst Wahliss had purchased the old 'Royal' Vienna moulds and he produced and marketed a later range of Vienna-styled porcelains which were often richly decorated. Porcelains of the type would have the old Vienna shield mark but some more commercial post-1900 products would bear one of the above printed marks. It would be expected that such imports would have ceased in 1914.

ALLEN LOWESTOFT
This wording occurs in handwritten letters on some Continental hard-paste porcelains made in the style of Chinese Export Market porcelain – usually decorated with armorial bearings. This type of 18th-century porcelain used to be erroneously called 'Lowestoft', 'Chinese Lowestoft' or 'Oriental Lowestoft'. Apart from one teapot in the British Museum decorated in a different

style on a Chinese porcelain teapot, this name mark only exists on later French reproductions or fakes.

ANGOULÊME

The Duc d'Angoulême Paris porcelain factory is usually referred to in Britain simply as Angoulême. The output of this Paris factory from April 1781 was large and became well known in England, one type of scattered floral design being termed the Angoulême sprig. John Flight of the Worcester porcelain factory purchased stocks of Angoulême porcelain for sale in his London showrooms in the late 1780s and early 1790s. From this period the Angoulême and other leading makes of Paris porcelain became extremely fashionable.

The factory was established and run by the Dihl & Guérhard partnership, the young Duke of Angoulême (only six years old in 1781) being merely the 'protector' or patron. The first address was in the Rue de Bondy. The original partners were Christophe Dihl (b. 1753) and Antoine Guérhard and his wife. Dihl provided the know-how, the Guérhards the funds. The undoubted success of the venture necessitated the move to much larger premises in 1789. Antoine Guérhard died in 1793 but his widow continued the firm with Dihl, whom she married. By at least the 1820s the firm had lost its place in the market and the partnership was dissolved in 1828 and the factory closed. Dihl died in February 1831, his wife in July 1831.

The Dihl and Guérhard 'Angoulême' porcelains in the 1790–1815 period were superb and were exported far and wide. The painters were highly accomplished, the gilding of the finest, all applied to novel and fashionable forms.

In June 1816 Harry Phillips the well-known London auctioneer sold a large selection of Dihl & Guérhard porcelain 'from the celebrated manufactory embracing several unique and matchless vases, painted by La Coste and de Marne … Several fine enamels on porcelains from celebrated Dutch pictures and an assemblage of fine porcelaine'.

The general standard of these Dihl porcelains was extremely high and some very good prices were obtained. Of the more modest lots it is interesting to see that single tea and coffee pots were being offered. This sale also included a large number of biscuit porcelain figures and groups but at least some of these may have been of Sèvres manufacture. However, the Angoulême factory certainly produced such unglazed porcelains and made good use of biscuit porcelain to contrast with glazed porcelain or ornamental articles, such as: 'An elegant Porte Fleurs, mounted in biscuit figures, richly gilt and pencilled in landscapes'. Other unglazed biscuit items included: 'Four biscuit vases with goats heads and 4 amours. £1 13s 0d; A pair of biscuit turns, of Etruscan shape. £1 5s 0d; A beautiful biscuit group, on a plinth, Instructing the Shepherd. £8 8s 0d'.

At least one contemporary early 19th-century visitor to the Dihl showrooms in Paris stated that the porcelains were far above that of Sèvres! On the evidence of some of these London sale records and surviving examples this was a fair statement. Some good specimens are illustrated in Régine de Plinval de Guillebon's superb book *Paris Porcelain 1770–1850* and some in Michel Bloit's *Trois Siècles de Porcelaine de Paris*. Some British museums include specimens, notably the Victoria & Albert Museum and Apsley House in London.

Most Dihl & Guérhard porcelain bears one of the standard factory marks. The first mark registered in 1781 comprises the initials GA in monogram form with crown above. The monogram was often in an oval frame. The Rue de Bondy address can appear with this mark:

A stencilled, incised or written mark, 'Manufre de Mgr le Duc d'Angoulême à Paris', can also occur in the pre-Revolution period. The incised mark 'Manufacture du Duc d'Angoulême, Paris' can occur on biscuit figures or groups. A simpler post-Revolution partnership mark found applied in stencilled or written form is 'Mre de Dihl et Guérhard, Paris'. On rare occasions the names were reversed, i.e. Guérhard & Dihl.

The single name Dihl can also occur, incised on biscuit porcelain or written on glazed wares.

ANTIQUE FAIRS

In recent years 'antique fairs' have multiplied and one now can pick from very high-class specialist ceramic fairs to such occasions as the magnificent Grosvenor House event, or to a host of smaller provincial fairs. The basic advantage of such events is that a number of dealers – running into hundreds at Olympia or the Birmingham Exhibition Centre, for example – bring their stock to one place, where one can view far more objects than can be seen in several days of travelling around various towns and viewing many individual shops or auctions.

Another advantage is that in most fairs the stocks have been 'vetted' by a panel of 'experts' to ensure that no fakes or reproductions have been included and that the pieces fall within the pre-set and published permitted period of manufacture. However, most fair organizers will include a disclaimer in the official catalogue or guide, pointing out that they are not responsible for the vetting! The system of in-house vetting, where the vetters are drawn from the exhibitors, can lead to problems but in general a vetted fair is safer for the new collector to one that does not boast this protection. At the same time the buyer should be aware that it is the responsibility of the seller to guarantee the goods he sells, and a detailed invoice or receipt should always be obtained.

Whilst the would-be buyer has the advantage of seeing a large group of dealers' stock within one building, he must expect to pay at least a small premium for this convenience. Remember the dealer has to lease an expensive stand, he also has to transport his stock and perhaps live away from his home. If he is wise he will also have taken out special insurance for the period of the fair.

Nevertheless, the antique fairs are extremely popular and tens of thousands of satisfied buyers have purchased interesting pieces at fair prices! Antique fairs come in all shapes and sizes and you must not expect too much of a one-day event in a village hall – although a great bargain may lie within and await the educated eye of a connoisseur. In a like manner the superb London antique fairs may not admit the less expensive late 19th- or 20th-century popular wares of the type featured in parts of this book.

Do, however, check the days and times that a fair is open to the public. Arrive early for the opening on the first day and expect a queue. Try to ensure that you have a ticket which is usually available from the organizer or from an exhibitor. At the large fairs expect to have to leave baggage, holdalls, sticks, etc., in the cloakroom, and ladies' handbags may even be searched.

AR MONOGRAM, see Augustus Rex

ART DECO STYLE
Art Deco is quite different from Art Nouveau, indeed it was probably a major reaction against the curved, rather feminine taste of Art Nouveau. It came to fruition in the mid 1920s and 1930s in the 'Jazz Age'. It was perhaps introduced at the 1925 Paris Exhibition and in England is associated with the chunky rather angular and brightly coloured Clarice Cliff designs.

On the continent the Art Deco style is to be seen more in the earthenwares (including stoneware) than in porcelain. Several French studio-type potters such as Emile Decoeur and other individual decorators worked in the Art Deco style. These individual examples are rarely seen in Britain and the mass-produced popular wares made for export seldom display this taste. A good, well illustrated book on the style is Alain Lesieutre's *The Spirit and Splendour of Art Deco*.

ART NOUVEAU
This style of decoration had its birth in France, as the name suggests. This was reputedly taken from a Paris shop *L'Art Nouveau* which opened in about 1895 and which displayed a new range

of designs in reaction to the ugliness of some industrial designs. Art Nouveau is characterized by sinuous designs and graceful curves derived from plant life.

The effect of the new style quickly made itself felt in a whole range of objects from buildings to posters and postcards. In even these later commercial creations, leading designers and painters were employed as the Art Nouveau movement seems to have heralded a reawakening in good, modern design. In practice, however, the porcelain manufacturers were slow to adapt their designs and shapes to the new fashion.

When one finds good quality Art Nouveau ceramics they are highly desirable; individually designed (not mass-produced) pieces can rightly be expensive now that the style has come back into fashion. However, this return of interest has led to the introduction of modern pieces in this style. To have interest to the collector an Art Nouveau object must be of its correct period c.1895–1910. Most good quality Continental Art Nouveau porcelain or pottery will have a maker's mark, so helping both identification and dating.

Several good, well-illustrated books are available on this style. These include *Sources of Art Nouveau* by Stephen Tschudi Madsen and *The Triumph of Art Nouveau, Paris Exhibition 1900* by Philippe Jullian.

ART POTTERY

We tend to associate 'Art Pottery' of the approximate period 1870–1914 with British potteries, some of which were quite small concerns. It would seem, however, that similar wares were being made on the Continent and indeed wherever earthenwares were being produced. Whilst it is true that most 'Art Potteries' catered for a local market, some of the larger producers may well have exported some examples. Other pieces would have been purchased by travellers to the continent and so found their way back to Britain or other homelands.

In general terms little is known of these smaller manufactories and they are not collected or highly valued outside their own countries or circle of admirers.

AUGUSTUS REX

This term originally related to Augustus II (1670–1733), Elector of Saxony and King of Poland, the patron of the Meissen porcelain manufactory. The name has since been given to a porcelain mark comprising the cursive letters AR joined and rendered in monogram form as shown on the upturned cup in Plate 39.

This monogram mark, which was usually painted in underglaze-blue, occurs on a very early and scarce type of Meissen porcelain. The original AR marked porcelains are usually decorated in the Oriental taste, often in the restrained Japanese Kakiemon style.

Plate 39. Decorative and typical Helena Wolfsohn bird-painted cups and saucer. Underglaze-blue 'AR' or so-called 'Augustus Rex' mark as shown on upturned cup. c.1860–80. (Messrs. Godden of Worthing Ltd)

The same blue monogram mark will, however, be found on quantities of colourful 19th-century German porcelains which have no relationship with Augustus II or with the Meissen factory. Most AR marked porcelains were made or decorated at the Helena Wolfsohn works (est. 1843) c.1860–90, but some other German decorators also used this mark.

The Wolfsohn examples can be of very good quality. They are certainly decorative and enjoyed a very large market. Cups and saucers of the general type shown in Plate 39 are the most commonly found objects but very decorative vases and other forms have versions of traditional Dresden designs. However, note that the AR mark was never used on such colourful patterns at the Meissen factory. On the cups and saucers, as well as other pieces, various ground colours, yellow, red, pink, blue, etc., were used and different subjects adorn the panels (see Wolfsohn below).

William Chaffers, Litchfield and other early writers reproduced the following carefully drawn AR monogram mark as the then modern Wolfsohn device but in reality it is much more clumsily rendered, although being hand-painted, many different renderings may be found.

$$\mathcal{AR}$$

BALDOCK, EDWARD

Edward Holmes Baldock (1777–1845) of Hanway Street, just off Oxford Street, London, first appeared as a dealer in ornamental china in the Post Office London directory of 1806. He continued in business until 1843.

Miss Rosalind Savill of the Wallace Collection writes at length of Baldock and the large class of porcelain that was known as 'Baldock-Sèvres', in her three volume work *Catalogue of Sèvres Porcelain. The Wallace Collection*. Miss Savill wrote: 'Few nineteenth-century collectors avoided acquiring some Baldock-Sèvres unwittingly' and she quotes several examples that are in the famous Wallace Collection. They fooled Victorian collectors and they still catch folk today.

Edward Baldock imported, or otherwise obtained, large quantities of white Sèvres (or similar), porcelain and it is believed that Thomas Martin Randall and Richard Robins (or Robbins) working in London were responsible for most of the Sèvres-style added decoration. However, there is little firm evidence on this partnership which seemingly was only in being between 1813 and *c*.1825. Several other painters were almost certainly also engaged in this trade as undoubtedly were other retailers including Mortlock. Although the Baldock pieces are strictly speaking fakes, they are certainly now antique, having been painted in the 1810–1843 period, often on genuine Sèvres porcelain blanks. The quality of the decoration and gilding is also superb, although not always in keeping with the original styles or with the date indicated by the Sèvres-style mark and its year letter.

Perhaps modern authorities have been too unkind in suggesting that he was responsible for all the redecorated Sèvres porcelain found in old English collections. The bulk of his trading seems to have been in genuine articles. He enjoyed an international trade importing articles from Holland and France. On his retirement this stock was sold by auction on the premises in May and July 1843. Much porcelain was included also glass, furniture, bronzes, tapestries, enamels, marble statuary, clocks, wood carvings, and so on. The porcelains included some hundred lots of Sèvres or Sèvres-style ware, also much Meissen and Berlin porcelain, some Oriental and some English wares – Chelsea, Derby, Worcester and Wedgwood.

Perhaps the term 'Baldock-Sèvres' should be linked with quality and decorative merit rather than be used in a derogatory sense. It is interesting to note that Frederick Litchfield, the author of several standard early 19th-century reference books for collectors, was the son of Baldock's assistant who apparently continued the business after Edward Baldock retired *c*.1843.

BAZAAR GOODS

From about the 1870s and well into the 20th century various manufacturers specialized in mass-produced, low-priced trinkets and ornaments especially for bazaars. Sometimes wholesalers who specialized in such goods would supply them on a sale or return basis. There were various grades of bazaars; some charity-linked special events might cater for slightly up-market goods, selling perhaps for five shillings or more, but in the main the goods were produced to sell for a few pence. Obviously quality had to be cut, and such inexpensive goods, which were normally of German origin, did not bear a maker's mark.

The best known class of porcelain novelties of this type are the so-called Fairings or Early to Bed small novelty groups, see Fairings below.

BEEHIVE MARK
This popular description is often applied to various marks similar to those shown below.

Such marks occur on late 19th- or 20th-century wares, made in the style of the popular Vienna porcelains. However, the true, pre-1864 Vienna mark is a shield; these copyists have incorrectly reversed the device and sometimes turned it into a beehive! In Chapter 1 some of the firms that sought to emulate the very decorative Vienna porcelains are discussed and listed. These copies were often made down to a price and, although often visually attractive, lack quality.

BERLIN PORCELAIN
The first name to be associated with Berlin porcelain is Wilhelm Kasper Wegely, who established the works in the early 1750s but this concern ceased in 1757. Obviously these Wegely Berlin porcelains are now very rare and are seldom seen outside museum collections. Various W marks are recorded.

In 1761 a Prussian financier Johann Gotzkowsky established a new factory at Berlin with the help of former Meissen workpeople. This was sold to Frederick the Great in 1763 so that the Berlin factory became a Royal or a State factory from 1763. Some Gotzkowsky period (1761–3) porcelains bear G initial marks, an initial not confined to these very rare porcelains.

The main period of Berlin porcelain commenced in 1763. The standard factory mark, a sceptre painted in underglaze-blue, occurs from this period and was used with variations well into the 19th century. The German title for the Berlin firm was Königliche Porzellan Manufaktur and the initials KPM were much used in the post-1820 marks. These initials can occur in large cursive form painted in underglaze-blue, often on mid to late 19th-century pieces, but are more often printed, as here shown.

Plate 40. A good quality Berlin porcelain plate showing a typical restraint of decoration. Underglaze-blue sceptre mark. c.1850–70. Diameter 9½ ins. (Messrs. Phillips)

KPM

KPM

In December 1792 on Christmas Eve, Joseph Lygo, the manager of the Derby factory's London shop wrote to William Duesbury in Derby: 'In this box have sent you four small comports of the Burlin [*sic*] China, painted with landscapes which are to be copied upon a pair of Ice pails, which hope you will succeed very well & have likewise sent you a Seave [*Sèvres*] plate …'

The royal factory was a major concern producing very good quality porcelains which were well decorated. Large and useful wares were produced, such as plates or cups and saucers, and these are not all that rare. Good and attractive as they can be, the Berlin porcelains, particularly the 19th-century examples, are not as highly valued as would be a similar Meissen piece. It is probably true to say that the Berlin porcelains are undervalued and neglected.

The shapes and styles of decoration vary greatly from very florid rococo forms to very simple classical shapes and styles of decoration (Plate 40). Many good-looking vase forms were produced and decorated in various styles. Some Berlin forms proved very popular and were produced over a long period.

Decorative as the vases, figures and tablewares may be, the Berlin factory is mainly known for two different types of porcelain slabs. Firstly, we have the 'Berlin Transparencies' or lithophanes which are thin, moulded, unglazed panels usually uncoloured. These panels, which were normally mounted to be viewed against a light-source, spring to light showing an often delightful picture (Plate 77).

The other type of plaques were very finely painted by leading artists, usually copying fine-art paintings in museum collections. These decorative porcelain plaques were made by many firms over a long period but as a class they are termed Berlin (or KPM) plaques. (See the following entry.)

The production of Berlin porcelain continued up to and through the First World War after which the name was changed to Staatliche Porzellan-Manufaktur Berlin under which name it still continues. The factory was destroyed in 1943, but much of the materials had previously been moved to Selb, and production returned to Berlin in the mid 1950s. The KPM crowned globe mark has been continued.

Some Berlin porcelains made from 1901 onwards bear impressed year-letters starting with A and proceeding to Z in 1925. Subsequently Greek letters were used Alpha in 1926 to Omega in 1954. From 1955 capital Roman letters have been used, F in 1960. Like all impressed date-markings these relate to the year of potting, not necessarily that of decoration and sale which can be later. A modern mark is here reproduced:

K P M

Most English-language books on Continental porcelain give at least a résumé of the history of Berlin porcelain. There is also a helpful article 'KPM – Classicism to Empire' by Melitta Kollensperger published in *Collectors Guide* of September 1987. The Berlin Museum is preparing a specialist catalogue of the Berlin porcelains of the 1835–80 period. Modern Berlin porcelains are

Plate 41. OPPOSITE ABOVE *One of a pair of Berlin ornamental condiments or table ornaments, rather in the Meissen style. Blue sceptre and double eagle mark. c.1840–60. 5 ins high. (Messrs. Godden of Worthing Ltd)*

Plate 42. OPPOSITE BELOW *Representative parts of a Berlin dinner and dessert service, closely following in forms and decoration some Meissen services. Blue sceptre and orb and 'KPM' mark printed in red. c.1850–70. Diameter of plates 9¾ ins. (Messrs. Phillips)*

well recorded in Margarete Jarchow's *Berlin Porcelain in the 20th Century*. This German work includes an English-language text.

It must not be thought there was only one Berlin factory, any more than there was only one Paris or London factory. There were, for instance, earthenware potteries in the 17th century, but such early wares are not met with in England. Likewise Karl Ludicke produced earthenwares in Berlin *c*.1756–79.

From about 1853 H. Schomburg & Son produced KPM-styled wares and this concern seems to have linked with the main factory in 1866 but it separated in 1904. Post 1904 marks incorporate the initials BPM for Berliner Porzellan Manufaktur. Other 20th-century Berlin porcelain manufacturers were Vereinigung Deutscher Porzellan Fabrikanten using a VDP mark, also Vereinigte Lausitzer Glaswerke AG with a VLG mark.

An earlier and quite important firm was M. Schuman & Son of Moabit (Berlin) working from *c*.1835 to at least 1850. Various marks include the name Schuman or the initial SPM. Specimens are, however, rarely found in Britain.

BERLIN PLAQUES
In the 19th century some superb paintings were painted on Berlin (KPM) porcelain slabs or plaques. In the main these were copied from oil paintings in the Dresden Gallery and other German museums. The best of these ceramic copies were signed and they were sold and intended to be used as paintings to be framed and hung on the wall. The finest quality Berlin porcelain plaques have in recent years been highly sought after and high prices have been given for the more desirable, attractive subjects.

Plate 43. OPPOSITE *A typically well-painted Berlin porcelain oval plaque. The subject taken from a Raphael original. Impressed sceptre mark with 'KPM'. c.1850–70. 9¾ x 7¾ ins. (Messrs. Phillips)*
Plate 44. ABOVE *A large and important Berlin porcelain plaque painted with the rape of the Sabine women after Rubens. Impressed sceptre and 'KPM' marks. c.1850–60. 22½ x 18 ins. (Messrs. Sotheby's)*

However, not all ceramic plaques are Berlin or of the finest quality, these being always expensive. Especially after about 1870, inferior mass-produced plaques were produced; these can hardly be compared with the finest paintings by leading German ceramic artists. (See also Plaques below and Chapter 7 of *Godden's Guide to European Porcelain*.)

Whilst the Berlin factory made most of the largest and best porcelain plaques, all were not necessarily painted by factory artists. There were many good ceramic painters working independently who purchased the Berlin blanks and painted them on their own account.

BERLIN TRANSPARENCIES, see Lithophanes

BING & GRÖNDAHL, see Copenhagen

BISQUE, BISCUIT
Bisque is the term usually used to describe Continental ceramics (normally porcelain) that were not glazed. The term 'biscuit' can also be applied, meaning a once-fired ceramic body before glazing. English parian ware has a rather similar matt appearance but is more creamy in tone.

Continental bisque occurs at all periods from the mid 18th century to the present day. It can be left in the white or tinted. It can be of very fine quality or more in the nature of mass-produced fairground or bazaar-type trinkets. The subject is vast and is dealt with in greater depth in *Godden's Guide to European Porcelain*, Chapter 8.

The high water mark is reached with the mid 18th-century French bisque figures and groups produced at the royal factory at Sèvres. The original models were sculpted by leading artists, such as Etienne-Maurice Falconet (1716–91) who was appointed Director of Sculpture in 1757. As with other ceramic figures the original models were used to produce moulds in which the various component parts could be produced separately by pressing 'bats' of pliable porcelain into the moulds. These separate pieces,

Plate 45. A typically high quality Gille bisque porcelain figure, the pair turn up to show the raised and tinted monogram 'JG' pad mark. c.1850–70. 8¼ ins. (Messrs. Godden of Worthing Ltd)

Plate 46. An important and high quality French bisque porcelain group. The meticulous decoration including silver as well as gold embellishments. c.1850–70. 12½ ins high. (Messrs. Godden of Worthing Ltd)

the head, hands, body and legs were then carefully assembled and mounted on a base to form a graceful copy of the original. All the mould marks and joints were then 'fettled' or wiped smooth before the piece was submitted to the kiln. In the firing, the figure, the outstretched hands, etc., had to be supported so that the composition held shape, as the whole contracted as it was fired.

The now rare 18th-century Sèvres white biscuit figures and groups can be charming (indeed some are still being copied today) and won universal acclaim. Various factories attempted to rival the Sèvres models, notably the Derby factory, but even in London the French examples were generally preferred.

From about 1780 various Continental factories attempted to produce biscuit groups some of which were very elaborate. The various Paris factories also made very good use of white biscuit porcelain in combination with glazed, coloured or gilt porcelain. These now scarce, Empire-styled wares are of fine quality.

From about 1850 many, mainly French, manufacturers produced well-modelled coloured bisque porcelains. The best of these figure models were produced by Jean Gille, who exhibited at the 1851 Exhibition. These Gille models (Plate 45) usually bear a raised oval initial pad mark, as shown below:

The fashion for white unglazed figures continued through most of the 19th century, as is evidenced in England by the large numbers of white biscuit figures, busts, etc., which were made by the Minton factory to name but one. After the introduction of the parian body in the early 1840s the fashion really took off. At the 1851 Exhibition excellent quality parian figures and other ornaments were exhibited by the following firms: Copeland; Minton & Co.; Wedgwood; Samuel Alcock; T J & J Mayer; Charles Meigh; T & R Boote; Keys & Mountford; Bell & Co. of Glasgow; and John Rose & Co. of Coalport. Minton was by this time experimenting with coloured and slightly gilt parian figures but in general the British firms did not favour this ornamented unglazed parian. They did, however, excel in using the white (or slightly tinted) parian in attractive contrast with glazed and decorated porcelain, rather as leading Paris manufacturers had so successfully done in the 1800–20 period.

Many other French and German manufacturers produced similar, coloured and sometimes gilt bisque porcelains in the 1850–80 period. One such firm was Vion & Baury who succeeded Gille *c*.1868 and used a VB monogram mark or a printed anchor device:

The Victorian bisque porcelains can be extremely decorative and charming. The best are deservedly costly, but from about 1880 the coloured bisque was mainly used to mass-produce cheap wares made down to a price. These later, almost fairground-type, products were slip-cast (by pouring liquid porcelain slip into the moulds) and are consequently much lighter than the earlier press-moulded types. Less care was taken in 'fettling' the seams and in general the modelling is not as fine or sharp as the earlier products. Some of these later examples can have a charm and may well be antique but they are very, very distant poor relations to the 18th-century models. The post-1880 specimens are seldom marked as they were made by the smaller, little-known, firms. Indeed marks are scarce on all types of bisque porcelain.

BLOCH & CO.

Bernard Bloch of Eichwald in Bohemia produced a wide range of useful and decorative earthenware and porcelain from at least the 1880s well into the 20th century. The Bloch company also had works at Hohenstein, which produced decorative earthenwares.

From about 1882 Bloch & Co. produced a range of copies of the blue Dresden onion pattern design using as a mark the word MEISSEN within an oval outline. The firm also used copies of the Vienna shield shape mark and a crowned capital 'E' device.

B. Bloch took a full page advertisement in *The Pottery Gazette Diary* of 1921. The factories were no longer in Bohemia, but in the new 'Czecho-Slovakia'. The company reported that:

> The factories are now again working and limited quantities of his world-famed 'Corinthian Ware' in the original 1125 colour scheme is the most popular shapes in pots, vases, bowls, jardinieres, fruit-stands and candlesticks are available for his pre-war customers only. Stock assortments of the above will be continually arriving at London, Grimsby, Newcastle, Leith and Bristol, from the end of September onwards. Orders can also be accepted for forward delivery of all shapes and all articles in a variety of colour schemes, a full range of which can be seen at the showrooms of the Anglo-Czecho Agencies Ltd, 55 Farringdon Street, London EC1, where can also be seen a fine selection of beautiful models in figures, groups & pottery from the Hohenstein factory in antique and modern styles and old Japanese bronze effect.

In 1938 the Bloch Company was retitled Eichwalder Porzellan und Ofenfabriken Bloch & Co. In post-war years the town of Eichwald has been renamed Dubi.

BOCH FRÈRES

The 'Keramis' factory at La Louvière (Hainault) in Belgium dates from the early 1840s, although the Boch family had been involved in various ceramic enterprises from the 18th century. Eugène Boch had founded the vast Villeroy & Boch firm.

Boch Frères produced a wide range of earthenwares and stonewares of all types, as well as some porcelains. Much British-styled wares were made, including a whitish 'cream-ware' and printed designs. The firm also produced imitations of antique, Delft-type earthenwares as well as near-Eastern wares.

Lady Schreiber, the great Victorian collector, visited the Boch factory in 1877 and remarked on the blue and white earthenwares produced at this 'large establishment'. She described 'some coarse china, after well-known patterns', by which she may have meant English-styled designs. She also noted that at that period the Bochs did not use any factory marks, a rather surprising observation.

Lady Schreiber also related that at this period in the late 1870s the Bochs produced copies of antique Tournai and Sèvres porcelains. These she noted were not decorated at the Boch factory – a quantity of pure white vases of the old Sèvres forms go to Paris and are there decorated for the dealers and are sold for fine genuine Vieux Sèvres'.

Various printed and impressed marks were employed despite Lady Schreiber's remarks in 1877. These incorporate the initials BF or BFK, the name Boch Frères, or the trade name 'Keramis'.

The firm, now titled MRL Boch SA, was a large and important one in the 19th century. However, these Belgian wares are not particularly sought-after by British collectors.

BOCQUILLON, PAUL

This Paris-based firm represents one of several porcelain manufacturers that produced copies of earlier highly collectable wares. Such wares, which can be of very good quality, are traditionally attributed to Samson of Paris, but he was only the leader of a very large pack.

As they were producing wares in imitation of earlier types, the maker's name does not normally appear on such reproductions as the firms were in general not publishing their activities. However, we know about Paul Bocquillon as he placed an illustrated advertisement in the British journal *The Pottery Gazette* of 1914 (Plate 27).

Bocquillon featured reproductions of various makes of collectable china and earthenware: Lowestoft, Chelsea, Derby, Worcester, Chinese, Sèvres, Meissen (termed 'Saxe' by the French), Moustiers, Chantilly, Rouen and Delft wares. At this period Paul Bocquillon was represented in London by Rene Luce of Hatton Garden, and these hard-paste French copies of English and Continental wares were widely available in this country. Seemingly they bore fashionable fake marks such as the Chelsea anchor in gold, desirable inscriptions such as 'A Trifle from Lowestoft' and often a date, such as '1795' also featured. Typical examples are shown in *Godden's Guide to European Porcelain*.

I cannot say when this firm commenced activities, possibly soon after 1900, but it continued into the 1930s and produced a large quantity of decorative reproductions, which are sometimes mistaken for genuine specimens. Even when offered as reproductions they are usually attributed to the better-known Samson firm – praise indeed.

BOHEMIA

The old Central European country of Bohemia was the home of many pottery and porcelain manufactories, mainly, but not entirely, catering for a middle price market. The name Bohemia can occur as part of several factory marks from about 1880. However, it should not occur after 1918 as Bohemia then became part of the new Republic of Czechoslovakia. Most Bohemian factories continued but in most cases the place-names were changed from German into Czech; for example Pirkenhammer is now Brezewa Plan.

Although small pioneer factories had been set up in the 1790s these were commercially unsuccessful and it was not really until the 1820s that good quality German and Paris-styled Bohemian porcelains started to be produced. These wares could, however, be very decorative if a little clumsy when compared to the products of the leading manufactories. A good range of illustrations of typical Bohemian porcelains is shown in Emanuel Poche's large-format book *Bohemian Porcelain*.

Much Bohemian porcelain is unmarked and can therefore be mistaken for French or German porcelains but the following place and personal names relate to Bohemian wares: ALTROHLAU, CARLSBAD, GIESSHUEBL, HAAS, KNOLL, LIPPERT, PRAG, and TANNAWA. Initial marks include: A, Al, AM, AN, B, BK, CF, DH, FL, F & M, F & R, HK, K, P P & S, R, TK, UD, and VP.

E. BOHNE & SON

Ernst Bohne (& Söhne) was one of many porcelain manufacturers in Rudolstadt Volkstedt in Thuringia. The hard-paste factory was established about 1854.

The porcelain mainly comprised figures, groups, decorative items and novelties. Some Capodimonte-styled wares were

Plate 47. A decorative and amusing yet inexpensive Bohne porcelain ornamental flower-holder or spill container, one of a pair. Blue anchor and 'B' mark with impressed 'EBS' initials, model number 2261. c.1875–90. 5 ins high. (Miss D. Flowers)

Plate 48. A very good quality Bohne porcelain figure, one of a pair. Some of the smaller little-known manufacturers could rise to quite high class productions. Blue anchor and 'B' mark, with impressed 'EBS' initials, model number 3311. c.1880–90. 11¾ ins. (Messrs. Godden of Worthing Ltd)

made and bear the crowned 'N' mark attributed to, but never used by, this Italian factory. (See Capodimonte and Naples below.)

However, most Bohne porcelains bear one of the factory marks which comprise a printed anchor mark (usually in under-glaze-blue) with the initial 'B', or 'EB', alternatively from the late 1890s 'EBS'. The 'B' and 'EB' anchor marks were first registered in 1878 and the earlier pieces may well have been unmarked.

The firm seems to have enjoyed a large export market and their products, mainly of the approximate period 1878–1900, are not uncommon in Britain. Most specimens are of modest size and the original cost was probably quite small. The attractive shoe and cupid ornament or flower holder shown in Plate 47 is typical of the Bohne porcelains; such pieces would have been sold in pairs. Good biscuit figures were also produced.

The value of the Bohne porcelain mainly rests on the decorative quality of each piece and on the desirability of the shape or model.

After 1945 the factory passed to Albert Stahl & Co.

BOXES

One of the Continental specialities was small richly decorated porcelain boxes. Superb examples were made at the Meissen factory in the 18th century but most European factories produced such articles. Sometimes an erotic scene was painted inside the lid or on a second, hidden inner lid (Plate 50).

These small dainty boxes have always been popular and consequently many copies were made in the 19th century. These can be of good quality and great caution should be used in buying such costly trinkets.

BRIGHT GOLD

Bright or liquid gold was introduced on the Continent late in the 19th century. From the manufacturer's point of view the great advantages were that while it looked good, it was cheap (containing very little real gold), was easy to apply and did not need hand-burnishing. It may not even have needed a separate firing, perhaps being fired with the overglaze enamel colours. All these points saved time and money.

However in use it has disadvantages; it is bright and brassy-looking, but is very thin and very prone to wear. It was in the main used only on very inexpensive objects originally sold for pence or shillings, rather than for pounds. It is difficult to describe but can easily be recognized on cheap resort or bazaar-

Plate 49. A superbly modelled yet simple Nymphenburg porcelain figure, showing the skill of Franz Anton Bustelli. Impressed shield-mark. c.1760s. 7½ ins high. (Messrs. Sotheby's)

type goods. Its presence will indicate a post-1880 product made down to a price, generally by a less than first division factory!

BUSTELLI

Franz Anton Bustelli (1723–63) was an extremely talented Swiss-born modeller of ceramic figures. He was appointed chief modeller at the Bavarian Nymphenburg factory in 1754. He produced a series of elegant, lively, models with sharp, well-defined, features. In a word they are a delight.

The 18th-century examples, however, are extremely rare and will be very costly. In many cases his models have remained in production or been reintroduced at various periods. Therefore again I must warn the non-expert reader to be on guard. There are more later editions than 18th-century specimens. The

Plate 50. Two well-painted German porcelain small boxes, one with concealed inner cover painted with erotic scene. c.1760s. 3½ ins long. (Messrs. Phillips)

comparatively modern productions can be regarded as charming decorative figures, but not as antique museum pieces. The Bustelli models are not signed but examples of any period will bear the Nymphenburg shield mark.

CANCELLATION MARKS

Some Continental factories, mainly Meissen and Sèvres used cancellation marks to denote that a previously marked specimen was sub-standard or that it had been sold in the white, undecorated state. In this case it follows that any subsequent decoration was added outside the factory.

Except for the early Hausmalerei decoration (carried out before cancellation marks were employed), examples bearing a cancellation device are obviously not as desirable as a piece of the first-quality, made and decorated within a major factory.

In the case of the Meissen crossed-swords mark one or more nicks are cut with a grinding-wheel across the middle of the device or at either end. A single nick across the centre of the mark indicates merely that the example was sold in an undecorated state. If the piece is still in this state, it is precisely as it left the factory. As a general rule the more nicks (up to four may be found) the more serious the manufacturing fault.

The Sèvres factory seemed only to use a cut cancellation mark on printed 19th-century marks, to indicate that the piece was sold in the white undecorated state.

Another form of cancellation mark comprises a gilt flower or leaf applied on the reverse of a piece to hide or cancel the mark of the manufacturer. These gilt flower marks, which vary considerably, were used by decorators who wished to hide the source of their bought-in blanks. Such marks normally denote a Continental origin and were mainly used from about 1890 onwards. The decorator's mark often appears on the piece.

CAPODIMONTE

Capodimonte or Capo-di-monte was a short-lived Italian porcelain factory near Naples. Its soft-paste porcelains bear little resemblance to the type of articles which are today called 'Capodimonte' (see next entry).

The original factory was established by Charles III of Spain and King of Naples in about 1743, perhaps just pre-dating our Bow and Chelsea factories. The whole concern was, however, transferred to Buen Retiro (Madrid) in 1759. Production there continued until 1808. Typical, but rarely found, examples are illustrated in the late Arthur Lane's book *Italian Porcelain*.

The true Capodimonte mark is a fleur de lis emblem, NOT the crowned 'N' device so often referred to as the Capodimonte mark (see Naples below).

CAPODIMONTE-STYLE

My heading is one of convenience only. No pieces bear this description, nor do the pieces really relate to true Capodimonte but nevertheless the pieces to be discussed are very generally believed to relate to Capodimonte porcelain.

Typically these 19th-century or later wares are relief-moulded with figure subjects (as the caskets shown in Plate 52) often with floral swag border designs. These are really copies of one type of Doccia porcelain. Even this type is not typical of the Doccia factory's output and is hardly featured in the standard books on Italian porcelain.

The huge market in the later objects which usually bear a version of the crowned 'N' mark of the Naples factory (see Naples below) seems to have been built up almost by accident but by the 1870s and 1880s these Italian-styled porcelains were being made at numerous factories including several in Germany. One typically Capodimonte-style cup and saucer is included in the Silber wholesale catalogue of the mid 1880s (see Chapter 3) amid a page of Dresden-styled porcelains which were probably produced at the same factory.

As early as 1856, these reproduction Capodimonte relief-moulded porcelains were being commented upon in England. Henry G. Bohn's lecture on his collection of pottery and porcelain, delivered in July 1856, included the caution: 'Capo di Monte is undoubtedly the most beautiful of Italian porcelain ... Owing to the high prices ... an inundation of forgeries has come in from the neighbourhood of Naples; so that it requires great caution not to be cheated.'

The most commonly found Victorian so-called Capodimonte reproductions are similar to the cup and saucer in Plate 51, which bears the crowned 'N' mark. Most cups have only one handle and are not as tall as this chocolate cup. Various figure subjects occur on the cups moulded in relief but the saucer pattern remains remarkably constant. These cups and saucers must have been made in vast quantities and they, with rarer forms, found a ready market.

Major G. Byng Hall in his amusing book *The Bric-a-Brac Hunter* (1868) remarked on these wares: 'a modern piece of china is of the last century – a cup known by a connoisseur to have issued but yesterday ... a piece of Ginori ... is always converted and guaranteed by oath, for Capodimoni [*sic*].'

At a slightly later period Frederick Litchfield the London dealer was reporting on these reissues in his little book *Pottery and Porcelain, A Guide to Collectors*:

> Of the modern Italian School of ceramics, perhaps the chief is the large manufactory of the Marquis of Ginori ... of the porcelain, the sharpness of the bas relief is inferior to that of the old

Plate 51. A typical relief-moulded Doccia Capodimonte-style cup and saucer of a popular and much copied type. Crowned 'N' mark in underglaze-blue. c.1850–70. Cup 3 ins high. (Messrs. Godden of Worthing Ltd)

Capo di Monti, and the colouring is harsher, but the shapes are excellent and the peculiar kind of twisted handles very pretty.

Very large quantities were produced at the Doccia factory before about 1890. All such pieces are now 'antique' with a decorative merit in their own right and must now have gained at least an element of respectability. At a reasonable price for Victorian decorative porcelain objects they are a fair buy as long as you regard the pieces as Doccia standard designs not as 18th-century Capodimonte!

The question of Capodimonte-style porcelains (and earthenwares) is, however, further complicated by the fact that several German and perhaps French firms have also used the crowned 'N' mark sometimes on relief-moulded Capodimonte-style (Doccia) porcelains and more strangely, on a range of figures, groups and other pieces that seem to have no relation to Capodimonte, to Doccia or to any Italian factory or model. It can even occur on copies of Derby or Chelsea models! The only link is the re-use or faking of the old Naples crowned 'N' mark.

The name Capodimonte seems to have been given, or acquired, near magic qualities. In post-war years it has been very freely used to describe some very well and intricately modelled figures and groups often in biscuit (unglazed) porcelain. These very Italian and often charming models appear to have been produced by more than one firm but all seem to have been marketed on the strength of a Capodimonte association.

CARLSBAD

Carlsbad in Bohemia was one of the centres for the manufacture of low to middle price late 19th-century porcelains. Several British wholesalers' advertisements mentioned Carlsbad wares.

The district included several firms with a large output, such as Springer & Co. of Elbogen and Fischer & Mieg of Pirkenhammer. After the First World War several of these firms formed associations to advertise and market their wares jointly, known as EPIAG and OPIAG. These descriptions or initials can occur in several post-1918 marks, as can the name Carlsbad or Karlsbad. As a general rule such articles are not of great age or of fine quality.

CASKETS

Porcelain caskets or decorative boxes were a speciality of the Continental manufacturers, mainly in the 19th century. They are to be differentiated from the usually earlier snuff or patch-type boxes which are much smaller. Many large caskets were decorated in the Dresden or Sèvres style or are copies of Capodimonte-type designs, as the examples here illustrated in Plate 52.

Such boxes, although they may not have been manufactured at the factory suggested by the design or by the mark, have a

Plate 52. A selection of Doccia Capodimonte-style relief-moulded caskets. Crowned 'N' mark in underglaze-blue. c.1860–80. 8¼ to 10¼ ins long. (Messrs. Sotheby's)

decorative value. This can be considerable but is guided by the size of the casket and the quality of the decoration.

CHANTILLY

This French 18th-century manufactory is one of the relatively few Continental factories to have produced soft-paste porcelain. It was established about 1725 under the protection of Louis-Henri de Bourbon, Prince de Conde, a collector of Japanese porcelains. Much of the now rare and costly pre-1750 Chantilly porcelain is Japanese (or Oriental) in inspiration (Plate 53), but they are quite different from their Oriental prototypes. The most important difference is that the Chantilly glaze was whitened with tin-oxide, it was nearly opaque, more like a faience or Delft glaze than the glass-like covering usually applied to porcelains. At the same time it felt warm and pleasing to the touch and helped to give the enamel decoration an added freshness. Most, but not all, pre-1750 Chantilly porcelains were tablewares, mainly teawares.

The standard factory mark is a curled hunting-horn device painted in red (or blue) enamel on enamelled wares and in underglaze-blue on blue and white porcelains. This mark, which was used up to about 1800, varies greatly as it was hand-painted. The place-name 'Chantilly' can also occur with the hunting-horn mark:

The mark was copied in the 19th century and occurs on many fakes and reproductions. It can also occasionally appear on Worcester blue and white porcelain of the 1770–90 period.

The standard Chantilly blue and white porcelains were

Plate 53. An early Chantilly soft-paste porcelain mug enamelled in the fashionable Japanese Kakiemon style. c.1740–50. 7¼ ins high. (Messrs. Phillips)

extremely popular and filled a great need. Whilst in England the blue-painted porcelains were mainly painted with mock-Chinese designs, the Chantilly porcelains were in the main painted with simple, internationally favoured, floral and grass-like motifs, of the type that could be painted rapidly by semi-skilled hands. One of the great attractions of such useful wares was the good potting of tasteful shapes.

Another type of simple Chantilly floral decoration which is firmly associated with this factory, and was widely copied by English porcelain manufacturers, are the enamelled (overglaze) coloured (not blue) floral sprigs or small sprays of cornflower-type flowers. Such motifs scattered over the surface of the porcelain were known as 'Chantilly Sprigs'. These French floral-painted porcelains were mass-produced and genuine 18th-century specimens still do not command high prices. English collectors will in most cases prefer the rarer English copies!

In 1792 the Englishman (and Paris porcelain manufacturer) Christopher Potter purchased the Chantilly factory and continued it until about 1800, after which it was closed. A second porcelain manufactory was, however, established at Chantilly in 1803 by M. Pigorny. He was succeeded by the Bougon & Chalot partnership (using 'B & C' initial marks) in the period c.1818–45. From 1845 to c.1870 the second Chantilly factory was owned by M. Aaron and his son, who sometimes used the 'MA' initial mark. The mainly useful porcelains produced at this factory can bear the old hunting-horn or the place-name 'Chantilly' apart from the initials 'P, B & C' or 'MA', according to the period of manufacture.

CHINOISERIE
The Western term given to ceramics and other objects decorated in the Chinese style, usually with mock-Chinese figures and landscapes. The European painters and designers had no direct knowledge of such things but invented new designs loosely based on Oriental porcelains, wallpapers, etc., imported from the East.

True Chinoiserie is confined to 18th- (and rarely to early 19th) century designs such as were produced at Meissen and some French factories. The style is, however, more commonly found on early English porcelains.

CLIGNANCOURT, see Monsieur Porcelains

COBURG
In the late 19th-century, advertisements for the cheaper type of porcelains featured in the British trade journal *The Pottery Gazette Diary* there are several references to Coburg porcelains. These German porcelains seem to have been well-known, at least to the trade buyers and sellers but the manufacturers' name was not quoted.

The leading Coburg porcelain manufacturer was Albert Riemann. The working period for this firm was c.1860–1937. The recorded marks relate to the post-1910 period and include the initials or monogram AR, with or without the initial C or the full name Coburg.

It seems that during the period 1860–1910 the Albert Riemann porcelains were either unmarked or bore one of several misleading devices in the hope that they would be mistaken for more fashionable wares. I have elsewhere suggested that the host of AR marked Dresden-style porcelains attributed to the decorating studio of Helena Wolfsohn may well have been manufactured at Albert Riemann's Coburg factory.

A later Coburg manufacturer was Ferdinand Kaule, with the approximate working period 1885–1900. His only recorded mark incorporates his name and town. Lastly we have the 20th-century firm of E. Speiser.

COFFEE SERVICES
While tea was the main drink in Britain during the 18th and 19th centuries, coffee and chocolate were still fashionable and the

London Coffee Houses were the original clubs and centres of trade. It follows that coffee pots and coffee cups or straight-sided 'coffee cans' were made by British manufacturers. Although more were made on the Continent where coffee was the main beverage, Continental coffee services tended not to be exported to England because our own manufacturers catered well for most buyers' requirements.

Services comprising a coffee pot and coffee cups without a teapot or tea cups are, however, likely to be of Continental

Plate 54. A typically good quality Angoulême Paris porcelain coffee can and saucer. Stencilled name mark. c.1805–15. Can 2¾ ins high. (Messrs. Godden of Worthing Ltd)

manufacture if they can be dated before about 1880. After that period one finds British after-dinner, small coffee-sets but still most true coffee services will be of hard-paste Continental porcelain.

In general terms the Continental coffee cups will be larger than the British counterparts. Our coffee cups or coffee cans are often of stupidly small size contrasting with the larger capacity German or French examples. Again, in general terms the British coffee pots (which are quite rare) have a long curved spout whereas the Continental examples often have a pouring lip. They look more like a covered jug. The Continental pots both for tea and coffee are more likely to have locking lugs added to the cover, which fit into and under the rim of the pot.

The most reliable method of identification remains the type of porcelain, hard-paste for the European examples, soft-paste or bone-china for the British. However, in the case of the more ordinary coffee wares bearing standard forms of decoration, the

Plate 55. A superb quality Vienna porcelain coffee service on tray, with typical rich gilding. Note the tall narrow coffee cups and the elegant tall-coffee pot and, of course, the absence of a tea canister. c.1805. Tray 16½ ins long. (Messrs. Sotheby's, Sussex)

mark will give a reliable indication of the source of manufacture. The exceptions are, as always, the Dresden and Sèvres marks which should be treated with caution.

The standard books on Continental ceramics listed in the Bibliography, will give illustrations of typical products and details of the manufactory and the marks. See also the general guide to dating in Chapter 5.

CONTA & BOEHME

This partnership at Possneck in Saxony is not listed in most books on antique Continental porcelains but it was a leading manufacturer of the cheaper types of ornamental wares exported in vast quantities to Britain, the USA and many other countries. The firm claims to have been established in 1790. They certainly exhibited at the 1851 Exhibition in Hyde Park and at this time had an English agent, J. Kendall of 8 Harp Lane, Great Tower Street, London.

The Conta & Boehme mark which was normally impressed, not printed, is of small size and comprises a raised arm holding a dagger all within a shield-shape outline. This mark, which may not have been used before 1850, is often accompanied by impressed model numbers. These had climbed into several thousands by the end of the century.

Plate 56. A selection of inexpensive Conta & Boehme German porcelain small figures. Impressed shield-mark, with impressed model numbers 3532 (centre) and 8031. c.1870–90. 5 and 7¼ ins high. (John Morris)

The firm's great speciality after about 1860 was what they called 'Bazaar Goods in all price ranges' and what has more recently been called 'Fairings'. The best known of these are the small size often humorous and risqué groups depicting titled domestic scenes, such as: 'The last in bed to put out the light'; 'Kiss me quick' or 'Married for money'.

These little moulded porcelain groups on average measuring only about four inches long and three inches high were extremely popular on account of their low cost and humorous nature. They are aptly described as Bazaar goods, for this was the middle or lower-class market at which they were angled. In their way, however, they are more interesting as social documents than the much more expensive Dresden-type groups of 18th-century style shepherdesses, etc. These Fairings were goods for the maids and servants rather than for their employers.

The earliest groups are noticeably heavier than the late 19th-century examples and have a better finish; they do not bear a factory mark or even a model number. Slightly later groups from the Conta & Boehme factory had the model number incised by hand before the porcelain body received its first firing. By about 1870 the demand for this type of inexpensive group necessitated mass-production methods. The model numbers were now impressed by a seal-type instrument, the weight of the articles is not as great, or the quality as good as those of the pieces made previously, while the gilding, if still present, is very thin and brassy, as is all German 'bright-gold' introduced at this period. From about 1890 the shield mark may be printed on the glaze and the word 'Germany' appears. In the 20th century the fuller description 'Made in Germany' was used.

The small bedroom type groups bear incised or impressed model numbers in two series, the first from 2850 to 2899, the second from 3301 to the 3380s, and several collectors have gathered together a large proportion of the known models. Other porcelains from this factory bear other series of model numbers. Many subjects depict themes of courting, marriage or parenthood; several groups have children and animals, while others include mirrors, either for their own sake or to suggest water. The amusing nature of most groups is underlined by the painted title on the front of the base.

Many of these groups were intended for use as match holders and strikers; a hollow container is worked into the design and the back or underside of the base is roughened to provide a striking surface. Others are in the form of boxes (Plate 57), the covers often being roughened and indicating that most of these two piece boxes were again match holders and strikers. Watch holders and candlesticks were also made.

These groups of German manufacture were sent to many parts of the world; indeed, Conta & Boehme claimed that their products were exported to all countries. Some examples have French titles, others German; reports from America show that

Plate 57. A pair of inexpensive German porcelain bazaar-type covered trinket boxes of the type originally sold for pence. Impressed Conta & Boehme shield-mark and model number 3575. c.1880–1900. 4½ ins high. (Mrs P. A. Wall)

the groups are widely dispersed in old homes, in villages and small towns. The firm showed their products at the Melbourne exhibition of 1880, a fact that underlines the extent of their export markets.

The Conta & Boehme porcelains included many larger more ornate articles. In the 1900s the partnership was advertising jardinières, mirrors, candelabra, figures, animal models, ashtrays, bowls, tobacco boxes and similar decorative 'luxury and fancy' objects, even china dolls' heads – a favourite German line.

The Conta & Boehme porcelains are still usually modestly priced but they can have a great charm. They are typical of the less expensive German export range of decorative porcelains and they bear a clear factory mark.

Owing to an error in attributing the shield-shape mark to Springer & Oppenheimer of Elbogen, these Conta & Boehme porcelains, particularly the humorous 'Early to Bed' type of small groups are sometimes incorrectly attributed to Springer & Co. or are simply called 'Elbogen'. Such descriptions are incorrect. (See also Fairings below.)

COPENHAGEN

The Danish Copenhagen porcelains are well known in Great Britain and the Royal factory had a showroom in New Bond Street from 1897; prior to that, the wares were available at The Danish House in Regent Street.

The original factory was established in 1775, although Louis Fournier had apparently produced a small quantity of soft-paste porcelain at Copenhagen in the period 1760–65. The main, hard-paste factory was started by Frantz Müller but in 1779 this pottery passed to the Danish Royal family, giving rise to 'The Royal Copenhagen Porcelain Manufactory' which still continues. However, the factory was sold to A. Falck in 1867, together with the right to continue the old title. The basic and famous factory mark of three wavy horizontal lines in underglaze-blue symbolizes Denmark's three great waterways – the Sound, the Great Belt, and the Little Belt.

This three-line mark was used without addition up to the 1880s, that is for over 100 years. Most pieces found today will be post-1840.

One of the most popular Copenhagen patterns comprises the underglaze-blue, formal, floral pattern divided into four compartments in the Oriental style. This was normally painted on fluted tableware shapes and may be said to have a timeless charm. It is variously called 'Blue fluted' or 'Design number one'.

In the early 1880s Philip Schou purchased the factory from Falck. In 1884 Schou moved the undertaking to the Smallegade quarter of Copenhagen where he had owned an earthenware factory since 1868. The new combined works were enlarged and modernized. Importantly, Arnold Krog was appointed Art Director of the new concern.

From this time, the new modern period of Copenhagen porcelain was born. New-style, freehand underglaze paintings done in range of high-temperature colours were painted on simple, usually handle-less, vase forms or bowls and were signed by the artist. These Royal Copenhagen porcelains breathed fresh air into ceramic design of the period, being quite different from the usually fussy styles favoured by other manufacturers.

In the 20th century the Copenhagen porcelains won many medals in various exhibitions and the wares were available from the better-class china retailers and in some art shops. Apart from the now traditional Royal Copenhagen painted designs, the factory experimented with and reproduced several Oriental-style glaze-effects and the so-called Craquelé porcelain, in which the surface on the glaze is broken up with fine cracks, this 'design' often being accentuated with colour.

The subdued pastel-like underglaze colours were also used on figures, groups and very many animal models. The production of these types continued for many years. The figures were, of course, moulded and mass-produced.

From c.1889 the old three-wave mark in underglaze-blue was amended; the words Royal Copenhagen with a crown were added within a circle above the three lines. Another overglaze circular mark was also used from about this period, comprising the crown above the wares with the country 'Denmark' below. Several printed marks were introduced in the 1890s and have been used subsequently but the three-wave mark normally appears in underglaze blue. A selection of these are reproduced below:

In addition, figures, groups and similar forms will bear an impressed, incised or painted model of shape number. One should also find painters' initials or other personal marks.

A good range of earthenwares and stonewares was also made by the sister factory with the English title 'The Faience

Manufactory Aluminia' which was established in 1868 and merged with the Royal Copenhagen factory in 1885. This branch also employed leading designers and artists. The standard marks are here reproduced. The country name 'Denmark' also appears with 20th-century marks.

Another major porcelain factory in Copenhagen was owned by Messrs. Bing & Gröndahl, having been established by the Bing brothers (local retailers) in the 1850s. The original partner was F. Gröndahl, a modeller from the Royal factory. Around the turn of the century Bing & Gröndahl products were attracting considerable notice in exhibitions.

Although these porcelains and stonewares display a typical Danish air, with clean lines and landscapes, etc., painted in pastel tones, they appear to the writer to be rather too close to the Royal Copenhagen products. The 20th-century wares are of very good quality and are very decorative. The two major Copenhagen firms were combined in January 1987 and now trade as Royal Copenhagen Ltd.

The basic Bing & Gröndahl printed mark is here reproduced:

CROWN DRESDEN
Crown Dresden is a self-explanatory term used to describe several types of showy German porcelains which bear painted marks comprising the word 'Dresden' under a crown device, in the period *c*.1880–1914.

These marks did not infringe the rights of the State factory, although the mark and the style of the pieces suggested to some buyers that they were purchasing true Meissen porcelain. Many owners still harbour this belief. The porcelains may have been made, or decorated, within the boundaries of the City of Dresden but their relationship to the products of the main factory is very distant! They can be of good quality – although this is very variable. They can also be very decorative, especially the pierced-edged dessert services. The floral printed dish shown in Plate 58 is of this 'Crown Dresden' type.

Although British dealers tend to attribute all 'Crown Dresden' decorative porcelains to Helena Wolfsohn, the Continental authorities more correctly attribute this mark to lesser-known

Plate 58. A German porcelain Dresden-style floral dish of a popular general type, now termed 'Crown Dresden'. Painted 'Dresden' mark. c.1870–90. Diameter 9¼ ins. (E. H. Lockyer)

manufacturers and decorators. These include Adolf Hamann; Donath & Co., Karl Klemm and Oswald Lorenz. The reader is referred to Chapter 3 of *Godden's Guide to European Porcelain*.

DAGOTY (DAGOTY & HONORÉ)

The Dagoty porcelain works was to become one of the most famous of the classic Paris manufactories. The three Dagoty brothers, who had been trained under Dihl & Guérhard, were Pierre Louis (1771–1840); Jean-Baptiste Etienne and Isidore. In about 1799 the brothers purchased Roger's porcelain works in the Rue de Chevreuse. The Dagoty firm prospered and produced a very varied and rich assortment of goods.

On 1 January 1816 the Dagotys formed a partnership with Edouard Honoré who by this time owned two factories, one in the Petite Rue Neuve Saint-Gilles, the other at St-Yrieix near Limoges. The partnership was dissolved exactly four years later, after which Edouard Honoré continued on his own account as did Pierre Dagoty.

Several Dagoty & Honoré shape and design books of the approximate period 1816–20 have been preserved in the library of the Musée des Arts Décoratifs in Paris. Some of these, including ornate cup forms and styles of decoration and novel inkstand models are illustrated in Régine de Plinval de Guillebon's standard work *Paris Porcelain 1770–1850*.

In July 1814 Harry Phillips, the London auctioneer held an eight-day sale of Sèvres and Dagoty porcelain. In *Godden's Guide to European Porcelain* I have quoted at length from this catalogue. These descriptions give a good indication of the type of Paris porcelain then being made by Dagoty. The descriptions in some cases give the name of the top artists employed by this manufacturer. I quote a few typical 1814 descriptions here:

A dessert service enamelled in imitation of Etruscan ware at Malmaison, gilt border, contents – 24 plates, a pair of Etruscan-shaped ice-pails, 2 ditto sugar urns and covers, 8 compotiers (four are on pedestals).
Total of pieces 40. 52 guineas.
A magnificent dessert service, richly gilt and embellished, containing two ice pails, liners and covers, two sugar urns and covers, two cream bowls, twelve shaped compotiers and twenty four plates, a two-tier corbeille, borne by bisquit figures.
£120 15s 0d.
An extensive costly and superlatively elegant dessert service richly and tastefully gilt and exquisitely enamelled in landscapes, marine views and fanciful decorations, comprising pair of ice or custard trays with urns to each, two sugar urns and covers, 2 ice pails, covers and liners, eight compotiers, 2 corbeilles or fruit baskets, on bisquit figures and 24 plates.
£132 6s 0d.
A singularly elegant Breakfast Service elaborately enamelled in sporting subjects of Hunting, Shooting and Coursing, contents 14 shaped basins and saucers, cream ewer and bowl.
£26 15s 0d.

The more fancy and elaborate Dagoty porcelain of the period included the following lots:

A superb dejeune with plateaux, jet ground, richly gilt and enamelled in birds, fruit &c. Contents tea, sugar and cream pots, 2 cups and stands.
£6 12s 0d.
A singularly elegant flower case on feet and plinth embellished with peculiar taste in groups of figures, festoons of flowers and antique devices in bronze and gold pencilling, executed in a masterly style.
Unsold £11 0s 6d.
A pair of large porcelain cases for environing flower pots, enamelled in romantic scenery with goats, sheep, &c. by Hue.
£6 15s 0d.

Various painted, printed stencilled marks include the name DAGOTY. These name marks relate to the 1804–15 period.

Several other marks record the partnership between P. L. Dagoty and Edouard Honoré and these devices include the joint names. These marks were used in the 1816–20 period, after which Honoré continued under his own name. Dagoty porcelains are always of good quality. They are now quite scarce and deservedly may be rather costly.

DAMAGE

It is difficult to give helpful advice on damage as it affects the desirability and value of Continental ceramics. The difficulty is that there are degrees of damage and so many different types of Continental pottery and porcelain.

In general, damage to 18th-century European porcelains affects the saleability and value to a greater extent than it affects British wares. For – again a generality – Continental collectors are very discriminating and being relatively wealthy, can disregard second-best or damaged specimens. This is not to say that minor damage to perhaps the applied flowers or leaves on a Dresden figure or group, will greatly affect its value. Slight faults to a very rare specimen will always be overlooked by most true collectors. With later pieces which might be purchased mainly for their decorative merit, some non-disfiguring damage may be acceptable particularly if the purchasing price has taken any faults into account!

There is a difference between what I term true collectors who are interested mainly in the piece for its beauty or interest and what might be called investment-collectors, who are concerned mainly with monetary profit. Those seeking a reasonably safe investment will (or should) shun damaged pieces and seek the best specimen available.

Damage over the years to fragile old porcelain can affect a high proportion of specimens. David Battie, one of the experts on the BBC's *Antiques Roadshow* has written, 'I would guess that under 5 per cent of all objects brought into Antiques Roadshows could be considered in perfect condition.' If this is correct, more than 95 per cent was faulty to some degree! (See also Repairs.)

DARTE FRÈRES

Joseph, Louis and Jean Darte formed a partnership in the mid 1790s to buy an existing porcelain works in the Rue de Charonne, but from 1804 the brothers owned two distinct factories. Joseph Darte had a shop in the Rue Saint Honoré and took over Maurice Dassier's porcelain works in the Rue de Popincourt up to *c.*1823. The two younger brothers Louis Joseph and Jean François Darte set up their own factory in the Rue de la Roquette, trading under the style Darte Frères from 1808. In 1824 Louis's now married son Auguste was taken into the partner-

Plate 59. A Darte Frères covered sugar bowl from a Paris porcelain coffee service painted with animals in landscapes. Red stencilled name-mark. c.1820–30. 6½ ins high. (Messrs. Godden of Worthing Ltd)

ship but this was soon dissolved. Louis was declared bankrupt in 1828 but he continued for at least a further five years. He died in 1843.

In the approximate period 1810–20 the Darte brothers produced a wide range of very high quality decorative Paris porcelain, much of which was exported. By 1810 they were employing 150 persons.

A good idea of the quality and scope of the Darte porcelains can be gauged from a consignment sold by Mr Christie in London in April 1815. The sale catalogue was headed:

A Catalogue of a truly elegant and splendid assemblage of Fine French Porcelain of the celebrated manufactory of Messieurs Darte Frères, comprising Extensive Table and Dessert Services painted with Ornithological and Botanical Subjects and of Barbeaux and other patterns. Sumptuous vases for flowers & Essence, déjeunes, tea and coffee equipages; a chimney piece of porcelain, ornaments for desserts, of beautiful devices.

This sale included lots such as:

A table [dinner] service, corn flower pattern, consisting of 1 soup tureen and cover, 6 round and 6 oval dishes, 1 square ditto, 2 casseroles and covers, 1 sauceboat and stand, 2 butter ditto, 4 radish dishes, 2 salt sellars and 36 plates.

A dessert service, Barbeau pattern, consisting of 2 ice pails, 12 compotiers, 2 baskets and a plateau, 2 fruit and 2 cream bowls, 2 custard standards and 12 custard cups, 2 sugar dishes, 2 salad bowls and 30 plates.

A pair of magnificent vases of Medici shape, 21 inches high, painted with historical subjects after A. Kauffman and on the reverse with Flemish Festivals after the paintings of Teniers, in very superior style of execution, the ornaments pencilled on richly burnished ground.

The standard Darte mark was the written or stencilled name 'Darte Frères' sometimes with the address of the retail shop at 21 Palais Royal. However, several variations may be found such as: Darte, Darte F, Darte Frères à Paris.

The brothers occupied various addresses which can be incorporated in rare marks. These mainly retail addresses, in date order, were:

Rue de Charonne	*c.*1795–1804
Palais du Tribunat	*c.*1804
Rue de la Roquette	to 1828
Rue Viviene	
Faubourg Poissonnière	to *c.*1833
Rue des Vinaigriers	

All these marks pre-date 1833. It is believed that the Darte brothers also decorated or at least marked and resold some porcelains made by other firms, such as Nast.

DÉJEUNER

This French word which is found spelt in various ways in old accounts describes one of the most delightful of ceramic objects. In essence it comprises a small tea set on a tray, in fact they are usually decorated in a very costly manner and often reflect the glories to which ceramic designers and decorators can aspire. Apart from tea sets, some were for coffee and other rarer types were for hot chocolate.

The leading 18th- and early 19th-century porcelain manufacturers all produced such trayed sets. They are rarely found in a complete or perfect state today and being originally costly objects, were never mass-produced, being more in the way of individual sets.

Several good examples with contemporary sale-catalogue descriptions are given in *Godden's Guide to European Porcelain*. It is impossible to describe typical sets in this book, as they vary so much. In general, however, the earlier tea sets comprise the tray, on which sat a small teapot and cover, a small milk or cream jug, a small sugar bowl and cover and two cups and saucers. The main units were of small size as the sets were mainly (but not invariably) intended to be used by two persons; waste bowls

Plate 60. A French hard-paste porcelain floral-painted part dessert service with armorial bearing in the borders. Painted Paris retailer's mark. c.1865–75. Diameter of plates 8¾ ins. (Messrs. Sotheby's, New York)

were seldom included. In coffee or chocolate sets tall pots replaced the generally globular teapots.

The mid to late 19th-century Tête à Tête sets also on trays were probably descended from the earlier Déjeuners but being mass-produced commercial lines the descent was very great!

DESSERT SERVICES

Every major, and most minor, 18th-century porcelain factory produced dessert services. These could be finely decorated for they were prestige goods made mainly for the wealthy. Today few survive intact and most sets have been divided up. Still an old Meissen or Sèvres dessert plate can be very desirable and costly, as can the fewer dessert dishes and the rare centrepieces.

In the approximate period 1800–20, the Paris manufacturers in particular produced sumptuous services. Many were exported to Britain and other overseas markets at the time, for the French porcelains were exceedingly fashionable. Some magnificent examples can be seen at Apsley House by Hyde Park Corner. Other fine Continental dessert services are on display at various stately homes, and sets or part sets turn up at the major London auction houses on a fairly regular basis. This is not to say they are common and they certainly are not cheap but they can be quite magnificent.

Sliding down the social scale, the various porcelain manufacturers at Limoges in France from about 1875 produced a large number of hard-paste dessert services for overseas markets. These can be very decorative but many bear printed decorations or printed outline patterns coloured in by hand. Many are rather subdued in colour. They were very popular and probably undersold our own bone china dessert services – at least those from our leading manufacturers. Many French and German dessert wares are featured in the various Silber & Fleming catalogues (see Chapter 3). Then as now, they represented good value for money, but they and the odd units from such late Victorian services are rarely of interest to a collector of antique porcelain.

Nevertheless, if you are seeking a decent dessert service to use on the table, a 1900-ish Limoges-type set, perhaps by Haviland or a similar leading Continental maker has much to recommend it. The old fashioned dessert services with twelve, eighteen or twenty-four plates and various fruit dishes and footed comports are not made today, at least not to match the quality and charm of the old services.

DINNER SERVICES

As with dessert services, every major 18th-century porcelain and earthenware manufacturer produced a range of large dinner services. Some, such as the state factory at Meissen, specialized and excelled in such sets, modelling special ornate shapes and forms. Many of the relief-moulded Meissen dinner plate designs were copied by British makers because they were decorative and fashionable.

Obviously, few if any, rich special Meissen services exist today but the later, rather plainer services which were produced in large numbers do come on the market from time to time. This is especially true of plates. Any soup plate or meat plate with a diameter of 9½ inches or more was originally part of a dinner service, as was any large platter. The value of a plate depends very much on the factory; on the style of decoration; on the quality of decoration; and on the general condition of the piece. It follows that one cannot lay down hard and fast rules. A Meissen plate of c.1760 could be hard to sell at £25 or a bargain at £250!

Continental 18th-century earthenware dinner services rarely survived in a reasonable state and seldom found their way to Britain, where we had our own manufacturers.

Meissen and other leading makers continued to sell dinner services in Britain in the 19th century but in general our own excellent bone china or earthenware services met the home market demands. Today any good and decorative dinner service will command a very fair price because of the cost of modern sets and the modern manufacturers' inability to match the charm and quality of an old dinner service.

The composition of a dinner service in the period 1760–1840 might have included the following articles:

Pair of ornately shaped soup tureens, covers and stands
Four smaller tureens for sauce, etc.
Ten or twelve circular or oval dishes, ranging in size from about 20 inches down to 8 inches or so
A salad bowl
A fish dish and strainer
Four sauceboats
Four or more salts
48 (to 72) dinner plates
24 soup plates
24 side plates

Some expensive Dresden services may also have sported decorative leaf-shape dishes or perhaps figures and groups with baskets or shells to hold various small sweetmeats, etc., and generally to dress the table.

Although the buyer could purchase just what he fancied to suit his needs and his pocket, any old dinner service would originally have contained twice or three times as many dinner or meat plates as the deep soup plates. The reason for this was that one would only have one soup course but there could well be two or three meat or fish courses necessitating fresh clean plates.

It follows that the large dinner plates unless rather special in some way will not greatly excite a buyer because even 18th-century examples are relatively common. A chip or crack will also greatly affect the price. When one comes to consider the tureens the opposite is the case, they are rare and decorative and in great demand, minor damage is to be expected and will not make the whole unit unsaleable. However, scarcity is not the whole answer for the soup plates, which were made in fewer numbers than the meat plates, are not as popular. The reason for this is that in general they are not as decorative, the deep well seems to detract from the visual appearance of the plate. However keen one is to collect porcelain you usually wish to display your collection and therefore its visual attractiveness is of great importance. Obviously there are a few exceptions to this rule, as when one collects a single object, perhaps pierced strainer dishes, where every variation can be a bonus overriding the visual appeal, but in general a pretty or attractive object will be more saleable than say a heavy-looking lump!

In the 19th century most British families purchased English dinner services often of the durable Ironstone or Stone China bodies. The position changed to some degree after about 1875 when services seem to have been imported in larger quantities.

Simple floral painted Dresden sets were fashionable as was the ever-popular blue onion-pattern design, but apart from these standard types, various French manufacturers in and around Limoges specialized in dinner services. In general these seem to have undersold our major porcelain manufacturers and therefore sold in fair quantities. Some were decorated with transfer printed or lithographic designs to cut cost and, where gilding was included, it tends to be rather thin and prone to wear. Being of hard-paste porcelain too the plates tended to chip and in general they do not seem as pleasant to use as a standard English bone china service.

Unless a post-1875 Continental dinner service is unusually well decorated, attractive and complete it will not be very valuable or desirable from a collector's viewpoint. However, any complete and reasonably perfect old dinner service will command a goodish price, as a modern service can be so costly.

DOCCIA

The Marchese Carlo Ginori established a porcelain factory on his estate at Doccia, Florence in Italy in about 1737 with the help of workpeople from Germany. The Ginori porcelains were very fine of their period and quickly established a wide reputation, but the early pieces made before about 1780 are very rarely found in Britain today. The early marks comprised various painted, gilt or incised star devices.

The Doccia factory remained in the hands of the Ginori family, Carlo's son Lorenzo succeeding his father and from 1791 Lorenzo's son Lepoldo Carlo Ginori until his death in 1837; the Ginori tradition continued into the 20th century.

The Doccia porcelain – softer than most Continental hard-paste porcelains – is often rather grey in colour and can also display tears or other minor manufacturing faults. One type of 18th-century Doccia porcelain is covered with a whitened tin-glaze, to give an improved surface texture and colour. The texture, colour and potting improved in the 19th century but these wares are rare in England and are not generally highly esteemed.

The Ginori family purchased many of the old Capodimonte factory moulds from about 1811 which they continue to use, marking the resulting productions with a crowned 'N'. (See Capodimonte.)

Apart from the porcelains, the Ginori factory in the 19th century produced a very good range of decorative earthenwares. Much of this was in the nature of copies of earlier wares but such pieces were extremely popular at the time and were widely distributed.

DONATH, P.

The Schlesische Porzellanfabrik at Tiefenfurt (in Silesia) was established by Louis Lovinsohn in about 1818. Probably in the 1880s it passed to P. Donath. Donath and presumably Lovinsohn before him had a large international trade in inexpensive novelties and useful wares. Although his products do not generally emulate in style or quality the Dresden porcelains, this Silesian porcelain factory at Tiefenfurt used a mark that can be mistaken for the crossed-swords device and the state factory took action in the 1890s to prohibit its use.

This version of the crossed-swords mark was probably only used *c*.1880–95. After the mark was withdrawn the Donath firm introduced several other marks. One incorporated the name Donath, including the initial 'S' either under a crown or a star-like device.

In about 1916 Donath passed control to Carl Hans Tuppack who traded as Schlesische Porzellanfabrik Tiefenfurt to 1919 and then as the Porzellanfabrik Carl Hans Tuppack. Some marks comprise or incorporate the initials TPM.

DRESDEN

There always has been, still is, and probably always will be confusion of the name or description Dresden as it is applied to porcelains. Dresden is the name commonly used in Britain to describe what should correctly be called 'Meissen' porcelain (see Chapters 1 and 2).

The Meissen factory was the first in Europe to produce fine quality true porcelains on a commercial scale and quickly to establish a national and an international reputation. It was natural that other manufacturers should endeavour to emulate the Meissen or Dresden wares, to copy many of the models, shapes, designs and the standard factory mark – the crossed-swords device. This mark was, of course, the easiest to copy and in the days before copyright or other such protection was very widely copied.

It was also difficult to stop the use of the word 'Dresden' for this was not used as a mark by the Meissen factory, near but not at Dresden. Various small firms and decorating establishments within the city of Dresden could correctly use that designation, to give their products an often unwarranted cachet. In the Staffordshire Potteries we had the Dresden Porcelain Company at Longton. Various other firms, including the great Minton Company, used the word 'Dresden' to describe the popular

Dresden-styled patterns. In the 18th century William Duesbury called his so-English Derby porcelains the 'Second Dresden'!

One useful rule is that the word 'Dresden' will never appear on a Meissen factory product.

HENRY DREYDEL & CO.

This company with premises at 44 Farringdon Street, London, were importers of a large range of inexpensive Continental porcelain and earthenwares of various types. The firm also claimed in their British trade advertisements to be manufacturers at Rudolstadt in Thuringia.

However, their goods often bear one of the following initial marks, not recorded in standard reference books. When found such goods will probably be of German or French origin and can be dated 1870 to 1900.

DUX, see Royal Dux

'EARLY TO BED' GROUPS, see Conta & Boehme, and Fairings

ELBOGEN

This name is often used in association with inexpensive late 19th-century Bohemian porcelains, particularly the small 'Early to Bed' type of Fairings. This designation really arose because the shield mark found on such objects was erroneously attributed to Springer & Co., of Elbogen, rather than to Conta & Boehme, see above. Unfortunately the name 'Elbogen' seems to have stuck although it can be correctly used in relation to the Springer wares, which are usually of an inexpensive type.

The Springer, or Elbogen, shield is shown on the left, the Conta & Boehme on the right.

MAX EMANUEL & CO.

Max Emanuel was a leading importer and London wholesaler of a large range of late 19th-century medium to low-priced ceramics. In a letter published in the *Daily Telegraph* in September 1896, he claimed to own a porcelain factory at Mitterteich in Bavaria (The Mosanic Pottery, formerly Lindner & Co.) which was financed by British capital. In this and a subsequent letter, he made interesting comments on the low costs prevailing on the

Continent and explained that the manufacturers there concentrated on this market:

> The German mechanic earns little more than one-half what the English mechanic gets, and German work has the advantage of cheap women's and child labour.
> It is therefore in the lighter fancy articles – bazaar goods – that Germany takes the lead, candlesticks, butter dishes, fancy jugs, ornaments, and the large assortment of wares that come under the denomination of vases; and why? Chiefly because their material and labour is best suited for this class of work.

The Mitterteich factory employed some 400 persons but the London store, no doubt, also stocked saleable goods from a variety of sources, for example, Max Emanuel advertised Klemm's 'Dresden China' in the 1880s. The trade mark was of three stacked rifles.

Max Emanuel also used the trade name 'MOSANIC' on late Victorian or Edwardian articles.

ENGLISH DECORATION
In the period 1795–1825 when the Paris porcelains were so fashionable in England, various very talented specialist ceramic artists embellished French blanks for resale in London and elsewhere. Thomas Baxter and William Billingsley were only two of many English decorators who painted and gilded imported porcelains. This rather specialist collector's subject is enlarged upon in *Godden's Guide to European Porcelain*, where some specimens are illustrated in Plates 10–21.

FABER
F. Faber of 13 Rue de la Madeleine, Brussels established a hard-paste porcelain factory supported by William I of Holland in about 1818.
    On the evidence of some scarce name-marked examples the forms and style of decoration closely followed the Paris porcelains of the period and the quality is extremely fine. A superb quality cabaret service and tray was sold at Sotheby's in London in February 1991, each piece finely painted with named views relating to the Battle of Waterloo.
    Written or gilt marks include: F. Faber à Bruxelles, and Faber, 13 rue de la Madeleine Bruxelles. The factory was later owned by Cappellemans, who exhibited at the 1851 Great Exhibition in London.

Plate 61. A selection of so-called 'Fairings' or 'Early to Bed' groups which were such popular low-priced novelties in the latter part of the last century. Impressed Conta & Boehme shield-mark and model numbers. c.1880–1900. Average height 3 ins. (Messrs. Godden of Worthing Ltd)

FAIRINGS

This modern name is often applied to inexpensive Victorian or Edwardian objects of the type that might have been sold or won as prizes at Fairs. The best known type of so-called Fairing is represented by the small porcelain groups made in Germany which typically depict humorous domestic events (Plate 61).

These originally inexpensive trinkets were the subject of a specialist book *Victorian China Fairings* by W. S. Bristowe, but the author originally incorrectly attributed the source of these popular novelties. They (or at least the marked specimens) were made by the firm of Conta & Boehme of Possneck. The impressed shield-shaped mark should not be confused with the crowned shield as used by Springer of Elbogen (see Elbogen above for examples of both).

Fairings were made over a very long period, from the 1850s to 1914. The early examples seem not to have borne a factory mark, although an incised model number can occur. From about 1870 the model numbers were neatly impressed using printer's type and the shield-shape device occurs. From about 1890 the country of origin, 'Germany' should be added and in the 20th century this was often expanded to 'Made in Germany'.

The early 20th-century examples are of poor quality; they are very light, being formed by the later slip casting method in which liquid slip is run into plaster-of-Paris moulds. The plaster takes up the water leaving a thin skin of china when the excess china clay is poured out of the mould. Such slip cast pieces show hollow arms, bodies, etc., when broken; whereas the old specimens are solid, being formed by pressing the soft clay into the moulds. The later titles are also printed, not hand painted, as are the early Conta & Boehme groups. As the price of these groups increases it is not inconceivable that some reproductions will be made, but these will lack the period charm of the admittedly mass-produced Victorian examples and almost certainly they will not bear the Conta & Boehme shield mark.

Today the search for these humour groups gives much pleasure and scope to collectors and others seeking relatively inexpensive decorative and amusing objects. *Victorian Fairings and their Values* by M. Anderson illustrates many of these novelties and indicates their comparative value.

FEUILLET

Feuillet was one of the leading Paris decorators c.1820–40s and his products normally bear his painted name mark. The address of the decorating establishment and presumably also of the retail showroom was 18 Rue de la Paix and had attracted patronage from the Duc de Bourbon and other influential figures.

In 1834 Feuillet took Victor Boyer into partnership and soon the Boyer name-mark replaced Feuillet's. Boyer exhibited under his own name at the 1851 Exhibition in London and he in turn was succeeded by others; Boyer, Paul Blot and Hebert, so the Feuillet tradition continued to c.1900.

The Feuillet name was also used by a nephew (from c.1834) who also practised as a decorator, and who was succeeded by Hippolyte Manoury in 1846. Manoury is associated with Sèvres-style porcelains sometimes mounted in ormolu.

Feuillet

FISCHER, MORITZ

Moritz Fischer took over Vince Stingl's failing pottery at Herend in Hungary in 1839. Some of the Herend porcelains were shown at the 1851 Exhibition and included vases and candlesticks as well as table wares. The Jury awarded Fischer a standard 'Prize Medal' and noted especially the embossed porcelain tablewares and the texture and colour of the white porcelain.

However, some at least of the vases shown in 1851 were copies of Meissen specimens and Joseph Marryat writing in 1857 noted that these Fischer exhibits 'attracted great admiration'.

In the 19th century the Fischers were mainly known to collectors for the clever copies of collectable wares made at the Herend factory, rather than for his useful wares for sale to the usual buyers of porcelain tea or dinner services. Of the unmarked Fischer reproductions of collectable wares Frederick Litchfield in his 1879 book *Pottery & Porcelain, A Guide to Collectors*, noted:

> A china manufactory was established at Herend by Moritz Fischer in 1839, and is at the present time carried on by his son Samuel. The speciality of the productions is the imitation of old Sèvres, and Oriental porcelains, and the finest specimens are so closely copied as to deceive any but the most experienced collector … The execution both in gilding and painting is very fine, and it seems a great pity that so much talent is applied to furnish specimens, that, in the hands of unscrupulous dealers, are the means of deception and fraud.

The Herend firm exhibited their wares at various international exhibitions, even some of the smaller ones such as Dublin in 1865. Often the Fischer porcelains received comment and it could be that the special exhibition pieces, shown to receive publicity for the maker, bore the Herend mark but I doubt that the close copies of Oriental and other collectable wares bore his name or the arms mark.

Lady Schreiber, probably the greatest and most experienced English collector of the period had other ideas when she saw the Herend display at the 1878 Paris Exhibition: 'Went to the Exhibition, loitered among the Continental productions. Fischer's imitations are wonderful, he was there himself, a quiet little man …' One of the great puzzles is where are all these Herend copies? We have a factory that reputedly specialized in copies of Sèvres, Meissen and other valuable wares for well over twenty-five years. Yet nobody attributes such porcelains to Fischer! Probably we call them all Samson but some pieces are Hungarian copies made well over 100 years ago.

The middle history of the Fischer firm is confused. Seemingly the firm failed in 1874 but various contemporary sources indicate that it was in being in 1878 and in the 1880s. It would appear that Moritz's grandson Jeno took over the concern in 1897. He reorganized the company in 1923 and it was nationalized in 1948.

The present firm produces high quality decorative table and ornamental wares. These very good quality Herend porcelains are now exported to over thirty countries and reputedly some 2,000 different forms or patterns are available. They still mirror 18th-century shapes and patterns but all bear clear Herend marks and they are made to be used and enjoyed. Herend porcelains can bear an impressed mark HEREND or the standard shield-mark, a 20th-century example of which is here reproduced:

FLOWER POTS
The French in particular specialized in decorative porcelain flower pots or 'Jardinières'. They would usually have had an earthenware pot inside to hold the earth and plants. These open-topped flower or plant pots were a great feature of Victorian interiors. Some had feet, others a neatly turned foot. Some had a decorative pierced rim and some were sold with (or were later placed on) special, often ornate, jardinière stands.

The post-1881 Silber & Fleming wholesale catalogue features a page of twenty-seven such decorative flower pots, only two of which appear to be British; these are Wedgwood jasper-ware pots. Each design was available in different sizes and background colours, usually black, green or pink. The average size mentioned in this trade catalogue was 7½ inches high. Pairs are more desirable than single specimens but they could be purchased singly.

Most French drawing-room china flower pots of the 1860 to 1900 period are unmarked and although they may not be collectors' pieces they are decorative and still fulfil a useful function. Not all examples are Continental but the imported examples outnumber the British.

FRANKENTHAL
Paul-Anton Hannong established a porcelain factory at Frankenthal near Mannheim, in 1755, under the protection of the Elector Palatine Carl Theodor. It passed to Hannong's sons in 1759 but was purchased by the Elector in 1762, under manager Adam Bergdoll. Simon Feilner succeeded in 1775 and in the mid 1790s the factory passed to Peter and Johann Nepomuk van Recum (when Frankenthal became part of France) and was closed in May 1800. However, it should be borne in mind that many of the moulds for figures and other objects passed to other factories and some Frankenthal models were reissued at later dates.

Plate 62. An attractive and good quality Frankenthal porcelain flower-painted sugar bowl from a tea and coffee service. c.1770–80. 4½ ins high. (Messrs. Godden of Worthing Ltd)

The standard reference books on 18th-century porcelain make great play of the finely modelled Frankenthal figures and groups and the number of different models issued, but in reality the more restrained tablewares now outnumber the figures. Even the late wares of the 1790s are now scarce in England.

The hard-paste German Frankenthal porcelains are well potted and trimly decorated. They normally bear one of the underglaze-blue or impressed marks reproduced overleaf and from 1770–88 the last numerals of the year were added below the CT monogram. In addition various workmen's marks or initials can occur:

It has been stated elsewhere that the Frankenthal Palatinate lion crest mark of the 1756–9 period (below) was copied or used on underglaze-blue printed New Hall porcelains. Although a somewhat similar mark can occur on English porcelains of the 1780s, it seems most unlikely to be an imitation of the Frankenthal factory mark:

FÜRSTENBERG
The porcelain factory in this German (Brunswick) city was established in about 1753 although the present management favour the date 1747. The early, pre-1770 Fürstenberg porcelains were probably seldom marked and are now difficult to find, especially in Britain.

The basic factory mark used well into the 19th century was a handwritten (usually in underglaze-blue) cursive capital letter 'F'. Being handwritten this initial mark can vary greatly.

From about the 1890s a simple crown device has been added and in the present century this crowned mark has generally been printed not hand-painted. The word Fürstenberg and sometimes the claimed date of establishment, 1747, is added:

Fürstenberg porcelains have always been of good quality and antique examples are in reasonable demand. A good range of figures as well as tablewares were produced. In recent years the Company has greatly favoured close copies of traditional 18th-century shapes and styles of decoration.

GÉRARD, DUFRAISSEIX & ABBOT
This partnership acted as the American agents for the Limoges firm of Gérard, Dufraisseix & Morel from the mid 1870s into the present century. Special printed marks (below) were used on Limoges porcelains sold by this agency:

These marks can be found on wares not exported to North America and they have been misattributed; one standard reference book giving the date of 1798 for such wares. This was perhaps a printer's error for 1898. On high class, richly decorated porcelains the letters within the wreath are printed in gold.

However, it would also seem that in about 1900 the American agent Edgar Abbot joined the Limoges parent company of Gérard, Dufraisseix & Cie, which then traded as Gérard, Dufraisseix & Abbot. This Limoges firm produced a good range of hard-paste porcelain. A Paris showroom was opened in 1902 but the GDA porcelains had earlier been carried by such well-known retailers as Samuel Bing – such specially commissioned Bing Designs can bear the 'Leuconoe' trade name. Other standard printed marks comprise, or incorporate, the initials GDA.

GÉRARD, DUFRAISSEIX & MOREL and GÉRARD, DUFRAISSEIX & CIE

These firms succeeded Charles Field Haviland at the Alluauds' former factory at Limoges, when Haviland retired in 1881. Morel retired from the firm in 1890 and the company traded as Gérard, Dufraisseix & Cie. The firm continued Haviland's large trade with the USA and it had a separate firm in New York, Gérard, Dufraisseix & Abbot, acting as agents. The wares made for America bore this partnership's initials 'GDA'.

It would appear that in about 1900 Edgar Abbot, the American agent, joined the Limoges partnership which then traded under the former American name Gérard, Dufraisseix & Abbot (see entry above).

The 1881–90 partnership used marks incorporating the initials 'GDM' usually with the old C. F. Haviland initials. These initial marks were perhaps continued to c.1900 but the initials 'GD&C' could have been used from 1890 to 1900.

The 'GDM' Limoges porcelains were of good quality but the standard tablewares are not highly valued.

GILLE

Jean Marie Gille of Paris is mainly known for superb quality decorative biscuit figures, groups and suchlike ornamental objects which were usually enhanced with colours and gilding. They are quite different from the white biscuit 18th- or early 19th-century models.

Bertrand and Jean Marie Gille reputedly established their works in the 1830s and by 1844 were employing some 200 workpeople and their products were being exported. Jean Gille won a Prize Medal at the 1851 Exhibition in London, where the Jury especially noted the figures and bird models 'executed with great delicacy and sharpness'. Some 1851 exhibits bear a special mark or inscription to this effect, as do models shown at later exhibitions.

The Gille biscuit and glazed porcelains are well modelled and produced, and they are decorated to a very high standard; of all makes of Continental biscuit statuary they stand supreme. Furthermore, the models are usually very attractive; perfect examples can be quite costly. However, they are usually purchased on their decorative merits rather than to form a collection of Gille wares, so that some forms, or out-of-favour subjects will still be neglected.

Most Gille porcelains bear a raised pad mark in a light blue tinted paste. This oval or circular pad bears a monogram of the initials 'JG'.

This initial mark would have been used c.1848–68. Jean Gille died in 1868 and the concern was taken over and continued by the Vion & Baury partnership. (See Vion & Baury below.)

GILT FLOWER MARKS
A prominent gilt flower or leaf can occur as a form of cancellation mark, used by independent decorating firms to hide the name of the manufacturer of the original blank, from about 1890 into the 20th century.

GINORI
The Ginori family name is probably the best known in the history of Italian ceramics, from the 18th century to the present. It is forever associated with the Doccia factory and the well-known Capodimonte style.

Although most specimens will be 19th- or 20th-century, the earlier examples were well known in Britain. The London *Public Advertiser* in May 1764 carried a notice relating to the stock in trade of John Crowther, a dealer mainly in Bow porcelain but we read:

> In the fourth day's sale will be sold a rich and elegant tea and chocolate equipage, of the curious and rare Tuscan manufactory. This inimitable superb set was first intended by the Marquis Ginogi [*sic*] for the late Grand Duke of Tuscany.

The Doccia factory had been founded by the Marchese Carlo Ginori in about 1735, but production did not start on a commercial scale until the mid 1740s. The factory passed down through

Plate 63. Representative pieces from a Ginori Doccia porcelain dinner service. 'Ginori' name-mark. c.1850–70. Diameter of plates 9½ ins. (Messrs. Phillips)

succeeding generations and tasteful modern wares are currently produced under the Richard Ginori trade name. (See also Doccia above.)

GRÄFENTHAL

Several porcelain factories were situated in or around Gräfenthal in Thuringia. The largest was that established in 1861 by Unger Schneider & Hutschenreuther. In 1885 the firm became Schneider & Hutschenreuther and in 1886 Carl Schneider. Generally inexpensive but decorative wares were produced including biscuit porcelain figures and groups.

The factory mark was the town initial, a capital 'G' pierced by a vertical arrow device. A double-lined arrow version was registered in 1879. This mark also occurs on 20th-century pieces usually with a model number running into several thousands.

GREINER

One of the many now little-known Continental firms that made inexpensive copies of collectable lines was Greiner or Greyner. However, we cannot be sure of the spelling or which firm was being referred to in contemporary advertisements, for several were in existence.

The *Stationery Trades Journal* of January 1882, for example, carried an advertisement for the London firm of importers and wholesalers, Henry Dreydel & Co. This featured 'Greyner Dresden Wares', including 'Reproduction of old Crown Derby, Old Dresden, Lowestoft and Copenhagen in plates and bowls'. This probably relates to the Dresden decorating studio of Julius Greiner & Son established in 1870. This firm also had a branch at Lauscha in Thuringia and the Dresden division may well have been little more than a convenient retail outlet for the firm's Dresden-styled goods. The reproduction pieces probably did not bear a Greiner mark but they may well have borne copies of original, fashionable marks.

The recorded marks of Julius Greiner & Son include the initial mark as reproduced below, but this is likely only to occur on standard productions, mainly decorative novelties:

GS

GROSSBAUM

Bernard Grossbaum & Son had decorating studios in Dresden and Vienna. His late 19th-century productions could consequently be described as 'real Dresden' or 'real Vienna' – so enhancing their saleability. This firm had showrooms in London and advertised in the *Pottery Gazette*, so their goods were widely available in Britain and no doubt also in North America.

The Meissen-styled goods can bear various 'Dresden' name marks, as that reproduced below left:

The 'GS' device was also employed from at least 1900 onwards. In general, Grossbaum porcelains, which date from about 1875, are decorative but were originally produced as inexpensive copies of popular Meissen designs or shapes. The Vienna shield-mark or a close copy of it can occur on Grossbaum's decorative Vienna-styled wares.

HARD-PASTE PORCELAIN

Whilst most British porcelains are of the type we call 'soft-paste' or later 'bone china', most Continental porcelains are of the type called 'hard-paste' porcelain. Apart from its basic make-up, this is fired at a higher temperature than soft-paste so that the item and its covering glaze will appear (at least to practised eyes) to be more glassy, cold and glittery.

There are certainly important exceptions in regard to some 18th-century French and Italian manufactories, such as Sèvres, where warm, soft-paste porcelains were produced, but when we come to the 19th century the hard-paste Continental bodies can be distinguished from the British bone china. Also most Continental copies of soft-paste English porcelains such as Chelsea or Derby will be in the hard-paste Continental mix.

It is more important to learn to distinguish between the two porcelain bodies, than to have the ability to look up a factory mark as this in itself can be misleading.

HAUSMALEREI

The German term is used for ceramics (usually porcelains) decorated outside the place of manufacture by a painter, or gilder working on his own account. This term should really only be

Plate 64. A Meissen porcelain teapot decorated by Johann Anterweith outside the factory of origin and therefore classed as 'Hausmalerei' decoration. Blue crossed-swords mark. c.1725. 4½ ins high. (Messrs. Klaber & Klaber)

applied to 18th-century Continental essays, where the often talented decorators were purchasing small quantities of perfect white blanks from Meissen, Vienna or a similar source. Usually, being early, such Hausmalerei decoration can be highly desirable and interesting; it can also be costly (Plate 64).

We do not use this term in association with the Paris porcelain blanks of post-1800, much of which was decorated independently for resale. The French term for such painters was 'chambrelan'; they were very numerous and often very talented. In regard to English porcelains decorated in the studios of James Giles or Thomas Baxter we refer to such pieces as Giles decorated, or from the Giles Studio. We also use the simple term 'outside decorated'.

The decoration of, for example, Meissen porcelain 'seconds' or discarded faulty wares by painters or decorators working in Dresden in the 19th century, must not be classified as Hausmalerei.

HAVILAND PORCELAIN

There were several members of the Haviland family decorating and making porcelain in the French ceramic centre of Limoges. The first was David Haviland (1814–79) who was born in New York. The Havilands were dealers in imported pottery and porcelain in New York, trading initially as 'D G & D Haviland' and later as Haviland Brothers & Co. They were in a large way of business, importing quantities of French, mainly Limoges, porcelains but the New York business failed in 1865.

The American author W. P. Jervis writing in or before 1897, noted:

It was in 1839 that Mr. D. Haviland conceived the idea of introducing French china into his market – an idea that with characteristic American enterprise he tenaciously held until accomplished. His search for the maker of a cup of exceptionally fine paste led him to Limoges – a visit that was destined to revolutionize the products of that city and to make its name more closely associated with French ceramics than that of Rouen itself. The existing shapes and decorations did not appear suitable for this market. New shapes were made for him, and organizing a large decoration shop, he, with the assistance of the ablest talent that money could command, eventually revolutionized the productions of Limoges, and gave them the distinctive character possessed by them until this day, and inaugurated a business destined to grow to colossal proportions. From decorating he turned to manufacturing, adopting all the newest processes; and the combination of labor-saving devices with the employment of an artistic element resulted in placing him easily in the front rank of ceramic manufacturers.

The American background to the French Haviland porcelains has assured the succeeding partnerships a firm foothold in the American market but their reputation is really world-wide. Of all the Limoges porcelain makers probably the best-known name is Haviland. I have treated the main Haviland firms separately in the following entries.

A useful, well-illustrated, exhibition catalogue was issued by the Haviland Collectors International Foundation of New York in 1992, titled *Celebrating 150 years of Haviland China.*

HAVILAND, C. F.

Charles Field Haviland (b. 1842) first worked for his uncle David Haviland at Limoges but later joined Richard Haviland at a decorating workshop where they decorated Alluaud porcelain blanks mainly for the American market. The firm of C. F. Haviland probably dates from 1870. He also ran another factory in Limoges producing good quality white porcelain.

In 1875 or 1876 he succeeded to the Casseaux factory at Limoges run by the Alluaud family until the mid 1870s. The Limoges hard-paste porcelains made under C. F. Haviland's ownership bear printed or impressed marks incorporating the name 'C. F. Haviland' or 'Ch. Field Haviland' or the initials 'CFH'.

Haviland retired in 1881 and the factory was taken by the Gérard, Dufraisseix & Morel partnership. The initials 'GDM' were added below the old 'CFH' initials, with 'France' being added from 1891:

```
C F H          C F H
GDM            GDM
             FRANCE
```

HAVILAND, FRANK

Frank Haviland (1886–1971) is a somewhat mysterious figure. He was the son of Charles Haviland (1839–1921) and his second wife was Madeleine Burty. His name is associated with a decorating studio in Limoges from approximately 1908 where Haviland & Co. blanks were finished. His own paintings were signed 'Frank Burty'. The recorded marks comprise the name Frank Haviland and the place-name Limoges.

However, a half-page advertisement in the *Pottery Gazette Diary* for 1915 carries the name and address Frank Haviland, 60 Faubourg Poissonnière, Paris. The photograph is captioned 'Visit of the President of the French Republic to Haviland's Works whose Table Services are renowned throughout the whole world'. Perhaps at this period the Paris retail establishment was in Frank Haviland's name. This same issue lists F. Trauffler of Hatton Garden as the London agents for 'Haviland Frères', an otherwise unrecorded trade name!

HAVILAND, THEODORE

After the dissolution of Haviland & Co. (see below) on 1 January 1890, Theodore (1842–1919) built a new factory at Limoges which opened in about 1893. W. P. Jervis writing in or before 1897 was already able to note that 'the quantity of the goods, the taste shown in the decorations, and the purity of style of the shapes quickly secured generous recognition and placed him in the front rank of Limoges manufacturers'.

In the present century the Theodore Haviland company enjoyed leading artists to design and decorate special wares. He successfully experimented with glaze effects. By 1906 the Theodore Haviland factory at Limoges employed about 800 hands. The main output comprised reasonably inexpensive table wares, often bearing simple printed designs, sometimes over-painted by hand. These standard Limoges porcelains are typical

Plate 65. A Theodore Haviland Limoges dessert plate decorated in an inexpensive printed style but produced for Harrods in London. Printed name and 'Limoges. France' mark with Harrods retailer's mark. c.1900–10. Diameter 8 ins. (M. Wade)

Plate 66. Representative pieces from a stylish mid 1920s Theodore Haviland blue and acid gilt service designed by Jean Dufy. Shown at the 1925 Paris Exhibition. Printed name-mark. c.1924–5. Diameter of plate 10 ins. (Messrs. Christie's)

of their period but are not now in special regard. The plate shown in Plate 65 is part of a dessert service sold by Harrods in London in about 1910. It bears the full name-mark 'Theodore Haviland Limoges. France' plus the Harrods Ltd retailer's mark.

Other marks incorporate or comprise the names 'Theodore Haviland', 'Theo Haviland' or the initials 'TH'. The name 'Mont Mery' also occurs.

Theo Haviland
Limoges

Theodore Haviland was succeeded by his son William, who had joined the family business in 1903. In the 1920s and 1930s the firm, still trading under his father's name, produced some very stylish Art Deco designs, often with very restrained tableware motifs. Leading French designers were commissioned to produce some shapes and patterns.

The company was renamed Haviland SA in 1941, and continues today.

HAVILAND & CO.

This respected Limoges porcelain company was established by David Haviland in 1840 or 1842. At first he may have only decorated blanks purchased from other firms but he quickly prospered and built up an international reputation for the quality and novelty of his output. His own porcelain production may date from 1853.

Frederick Litchfield writing in or before 1880 noted in his book *Pottery and Porcelain, A Guide to Collectors*:

Plate 67. A rather fancy Haviland & Co. plate, part of a service designed by T. R. Davis for President Hayes of America. Printed mark. c.1877–80. 9¼ ins. (Messrs. Phillips)

... in 1840, David Haviland, of New York, purchased a small atelier at Limoges, and since then a considerable trade has been gradually built up by him, especially for export to America. The speciality, however, of the firm of Haviland & Co., is the manufacture of a coarse but artistic pottery, and decorated in a quaint and original manner, sometimes with figures in Spanish costumes, or nearly nude, and sometimes with a vigorous and bold application of argillaceous pigments to the surface, that bears a slight relief. It is worthy of remark, too, that some of the pieces when decorated are signed and numbered by the artist, who undertakes to make no duplicates, so that the number will serve to show the approximate date of the specimen, and is also a sort of guarantee of its being unique in its way. The mark of the manufacture is HAVILAND & CO., impressed in soft clay, in addition to the painter's sign.

In 1879 Charles and Theodore Haviland succeeded their father but the now-large firm still traded as Haviland & Co. David Haviland's connections with the American market (he was a New York importer until 1865) helped the Company to specialize in exports to that vast market. In the main such porcelains were low-priced tablewares decorated with simple painted patterns. For example, the 1895 American mail-order catalogue of Montgomery Ward & Co., featured such items as floral pattern tea and coffee and dinner services described as:

> This beautiful pattern is genuine Haviland china, every piece marked Haviland & Co. Limoges. We call special attention to the handsome shape which is the latest production of this celebrated maker. It is artistically hand decorated [over a printed base] with delicate sprays of cornflowers in soft tints of pink and blue. The handles are richly finished in gold clouded effect ...

The pieces were available separately, a teapot being priced at $1.95 at a time when there were four dollars to the pound sterling.

The Haviland porcelains were also widely available in England and in other markets and the following two basic printed marks were featured in the British magazine *Pottery Gazette* in the 1870s and 1880s, the left-hand for decorated porcelains, the right-hand for the white undecorated wares for which there was a large demand.

Other variations occur but all Haviland & Co. marks incorporate the name Haviland & Co. or the initials 'H & Co.' sometimes with 'L' for Limoges.

W. P. Jervis in his helpful 1897 publication *A Book of Pottery Marks* noted that:

> ... the body was equal to any produced at Limoges, the decorations characterized by an artistic restraint, never overlooked with colour less beautiful than the glaze but in strict harmony with it. The chrome-lithographic process of printing in colours, whereby very soft and harmonious effects are produced, found capable exponents here. Nor was the higher artistic element wanting, the best modellers obtainable furnishing forms on which skilful artists expended all that careful training and their artistic talent suggested.

Jervis was writing in the past tense, for Theodore Haviland had taken over Haviland & Co. after the dissolution of the partnership in January 1890. The name Haviland & Co. seems to have continued in use, as there were several firms with the Haviland name, until eventually merged back into Haviland SA (see Theodore Haviland), whose address today is Avenue P. Lebon, Limoges.

In general terms, although the Haviland & Co. porcelains are of good quality, the standard tablewares are not costly collection pieces. Of course an attractive and reasonably complete dinner, dessert or tea service will have a good resale value but odd pieces from the printed sets will not cause any great excitement!

Over the years the Haviland Company published many catalogues: that produced at the time of the 1878 Paris Exhibition had a text and price list in French, English, German and Spanish, so covering most of the major markets of the world.

HEREND, see Fischer

HEUBACH BROTHERS
In 1840 Christoph and Philipp Heubach purchased a porcelain factory at Lichte in Thuringia and traded as Heubach Brothers. From about 1850 into the 20th century the firm specialized in inexpensive novelties made in porcelain and biscuit porcelain as well as in a refined porcelain-like earthenware. Dolls' heads were a speciality of the firm and the Heubach Brothers supplied tens of thousands of these to the doll makers.

The firm was remodelled in 1898 and some more worthy productions were undertaken including animal models by talented modellers of the period. These German porcelain animals and small figures often have the appearance of the better known Royal Copenhagen models. Yet in the main the firm is known for its inexpensive ornamental and novelty goods.

Various printed and impressed marks are recorded incorporating or comprising the initial 'H', 'GH' (in monogram form) or the name Heubach. The most common marks incorporate a sunset (or sunrise) design with the 'GH' monogram and often with the words 'Schutz-Marke' or the English equivalent 'Trade Mark'. Several designs were registered and these can bear the 'DEP' sign.

An interesting series of six articles on the products of 'The Brothers Heubach' appeared in the American collectors' magazine *The Spinning Wheel* of February and May 1967, December 1968, May, June and September 1970. These articles by Genevieve Angione show both the range of the brothers' middle-market decorative items and also the wide area in which they can be found.

HILL-OUSTON CO. LTD

I have included a brief entry on this 20th-century firm of importers and wholesalers because in my experience the type of ware that they were importing is widely spread and relates to a large degree to many of the reproductions of Chelsea, Derby and Meissen (Dresden) type reproductions or fakes that abound. The Hill-Ouston company were not, however, manufacturers and their name will not occur on the wares which they marketed.

They were not alone in this trade but they are of special interest, as a range of their stock is featured in catalogues, such as the illustrated copy in my possession, which is not dated, but is numbered eleven and would have been issued in the 1930s. In regard to the articles which were produced in England, mainly in the Staffordshire Potteries, the Hill-Ouston reference numbers

Plate 68. Three 20th-century hard-paste Continental groups, incorrectly described as based on Derby models. Priced for retailing at 25/- each. c.1920–30. 7½ to 6¼ ins high. (Messrs. Hill-Ouston Company, catalogue No. 11)

1279
DERBY GROUP
Height 7½"   Width 6"
25/- each

1278
DERBY GROUP
Height 7½"
25/- each

9880
DERBY GROUP
Height 6¼"
25/- each

9974
REPRODUCTION DRESDEN CHINA GROUP
Height 9"
Length 12"
£18 0 0 each

9973
REPRODUCTION DRESDEN CHINA GROUP
Height 10"
Length 15"
£21 0 0 each

Plate 69. Two large and ornate Continental mock-Dresden (Meissen) groups. Priced at £18 and £21 each. c.1920–30. 12 and 15 ins long. (Messrs. Hill-Ouston Company, catalogue No. 11)

have the prefix 'E', so that articles without this initial will have been imported – mainly, it would seem, from Germany.

The trade terms or discount offered by this Birmingham-based firm (with additional London showrooms in Newman Street, in the West End), illustrate the commercial advantages of stocking this type of reproduction. A basic 50 per cent discount was offered from the quoted price, with a further 2½ per cent for payment within thirty days. It was a trouble-free purchase permitting the retailer at least 100 per cent mark-up on the cost price.

In this book I am only concerned with the Continental ceramics, although the catalogue takes in many other types of goods, particularly glass ware which was one of the company's specialities. The Continental ceramics include many small models of animals and birds. Some family sets of five were listed at only two shillings (10p), less the generous discount.

There are also small figures and groups, rather similar to some later Doulton models, and Hummel-type children figures. There are several pages of typical models of the 1930s; dancing females, naked or semi-dressed, under the page heading 'Coloured China Viennese Figures', mostly priced between £3 and £6 each. These are once again very fashionable, and sixty years on have become collectors' pieces. There is also a good range of colourful 'Italian Pottery', which is generally rather broadly painted in an antique style, on a tin-glazed earthenware body. These wares, in the manner of old Italian faience, were apparently extremely popular in the 1930s, but do not now attract the attention of collectors, although they are good decorations.

The most interesting pages of the catalogue are those which illustrate 18th-century styled figures and groups. These pages bear the clear heading, 'Reproduction Dresden and Chelsea Figures', but the objects mainly bear copies of the original factory mark, such as an anchor in gold – a well known device used by the Chelsea factory c.1756–69. Such objects may or may have been retailed as productions but today's owners almost, without exception, believe their pieces to be genuine Chelsea or old Dresden. They also place an inflated value on such novelties based on their incorrect attribution!

Godden's Guide to European Porcelain shows a range of illustrations taken from this Hill-Ouston catalogue and a few more sample illustrations are shown here, in Plates 68 and 69 to warn readers of the types of German porcelain figures and groups which were widely available in the pre-war period.

Like most fakes and forgeries the mock marks are rather larger and more prominent than they are on the original. To be on the safe side you should regard all gold anchor marked pretty figures, animals and novelties as late 19th- or 20th-century Continental reproductions. For the more knowledgeable, the porcelain body on these reproductions will be of hard-paste porcelain with a glittery glaze and appearance. They will probably also have a small pinhole-type vent, a feature not found on genuine English soft-paste examples.

HÖCHST

This German (Hesse) porcelain factory is purely an 18th-century one. The factory was established in March 1746. It is felt in some circles that only tin-glazed earthenwares (faience) were made up to 1749 when Johannes Benckgraff became the manager. After financial difficulties the concern became a joint stock company in 1765. In 1778 ownership passed to the Elector of Mainz, Archbishop Friedrich Karl Joseph, Freiherr von Erthal, but the factory was closed in 1796.

The hard-paste porcelains of the later period c.1775–96 are reasonably common especially tablewares. However, the speciality of the Höchst factory was figures and groups. A charming series of small-scale figures, often of children, is notable. The heads of such figure models often appear overlarge. The chief modeller of these was Johann Peter Melchior.

The basic painted Höchst mark is a wheel device, sometimes with an outline added; below are two average examples.

Plate 70. A typically charming but small Höchst porcelain figure. Wheel-mark in underglaze-blue. c.1770–90. 6¼ ins high. (Messrs. Sotheby's)

After the closure of the factory the figure moulds passed to Muller of Damm who proceeded to issue mainly earthenware editions of the old Höchst porcelain figures. The old Höchst wheel mark was used on these 19th-century products, usually but perhaps not always with an additional 'D' for Damm.

Muller sold the factory to Marzall in 1860 who continued to c.1884. He also used the old Höchst figure moulds and wheel-marks. Other copies of Höchst figures and other wares were produced from the original moulds by the Passau firm of Dressel, Kister & Co. from the 1840s. This German firm probably copied the Höchst wheel-mark on such reissues. Franz Hehlem of Bonn is also believed to have produced copies in the 19th century but these may have been in earthenware rather than porcelain.

Obviously the reissues are not as desirable and valuable as the original examples but all are now 'antique' and have decorative merit.

HONORÉ

Edouard Honoré joined in partnership with the Dagoty brothers in January 1816 until 1820, in which time some superb quality hard-paste Paris porcelain was produced. These wares sometimes bear the two names Dagoty and Honoré.

From 1820 Honoré continued alone although from c.1824 the Paris works were in effect a decorating establishment embellishing blanks made elsewhere. Edouard Honoré was succeeded in 1855 by his son Oscar who continued until 1865.

The Honoré Paris porcelains of the 1820–40 period are usually of very good quality and taste. Specimens sometimes bear simple name marks.

'HUMMEL' FIGURES

The so-called 'Hummel' small figures were produced at the W. Goebel factory at Ceslau (Upper Franconia) from the mid 1930s. The charming and very popular models of young children were based on drawings and models made by Sister Maria Innocentia (Berta Hummel 1909–46) a Franciscan nun. These figures were mass-produced and originally inexpensive. They are however earthenware not porcelain.

The Goebel Porzellanfabrik continues today at Rodenthal in Germany, with an agency in the United Kingdom. They are very collectable in North America and Carl F. Luckey's standard book *A Collector's Identification and Value Guide. Luckey's Hummel Figures and Plates* (Books Americana, Florence, USA), had run to nine editions by 1992.

INCISED MARKS

There is often confusion over the terms incised and impressed in relation to marks; catalogue descriptions and some authors can give misleading information.

An incised mark is drawn or scratched by hand into the still-soft, unfired clay. The incised mark normally shows hasty, uneven but flowing letters, numbers or signs, often with slightly ploughed-up edges. The effect is as of drawing into cheese or butter with a matchstick.

An impressed mark is one in which the model number or initials or other device has been formed by pressing a seal or die into the unfired body. These are altogether neater in appearance and can be a later form of marking. Most impressed marks are indented into the body, but some can be in relief, raised on slight pads applied to the body, as with the Gille initial mark (see Gille above).

INVOICES

One of the collector's greatest protections is to obtain a full invoice or receipt for purchases. This will be given as a matter of course by a respectable, knowledgeable dealer but it may be more difficult to obtain such a document from a part-time or casual trader at a small fair or Antique Market. It will be almost impossible at a car boot sale, jumble sale or similar exercise.

A simple description such as: 'An old figure. £50' does not comprise a full description or invoice. If the figure has been offered to you and purchased as being German and antique, the invoice should include and confirm these claims. Furthermore if no mention of damage or repairs has been made, the invoice should reflect the unblemished state of the object.

An invoice description such as 'An antique Berlin porcelain figure of a standing classical female figure, in perfect, unrestored state. German c.1830' might well represent a better buy at £500 than the 'old figure' sold for £50, that later turned out to be of the 1930s and extensively repaired. In the event of any subsequent dispute on the genuiness of a piece, the detailed and signed invoice can be offered in evidence of the statements made at the time of purchase. The other very brief statement will be useless except to prove the price paid.

If the seller will not give a detailed receipt the buyer should surely be very much on guard.

JEWELLED PORCELAINS

Some superb very decorative Continental as well as British porcelain is enriched with mock-jewels, of the type shown bordering the panels of the Sèvres-marked dish illustrated in Plate 71.

Such quite realistic jewelling was introduced at the Sèvres factory in the 1780s. However, such genuine 18th-century jewelled

Plate 71. A superb quality mid 19th-century Sèvres-style jewelled oval dessert dish. Sèvres crossed 'L' mark (with unrecorded year letter). c.1860–70. 9½ ins long. (Grosvenor Antiques Ltd)

porcelain is very scarce. The reader would be very well advised to regard all examples as 19th-century and to doubt any Sèvres attribution. Any copy of the Sèvres crossed 'Ls' device should be disregarded. Certainly any example bearing this mark and a single-letter year mark cannot be genuine.

Many quality jewelled porcelains were produced in the Sèvres manner in the middle of the 19th century. They will be French, now 'antique' and very decorative. Specimens may well be costly and rightly so.

A further word of warning, do be careful of the added jewelling, it is prone to shucking off, especially if the piece is washed.

JONROTH

The trade names and marks 'Jonroth' and 'Jonroth Studios' can occur on French and German wares (as well as British and Oriental articles) made to the order of the American firm of John H. Roth & Co. in the 20th century. Marks incorporating the monogram JHR & CO. also relate to this firm.

KAUFFMAN, ANGELICA

A signature does not in itself guarantee that the piece is by that artist, nor that it is a unique painting or even that it is hand

Plate 72. A good-looking but inexpensive Vienna-style plate. The figure subject panel is printed, not hand painted and bears the mock signature of Angelica Kauffmann (with an incorrect double 'n'). Unrecorded monogram mark. c.1890–1910. Diameter 8¾ ins. (Miss E. Chubb)

painted at all! This is certainly true of the thousands of ceramics that bear Angelica Kauffman's signature.

Very many items of mainly Continental pottery and porcelain bear on the figure subject decoration the mock-signature Angelica Kauffman or A. Kauffman. The name is sometimes erroneously rendered with a final double 'n'. I am able to write 'mock-signature' as it is almost certain that this internationally famous artist never painted a piece of porcelain in her life – which ended in 1807.

The subjects to which this name was later applied may be taken from her original work, or be in her well-known style, but the vast majority will date from the 1880s or later. It is also almost certain that such 'signed' work will be a mass-produced design based on a printed outline or other means of mass-production. If you have pottery or porcelain bearing the name Angelica Kauffman, regard it merely as a decorative novelty.

KRISTER

Carl Krister of Waldenburg in Silesia produced a wide assortment of generally low-priced porcelains which were largely exported. His late Victorian English advertisements featured such articles as view china, fancy cups and saucers, moustache cups and saucers, children's mugs, shaving mugs, egg cups as well as tea services. The Krister porcelains can be novel and decorative (Plate 73) but they are not specially valuable.

Plate 73. A decorative Carl Krister porcelain table ornament or centrepiece. Blue 'KPM' and cross mark, model number 975. c.1870–80. 6½ ins high. (Messrs. Frank Wilson, Worthing)

The mark employed at this post-1880 period comprised the initial 'KPM' usually with a vertical line above. The difficulty is that these initials were also used by the Berlin factory usually on earlier and better-quality objects.

LA COURTILLE

The Paris porcelain factory named after its location in the rue Fontaine-au-Roy, at La Courtille, was established by Jean-Baptiste Locré in 1773. The original mark usually painted in underglaze-blue, comprised crossed torches; these devices later tended to be rendered as crossed arrows. The two basic marks are here reproduced.

La Courtille porcelains were of very good quality and many shipments were sent to London; various lots sold at Christie's auction room are quoted in *Godden's Guide to European Porcelain*. Apart from the fully decorated examples, white La Courtille porcelain blanks proved very popular with early 19th-century English porcelain decorators, such as Thomas Baxter and William Billingsley.

The La Courtille factory had been taken over by Laurent Russinger in about 1787, but in the early 1880s it passed to François Pouyat of Limoges. It later had many different owners, listed under 'Porcelaine de Paris' below.

LACEWORK

Mock lacework is to be found on several types of porcelain figures or groups. This can look very attractive when not carried to excess, and many owners of such pieces marvel at the apparently fine workmanship.

The delicate effect is in fact easily obtained. Special lace-like openwork material is merely dipped in the liquid 'slip' (the porcelain body diluted to the consistency of thin cream) and the coated lace cut to shape and applied to the figure before firing – as one might dress a doll. The fabric is still pliable, and can readily be shaped and pressed onto the solid foundation of the figure. Once the piece is fired, the fabric base is fired-away, leaving only the delicate pattern in white porcelain.

The great difficulty is that the lace effect is now *extremely* fragile and brittle. Hand or finger pressure will break the lace and being so fine it can never be satisfactorily repaired. Be warned, if you have a lacy porcelain figure, pick it up by the solid base, keep well away from the embellishments.

Although the process was introduced in the 18th century, probably at the Meissen factory, you will be well advised to assume that all such specimens are 19th-century or later. In the present century some quite inexpensive novelty figures have been produced with an excess of porcelain lacework. It can look charming on graceful dancing figures but the lace does not necessarily indicate a costly, high-quality production.

Plate 74. An elaborate Continental dancing figure over-embellished with ceramic lacework. c.1920–30. 11½ ins high. (Dr. J. McDonald)

Certainly mock lacework can occur on genuine Meissen figures where it was generally used in a restrained manner, but the technique was also widely used on copies of the German originals. Some of these Dresden-style lacy figures were produced in England, at, for example, the Derby factory, where it was in use by 1771. Some fine quality white biscuit (unglazed) porcelain and parian figures were also embellished in this manner, but most lacy figures will be of Continental origin.

It is a good general rule that the more mock-lace there is, the later will be the example. That shown in Plate 74 is certainly a 20th-century specimen, probably produced in the 1920s. Decorative and novel but not antique.

LAMM, A.
Lamm owned a porcelain decorating studio in Dresden where various decorative wares were enhanced with designs in the old Dresden or Vienna styles. This Dresden decorating establishment seems to have been established in the mid 1880s and it continued to produce mock-Dresden porcelains into the 20th-century.

His marks comprise a pensive-looking angel over the words 'Dresden. Saxony' or more usually the word 'Dresden' under a standing lamb. The initial 'L' within a shield can also occur.

Dresden
Saxony

dresden.

LENCI
Very little seems to be recorded of this pre-war Italian manufactory at Torino (Turin). Most books do not mention it at all and yet an Art Deco-style figure of a naked young girl sitting on a globe was sold by Christie's of Glasgow in 1991 for £4,200. A large female nude study (Plate 75) had been sold in 1989 for £6,000.

The Lenci wares were certainly available in this country in the 1930s. High-class art-dealers in Worthing, Messrs. Aldridge Brothers, held an exhibition of 'Lenci coloured porcelain' (and Lalique glass) in November 1933. The advertisement then stated that this was 'the first time these remarkable models have been shown south of London'.

The Lenci ceramics date from c.1928. The first catalogue was issued in 1933, others were issued later. In the 1960s an Italian book was issued under the title Le Ceramiche Lenci. This gives details of the various modellers employed, several of whom later opened their own studios and produced wares under their own names (see Turin below).

The Art Deco-styled Lenci ceramics, useful wares as well as figures bear various marks, all of which incorporate the name Lenci: 'Lenci. Made in Italy', 'Lenci. Torino', 'Lenci. Torino Italy'.

156

Plate 75. A rare Italian Lenci porcelain figure. Painted Lenci name-mark. c.1930s. 8½ ins high. (Messrs. Christie's)

Many marks incorporate the date of production, i.e. 5-37 for May 1937 or 22.2.32 for 22 February 1932.

The Lenci wares are rarely found in this country and they are commercially desirable.

LIMOGES

Limoges (or Haute-Vienne) is to France as Stoke-on-Trent is to England – the centre of the ceramic industry. It owes its prominence in the field of hard-paste porcelain production in France to the discovery of rich high-grade deposits of the all-important kaolin; in this it had a distinct advantage over Stoke which has no nearby china stone or china clay, only coal and clay. The Limoges kaolin and ready-mixed porcelain bodies were supplied to many of the Paris-based porcelain manufacturers before the local industry really became established in the 19th century.

Plate 76. A tinted (Worcester-style) Limoges serving dish decorated with printed floral motifs. Printed mark 'Made by R. Delimeres & Co, Limoges for Haynes & Co. 15 Exchange Street, Manchester. D & Co. Limoges'. c.1900–10. 11½ x 11 ins. (J. S. Woods)

Although some porcelain was made at Limoges from the 1780s by Massie, Fourniera & Grellet working under the protection of the Comte d'Artois (using 'CD' initial marks), the vast majority of Limoges porcelains were made after 1850. From about this period into the 20th century a large number of manufacturers and decorators were situated in and around Limoges. One cannot, in a general work, list all these and many were of a small size with a small output, but the standard Continental mark books give good coverage. As a general rule marks incorporating the place-name 'Limoges' can be dated to 1860 or later. Marks also incorporating the name 'France' should date from 1891 onwards, whilst the longer description 'Made in France' suggests a post-1914 dating.

In general terms, and certainly excepting the Haviland porcelains, the Limoges porcelains found in Britain are of medium price range. Dessert sets, in particular, would have undersold the British bone china sets but most British porcelains were hand-painted whereas the Limoges manufacturers tended to use printed outlines or entirely printed designs.

The Limoges hard-paste porcelains were certainly popular but this was probably on account of its low cost – it was durable, decorative and good value. The excellence of 'Limoges porcelain' or 'Limoges China' as it was more popularly known, was acknowledged on a world-wide basis and in the 19th century it was particularly popular in North America.

Whilst in the vast majority of cases the inclusion of the word 'Limoges' in a factory mark will indicate that the piece was made or decorated there, sometimes the description was perhaps used to indicate the type of body or style. The mark reproduced below was used by the Staffordshire firm of Sampson Bridgewood & Son of Longton from about 1870 onwards. The initial 'PG' relates to this firm's durable ironstone-type body which they designed 'Parisian Granite'.

The standard book on the later Limoges porcelain manufacturers is *The Collector's Encyclopedia of Limoges Porcelain* by Mary Frank Gaston.

LITHOPHANE
Lithophane and the lithophanic technique of moulding in relief to show graduations of light or shadow when lit from the back, were extremely popular in the Victorian period. The French process was patented in 1826 and the rights were sold to various Continental and English firms in a type of franchising operation; the details of the Patent and the process are given in *Godden's*

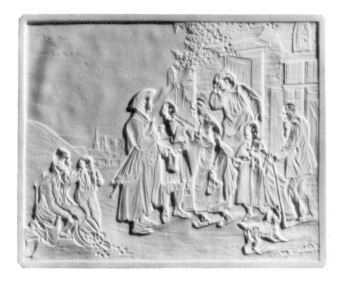

Plate 77. Top, an unlit relief-moulded Berlin lithophane. Below, the same slab lit from behind to bring the picture to life according to the thickness of the porcelain. Impressed 'PPM' initial mark. c.1860s. 7 x 5 ins. (Messrs. Godden of Worthing Ltd)

Guide to European Porcelain. Lithophanes were often known as Berlin Transparencies, probably because most of the better examples were made there.

Tens of thousands of small thin porcelain plaques were moulded and hung in windows, made up into shades or other articles which would permit the transmitted light to bring the usually white plaque to life. Plate 77 shows a typical German example, lit and unlit.

Not all lithophanes were left in the white however, some are delicately tinted. These are scarce and desirable, but whilst large collections of lithophanes have been built up, they are not generally expensive or particularly saleable, as they are difficult to display in quantity. The novel forms that were sometimes made introducing the lithophanic technique can nevertheless be desirable.

The panels often bear the maker's initials impressed near the lower edge, together with the reference number for that design. The Berlin examples – some of which were shown at the Great Exhibition of 1851 – bear the impressed initials 'KPM'. The Berlin numbers had exceeded 200 by 1851.

Some quite inexpensive novelty cups or small mugs can have moulded portraits or other motifs in the base. These designs come to life as the vessel is drained and tilted to the light-source. The two 1902 Coronation mugs shown in Plate 78 have portraits of the new King Edward VII and Queen Alexandra in the bases, but they were mass-produced German items made to be given away to the young folk of Garston, in Lancashire.

Plate 78. A pair of Continental porcelain Edward and Alexandra Coronation mugs with lithophane portraits in the bases. Dated 1902. 2¾ ins high. (B. Jacobs)

LLADRÓ

The undoubted success of the Lladró brothers porcelain venture in Spain is one of the great commercial stories of modern times. The brothers José (b. 1926), Juan (b. 1928) and Vicente Lladró (b. 1933) set up their first small workshop at Almacera (near Valencia) in 1951, producing earthenwares at first. Porcelain production started with hand-modelled flowers, later decorative Dresden and Sèvres-styled ornate vases and ornamental wares were made. Initially Vicente, the youngest brother, was responsible for the modelling whilst his elder brothers were mainly responsible for the painting.

The first specialist Lladró shop was opened in Valencia in 1955. Three years later a large new purpose-built porcelain factory was laid out at nearby Tabernes Blanques, employing some 1,500 craftsmen. It is amazing that the international reputation of 'Porcelanas Lladró' has expanded so rapidly. Perhaps not so amazing when one views the range of superb quality decorative, tasteful and charming figures, groups, animals, vases and countless other wares in stockists' shops or in one of the several specialist Lladró shops in Spain. These porcelains with their subtle colours under a glossy glaze (rather like some Copenhagen wares), the unglazed or bisque porcelains, and the stoneware models are all magnificent and strongly typical of the Lladró concept.

The Lladró wares, with their clear house-style, hardly need a trade mark but several have been employed. The simplest is the word 'Lladró' usually with 'Espana' or 'Made in Spain' added. The standard printed mark is here reproduced.

The Lladró team are great publicists, there is a Lladró Collector's Society, a house magazine titled 'Expressions' and a Lladró Museum in New York on fashionable 57th Street. The Lladró porcelains are now available world-wide and to date two extremely well illustrated specialist books have been published, *Lladró. The Art of Porcelain* and *Lladró. The Magic World of Porcelain*. Both works are available in English-language editions.

LUDWIGSBURG

Hard-paste porcelain was established by Duke Eugen of Württemberg at this German centre in about 1759. The director of the factory during most of the 18th century was Josef Ringler. The original factory was closed in 1824.

Although the porcelain body tends to be rather greyish some finely modelled figures and groups were produced (Plate 79) as well as decorated useful wares (Plate 80).

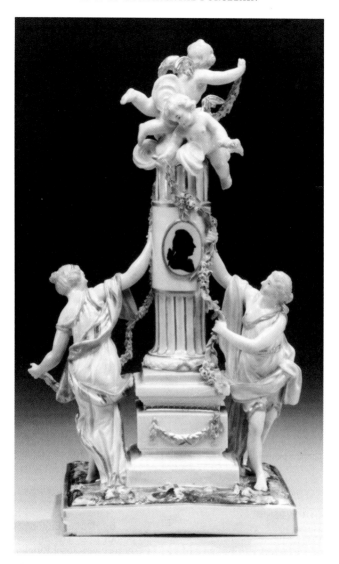

Plate 79. An elaborate 18th-century Ludwigsburg centrepiece showing the quality and diversity of the products of some of the smaller Continental manufactories. Crossed 'C' mark in underglaze-blue. c.1775–85. 10¾ ins high. (Messrs. Sotheby's, New York)

Plate 80. A good quality Ludwigsburg porcelain oval tureen and cover, originally part of a complete dinner service. Crowned crossed 'C' mark in underglaze-blue. c.1770–80. 11½ ins long. (Messrs. Sotheby's)

Various marks were employed but the best known and the most common comprise crossed 'C's, with or without a crown above. The difficulty is that this mark has been widely copied on later wares made in the old style, often from the original moulds. A later post-1948 manufactory at Ludwigsburg has used some of the old marks together with the place-name 'Ludwigsburg'.

The original 18th-century products are rarely found in Britain today. The manufactory was relatively small and few of its products found their way abroad.

MARCOLINI PERIOD OF MEISSEN

The Marcolini period of Meissen porcelain covers *c.*1774–1813, when a small star-like device was added to the basic crossed-swords factory mark:

Plate 81. A Marcolini period Meissen porcelain coffee jug and cover, well-painted with landscape and flowers in a typical, middle-market, manner. Crossed-swords and star mark in underglaze-blue, number 83 impressed. c.1774–85. 10 ins high. (Messrs. Godden of Worthing Ltd)

As explained in Chapter 1, the old authorities tended to dis-credit this period of the factory's history. However, while some of the old life may have gone, these Meissen porcelains are still of a very superior quality and excel over most other porcelains being produced at that time. I regard Marcolini Meissen as very collectable and decorative and certainly important examples can be quite costly.

MATCH-HOLDERS

The safety match is a comparatively recent invention. In the second half of the 19th-century, when electric lighting was not available, the friction match was in great demand.

Hundreds of ornamental match-holders were produced, mainly by the Continental producers of novelty-type porcelains. These ornaments were usually perhaps less than three inches long and quite low for stability, incorporating a holder for the wood or paper match and a roughened surface at the back or underside to provide the required friction to light the match.

These little ornaments are however seldom correctly identified as Victorian match-holders, they are merely regarded as ornaments. Many of the Conta & Boehme ornaments were in fact match-holders.

Another ornament incorporating a container or other receptacle, was the spill-holder, containing various types of spill so that a light could be taken from a fire to light a candle or a gas light.

McKINLEY TARIFF ACT

It has often been stated that the US McKinley Tariff Act of 1890 led to manufacturers adding the country of origin to all marks. It has been assumed that any mark with, for example, 'France' or 'Germany' appearing as part of the mark denoted a date after 1891 and that the absence of such a country name suggested a date prior to this Act. Section 6 of this Act read in part:

> That on and after the first day of March eighteen hundred and ninety one, all articles of foreign manufacture, such as are usually or ordinarily marked, stamped or branded, or labelled … be plainly marked stamped branded or labelled in legible English words, so as to indicate the country of their origin …

However, this Act only applied to goods shipped to the USA by way of trade and any firm not selling to that market did not have to comply. Conversely, there was nothing to stop a firm adding the country of origin to a trade mark before this Act came into operation.

The presence or absence of the country of origin is therefore a most unreliable method of dating, although in general terms a country of origin will indicate a date after about 1880. The fuller description 'Made in France' or 'Made in Germany' will almost certainly suggest a 20th-century date. The absence of such a designation will not, however, prove an earlier dating.

Various countries had their own import restrictions and tariffs and the subject is a very complex one. Further information and guidance is given in the dating section.

MEISSEN

The true name for at least early Dresden porcelain. Details have been given in Chapter 1. The Meissen factory was a state concern and the products have always been of very good quality. However, some showy, relatively inexpensive porcelains and even pottery can bear the name 'Meissen', a designation not used by the state factory, see the following entry.

MEISSEN NAME MARKS

Several Victorian and 20th-century wares, both porcelain and earthenware, can bear various marks which comprise or incorporate the name MEISSEN. Almost without exception, these late showy wares have no direct relationship with the state factory which was established at Meissen, near Dresden, early in the 18th century.

Some British pottery and porcelain can bear this name, but in these cases it is only the name of the pattern or shape which may bear some resemblance to a German design or form. Such wares are unlikely to deceive collectors.

Far more examples are of German hard-paste porcelain decorated in a colourful mock-Dresden style bearing various marks comprising the word Meissen alone or under various devices:

The above Meissen and star device was used by B. Bloch & Co. of Eichwald in Bohemia, mainly on its copies of Dresden blue onion pattern wares, which seemingly were produced with the permission of the main Meissen factory. This mark was used from the 1870s into the 20th century but the examples are not highly regarded by collectors.

The main point to remember is that porcelains bearing the Meissen name as the mark, or part of a mark, were not made at the main Meissen porcelain factory.

MENNECY

The Mennecy soft-paste French porcelains are counted amongst the earliest and most charming of European porcelains. The history dates back to the 1730s when Louis-François de Neufville, the Duke of Villeroy, set up a small factory in Paris. This was moved to Mennecy in 1748 where production continued to c.1773. At that time the factory, then owned by Joseph Jullien, was moved to Bourg-la-Reine where it continued to c.1806 but in the later period only earthenwares were produced.

The delightfully simple Mennecy porcelains, often rather in the style of Chantilly, sometimes emulate Oriental designs – although European floral sprays were much used. Good figures

Plate 82. Three Mennecy soft-paste porcelain small items, painted in a typical middle-market manner, without gilding. Incised 'DV' marks. c.1755–65. Vase 4¼ ins high. (Messrs. Klaber & Klaber)

and groups were also produced. Most general books on Continental porcelains illustrate a representative range of Mennecy porcelains which are also included in major museum collections.

The basic Mennecy mark of the 1748–73 period comprises the initials 'DV'. These are usually incised into the body before firing but painted versions also occur. However, the mark has been copied by later firms and the reader should bear in mind that old Mennecy is soft-paste, it is 18th-century and genuine specimens are rare and costly, hence the later copies.

DV

METZLER BROS. & ORTLOFF

This late Victorian and 20th-century partnership at Ilmenau, in Thuringia, from the 1870s produced an assortment of inexpensive but often decorative novelties and useful wares.

Various marks were used incorporating the initials 'MO' or 'M & O'. The printed mark here reproduced is the most commonly found:

MEYER & SON

This Dresden-based firm produced or decorated Dresden-style porcelains in the second half of the 19th-century. They used a version of the Dresden crossed-swords mark but with the initial 'M' below the hilts, as here drawn:

Frederick Litchfield was the source of our scant information on this firm. He wrote in 1917:

> Meyer and Sohn … also brought faulty white china from Meissen, which they decorated in various styles: they also procured white china from other factories and marked it with the crossed swords and the letter 'M' … Chandeliers, candelabra and cabinets made of ebonized wood with elaborate ornamental columns, feet and galleries of porcelain, the front and sides decorated with Dresden plaques, were specialities of Meyer …

The additional 'M' under the crossed-swords device was probably reserved for their own products or for blanks made especially for the Meyers' decorating trade. The Meyer Dresden porcelains were of good quality and are certainly much rarer than most types of reproduction Dresden. The reason for this may well be the more restricted working period of the studio; this is usually given as merely c.1880, although the period might have been 1860–85.

MONKEY BAND

This set of monkey figures (or Affenkapelle) dressed in human costume and playing various instruments is amongst the best known porcelain sculpture, see Plate 83. The band and its conductor was introduced at the Meissen factory and was modelled by Kändler, possibly in the 1740s, copied at the Chelsea factory by the 1750s, and by practically every other factory thereafter!

The genuine early Meissen and Chelsea examples are extremely rare and costly – hence the later copies. The Meissen factory at various periods reintroduced these popular models which are always of far superior quality to any other make. These modern examples were featured in Litchfield's 1884 'Dresden Gallery' catalogue at 10/6d each, with the bandmaster priced at 12/6d.

The examples you are most likely to come across will be late 19th-century or even 20th-century specimens, made at the lesser German factories or by those manufacturers specializing in reproductions.

Monkey band figures occur with all sorts of marks, most of which are misleading! These once inexpensive copies were made

Plate 83. Three would-be members of the famous Meissen monkey band but in this case 20th-century copies made by one of the lesser German manufactories. These lack the quality and verve of the originals and have the tell-tale description 'Foreign'. c.1920s. 4½ and 4¾ ins high. (Present ownership unknown)

because there was a demand for such amusing novelties. The original Meissen monkeys have been much aped!

MONSIEUR PORCELAINS

The Paris porcelains sometimes called Monsieur (after Monsieur, Comte de Provence) are also classed as Clignancourt, after the location of the factory, in Montmartre. The factory had a short duration from about 1771 to 1799. The founder was Pierre Deruelle, but in 1792 the concern passed to his son-in-law Alexandre Moitte.

The Monsieur porcelains were well known in Britain and a selection was sold by Mr Christie in 1790. This selection (shown in *Godden's Guide to European Porcelain*) included many very ornate cabinet pieces as well as dessert and dinner services. Good quality white biscuit porcelain figures and groups were also produced.

Various marks were used, but slight variations may occur.

 CLIGNANCOURT
M

Plate 84. Part of a Naples porcelain coffee service attractively painted with figures in landscapes but not as meticulously as would have been the case at the Meissen factory. Gilt and impressed star marks. c.1790–1800. Covered sugar bowl 5¾ ins high. (Messrs. Godden of Worthing Ltd)

NAPLES

The Capodimonte factory was near Naples but those wares are normally referred to as Capodimonte not as Naples. The true Capodimonte porcelains were produced in the short and early period *c.*1743–59 (see 'Capodimonte' and 'Capodimonte-style' entries).

Another factory was, however, established at the Royal Villa of Portici, Naples in 1771, and two years later this factory was moved to the Royal Palace where it continued into the 19th century. In 1806 the French occupied Naples and production ceased. In 1807 the factory passed to the French firm owned by Giovanni Poulard Prad and was moved to a new site. It was then subdivided and owned by several persons until it was finally closed down in 1834, although it is believed that production had ceased well before this date.

The porcelain body is a type of soft-paste, sometimes with white tin-glaze to hide defects in the body and to assist the painted decoration. From 1780 the forms and styles of decoration tended to be classical, with some attractive figure painting, and the Etruscan style of decoration was also favoured. Modelled figures and some groups were made – some in white biscuit porcelain – but all are quite rare. Some good and typical examples can be seen in the Victoria & Albert Museum.

Two basic forms of mark were employed. The initials 'RF' under a crown or the monogram 'FRF' under a crown. These initials relate to Ferdinand IV of Naples, and relate to the first part of the factory's existence before the occupation by the French. The second standard mark was the capital initial 'N' under the crown. This and the 'RF' marks vary greatly in detail as they were hand-painted.

It was the crowned 'N' device which was later widely copied and became, incorrectly, associated with the Capodimonte factory.

Good and typical examples of Naples porcelain are illustrated in Arthur Lane's specialist book *Italian Porcelain*.

NAST (FRÈRES)
Jean Nast came to Paris in the early 1780s, where he established two porcelain factories. The typically well decorated tasteful Nast porcelains mainly date from about 1800. Jean died in 1817 but the factory was continued by his sons Henri and François until the early 1830s.

Various painted, printed or stencilled name marks occur, two typical types are shown below. The Paris address can also be added or the single name could be amended to 'Nast frères'.

NAST
à
Paris   *Nast à paris.*

Typical Nast porcelains are featured in Régine de Plinval de Guillebon's book *Paris Porcelain 1770–1850*.

NESTLE & HUNTSMAN
This firm was one of several importers of Continental goods in London. The printed bill head of the 1850s gives the address as 6 Great Trinity Lane and 2 Little Trinity Lane in the City of London. The business was described as follows: 'Importers of Foreign Manufacturers – Glass, China, Lava, etc.' The firm moved to Bohemia House, 157 Commercial Street, Shoreditch about 1868 and continued to c.1888.

When a new china and glass dealer commenced business in Devizes in the late 1860s all his Continental (Bohemian) glassware and china seems to have been obtained from this firm of London retailers. Such inexpensive initial purchases included '6 China assorted inkstands' at 8d each, and numerous candlesticks at 9d.

On 15 April 1878. Nestle & Huntsman registered various ornate and decorative figure models at the London Patent Office, under the parcel number 11. These models included a pair of female figure models. A pair of girls with baskets, a decorative pair of Chinese-style figures with candelabra arms and a lady with children in a pram. These models sometimes bear a blue monogram mark comprising an 'E' over a sideways placed 'O' or egg-like device.

Marked earthenware plates are recorded bearing portraits of Princess Alexandra and the Prince of Wales, made to commemorate their silver wedding in 1888. Other marked late examples depict William Gladstone.

The firm's full name or the initials 'N & H' probably occur on some Continental porcelains imported by this London firm for resale in Britain.

NIDERVILLER

This French earthenware and porcelain manufactory in Lorraine produced hard-paste porcelains from the mid-1760s. The factory had several owners from this period into the early years of the 19th century when the production of porcelain seems to have given way to earthenwares.

The best known Niderviller products are the white biscuit porcelain figures and groups and the generally later glazed and coloured figure models usually mounted on a simple gilt base. These figures and groups sometimes bear the impressed mark NIDERVILLE or NIDERVILLER. The glaze appears very hard and glossy.

NODDERS

The name given to generally late 19th-century novelty figures in which the head is made separately and weighted so that it swings on pivots to give a nodding effect.

The Meissen factory made some, now very rare, early examples and reissued larger examples in the 19th century. However, most French and German examples were made down to a price as toy-like novelties for children. Most examples are unmarked and were made by the smaller Continental firms. A typical pair is here shown (Plate 85).

NOVE (LE NOVE)

At Nove (Venetia) in Northern Italy, Pasquale Antonibon, the owner of a maiolica factory, started to produce porcelain in the early 1750s. The early experimental, largely unsuccessful wares have a primitive appearance and are very scarce. By 1760 reasonable porcelains were produced, but the factory languished in the mid 1760s; however it continued at least on a small scale until the early 1780s when the works were leased to Francesco Parolin. After 1802 the Nove factory was taken over by Giovanni

Plate 85. A pair of originally inexpensive German porcelain 'nodder' novelty figures, with loose heads which nod. c.1900–10. 6½ ins high. (Mrs Mary Topping)

Baroni who continued to c.1825, when the factory returned to the Antonibon family who continued to about 1835.

The Nove porcelain has a very glossy glaze, similar to that of the Cozzi Venice porcelains. The Nove British-style creamwares are probably more noteworthy than the porcelains.

The standard Nove mark is a star device which can vary considerably in its rendering and it should be remembered that a star-like mark is not exclusive to this Italian factory.

The place-name 'Nove' appears as a mark, this too is painted or incised in various renderings, but at least the mark is a clear one, which did not seem to be used elsewhere.

Although the production of porcelain ceased in the mid 1830s, earthenwares continued to be produced. Lady Schreiber noted in 1869 that the Nove factory was producing copies of old wares for Rietti, the Venetian dealer.

NYMPHENBURG

Nymphenburg, Bavaria, was the celebrated Bavarian royal porcelain manufactory, but its early products are rarely seen and will be costly. The more plentiful 19th-century wares are usually of very high quality, especially the porcelain plaques.

The manufactory was established in about 1753 and its early success is due to the technical skills of Joseph Ringler. However the name rightly associated with Nymphenburg was Franz Anton Bustelli (1723–63) who was a very gifted Swiss modeller.

In 1754 Bustelli was appointed chief modeller at the Nymphenburg factory, where he modelled sharply worked, elegant, lively figures rather in the style of wood carvings. His male figures are inclined to appear rather effeminate but he can still be regarded as one of the leading ceramic modellers of all time.

Like other 18th-century modellers, his work is not signed but it is extremely characteristic and can hardly be mistaken. His models have stood the test of time and have been produced up to recent times from old moulds. Often his models are left in the white (undecorated) state, the better to show off the line and crisp modelling. Care must be taken not to purchase a relatively modern example as a costly and highly desirable 18th-century piece, although the later examples are charming as decoration.

Apart from the superb Nymphenburg figures and groups, some of which were left in the unglazed, biscuit state, the Bavarian Royal Porcelain Manufactory also specialized in the production of very finely painted porcelain plaques or pictures. The subjects were in the main copied from old masters in the King of Bavaria's Royal collection at Munich and are often referred to as Munich plaques.

There are several contemporary references to these plaques, including M. L. Solon's 1886 note:

> In the year 1809, the Prince Ludwig of Bavaria conceived the idea of causing the masterpieces of the Royal Museum of Munich to be painted on porcelain to bequeath to posterity reliable and unalterable copies, when time had defaced or destroyed the originals.
>
> The paintings were executed in the Royal Manufactory of Nymphenburg, first on a series of dessert plates and subsequently on plaques of various dimensions. For 57 years the work gave employment to many artists of the Royal Manufactory. The collection is now composed of 72 plates, 2 vases and 207 plaques, exhibited in a special room.

Joseph Marryat in his book *Collections towards a History of*

Plate 86. A graceful German Nymphenburg porcelain figure, the original modelled by Franz Anton Bustelli, in his appealing simple style. Impressed shield-mark. c.1755–65. 7¾ ins high. (Messrs. Sotheby's)

Plate 87. OPPOSITE *A superb quality costly Nymphenburg porcelain handled tray, signed 'J. G. Neyerhuber, 1813'. Impressed shield-mark. 1813. 15½ ins long. (Messrs. Sotheby's, New York)*

Pottery and Porcelain, commented on the Nymphenburg porcelains: 'The colours and gilding of this porcelain are excellent. The landscapes, painted by Heintzmann and the figures copied from the best pictures in the gallery at Munich by Adler, are very superior to any other of the paintings of this manufacture.'

Frederick Litchfield, writing of the Nymphenburg wares in or before 1879, noted in his little book *Pottery and Porcelain, A Guide to Collectors*: 'Its present productions appear however, to be chiefly white, and very little energy is apparent, though a few plaques well decorated in "Murillo" subjects may occasionally be bought ... ' Further details of this aspect of the factory's products are given in *Godden's Guide to European Porcelain*.

The factory sent a good general selection of its products to the 1851 Exhibition in London. The official catalogue introduction to the Bavarian section drew attention to the 'fine collection ... of objects of high interest as works of design and as specimens of the ceramic art ... A number of finely-painted vases and some pictures on porcelain, are shown.'

The Nymphenburg plaques and other porcelains should have borne the standard mark of the Bavarian shield device with cross-hatching (really oblique lozenges). In the 1850–62 period a star device appears above the shield. This impressed mark was often very small and can be quite difficult to see.

NYON

A hard-paste porcelain factory was established at Nyon, near Geneva in the early 1780s and the production of porcelain continued to *c*.1813, after which earthenwares only were produced.

Plate 88. A simple Swiss Nyon porcelain tea bowl and saucer painted with neat inexpensive Paris-style floral pattern. The saucer turned to show underglaze-blue fish-like mark on reverse side. c.1790–1800. Diameter of saucer 5¼ ins. (L. R. Rogers)

The porcelain, which mainly comprised useful tablewares, are rarely found but many later reproductions were made and marked with the Nyon fish mark painted in underglaze-blue. Like all hand-painted marks the fish is rendered in a variety of ways. A typical simple, formal rendering is shown on the reversed saucer shown in Plate 88. The simple sprig decoration is typical of several factories of the 1790–1810 period, attractive but not commercially the most desirable.

OHME, HERMANN

The Hermann Ohme porcelain factory at Niedersalzbrunn in Silesia dates from *c*.1882 and continued at least into the 1930s. There was also a branch factory at Waldenburg. The Ohme works produced a wide range of inexpensive decorative and useful porcelains, including the Crown Dresden type.

The usual impressed or printed post-1883 mark is reproduced below left. This device can also be incorporated in other more fancy marks which may include the name 'OHME' and on later examples the country of origin 'Germany', as shown on the 20th-century device below right.

The painted or printed crowned 'Saxe' mark was also used and denotes a post-1882 period.

ONION PATTERN

The quite simple underglaze-blue formal floral design which is widely known as the 'Onion Pattern' is mainly associated with the Meissen factory although it has been much copied, even by 18th-century British porcelain manufacturers.

This design, shown in Plate 10, was originally much used for relatively inexpensive Meissen dessert and dinner services, so that plates and dishes are quite common. However, particularly from the 1850s onwards, as the design became more and more popular, the underglaze-blue pattern was added to a variety of ceramic forms. Figures were even decorated in blue to match the onion pattern tablewares.

Nineteenth-century or later Meissen onion pattern plates, cups and saucers and such standard objects are not rare or valuable, but the more unusual or important articles (such as centrepieces) are certainly in demand. Many people collect only this one pattern so that rare examples or forms are very desirable.

As with other standard patterns, it is possible to build up quite a large collection of that one pattern, to fill a dresser or display case or to match up pieces to form large useable services. Such matchings may, however, vary in period and shade of blue.

From about 1893 most true Meissen examples of the onion pattern have the factory's crossed swords device incorporated in the front of the design. The mark also occurs in the normal position on the reverse of the plate. In the last century Frederick Litchfield listed the merits of this pattern as being its 'pretty simplicity and very low cost'. It may not be so inexpensive today but its charm remains.

PARIS PORCELAIN

This is a vast subject and *Godden's Guide to European Porcelain* Chapter 6 gives much background information and quotes many references to fine quality Paris porcelain that was sold in London during the period 1790–1825.

In general the term Paris Porcelain is applied, or misapplied, to all showy looking, good quality French porcelain particularly those types that show the French Empire influence; the equivalent in Britain would be the Regency style. This mass grouping of many unmarked porcelains is, however, largely one of convenience.

It is probable that several other non-Paris and even non-French porcelains are herded within this designation. Certainly the major Paris manufacturers set the style that others sought to follow, because it was fashionable and saleable – the object of the exercise.

In this alphabetically arranged section I have included details of the main makes of Paris porcelain. These major firms or partnerships are:

Angoulême (includes Dihl & Guérhard)
Dagoty
Darte Frères
Feuillet
Gille
La Courtille
Monsieur
Nast
Jacob Petit
Porcelaine de Paris
Potter
Stone, Coquerel & Legros

Whilst some Paris hard-paste porcelains bear relevant name or monogram marks, much is unmarked. However in most cases it is the overall decorative merit of the piece that is all-important from a commercial or a collector's point of view. A tasteful well-gilt quality vase from a small Paris firm might well be more highly regarded than a sparsely decorated example from a larger manufactory.

It must be understood that much Paris porcelain was outside decorated, that is not by the actual makers. This is no bad thing for the decorators (or 'chambrelans') and decorating firms were specialists. It merely complicates the position to some degree.

The influence of the Paris porcelain manufactories tended to wane after the 1830s perhaps as the influence of the English bone china manufacturers increased in world markets. This is not to say that there were no porcelain factories in Paris after 1830 but their numbers had certainly decreased and the old Empire style had become outmoded by more fancy rococo forms – as seen in the colourful Jacob Petit porcelains.

Several illustrated books on European porcelain will feature some Paris porcelain but the true magnificence and range of products can best be gauged by consulting Régine de Plinval de Guillebon's magnificent work *Paris Porcelain 1770–1850*.

PÂTE-SUR-PÂTE

This French term 'paste on paste' or body on body, aptly describes the most expensive and painstaking of ceramic decorative techniques. The relief decoration is normally in a white semi-translucent porcelain body laid on a darker ground and slowly built up, tooled, sculpted and refined until the design is perfected to show, when fired, a pleasing, correct rendering of the required, usually unique, semi-translucent design. There are several contemporary (or near contemporary) accounts of the process, such as M. L. Solon's 1901 explanation which is quoted in *Godden's Guide to European Porcelain*.

In Britain the English pâte-sur-pâte wares, usually worked on a glazed and tinted parian body, are more often met with than the Continental essays. These are usually of a lighter ground colour than the English pieces. Sèvres specimens are of the finest quality and, of course, these should bear clear Sèvres marks. The Museum at Sèvres, the Victoria & Albert Museum and the Bowes Museum at Barnard Castle contain good signed examples which were highly thought of and costly at the time. At Sèvres the major pâte-sur-pâte artist was Taxile Maximin Doat (1851–1939). Seemingly he was allowed special privileges, being permitted to sell his own work even though this was carried out at the Sèvres factory. The Doat pâte-sur-pâte decorative pieces were signed and sometimes dated and they are well worth looking for.

Various French factories produced some pâte-sur-pâte porcelain. Several in the Limoges district made decorative examples including a range of oil lamp bases bearing mainly floral designs in white relief on a celadon ground.

Some decorative French pâte-sur-pâte bears the printed initial mark 'CP'. This mark related to C. H. Pillivuyt & Cie of Foëcy and Mehun. The pieces I have seen with this mark were attractive but of rather commercial quality; probably many of the motifs were stock designs whereas the leading workers in this style produced one-off ceramic sculptures. Other examples bear the 'G & Cie' mark used by Gibus of Limoges or the name or initials of C. Tharaud also of Limoges.

The Meissen essays in this technique are, as one would expect, of very high quality and bear the standard crossed-swords mark in underglaze-blue. The Meissen or Dresden examples date from the late 1870s. Julius Hentschel was the leading artist in this style, another was E. Andersen. Large and elaborate examples were made to display at various international exhibitions but the less expensive smaller pieces are usually more attractive. These pâte-sur-pâte examples should not be confused with the delicately painted graceful figure compositions on a dark blue ground, painted in white (or slightly tinted) enamel.

The Berlin factory also produced fine quality pâte-sur-pâte vases and other pieces in the period 1875–1900. These examples bear the printed orb mark with the initials 'KPM'.

Some pâte-sur-pâte pieces usually with a chocolate ground bear the signature Schenk. In most cases these are English pieces made at the George Jones Crescent Pottery at Stoke, see Geoffrey Godden's 1961 work *Victorian Porcelain*. However, by far the most complete and up-to-date account of this costly technique with good illustrations of all types is Bernard Bumpus's large standard work *Pâte-sur-Pâte*. He also published an article 'Layers of Perfection', in *The Antique Collector* magazine of October 1992.

PÂTE TENDRE

This is a French term for soft-paste porcelain as made by several Continental factories such as those at Vincennes (Sèvres), St Cloud, Chantilly and Mennecy. In England such soft porcelains were made at Chelsea, Bow, Derby, etc. and with these we use the term soft-paste porcelain.

PETIT, JACOB

Jacob Petit (1796–1868) was one of the best known and most prolific of all the Paris porcelain manufacturers, although his wares are rather later than most, and the forms tend to be more fussy, indeed most examples were produced in the early Victorian period. The Jacob Petit porcelains, produced in the Rue de Bondy, date from the mid-1830s. He was temporarily bankrupt in 1848 but survived until about 1862. Reputedly Petit produced his ornately designed white porcelains in a large range of fancy forms for many other French manufacturers, although most specimens will have been entirely made and decorated at his large manufactory.

The porcelains normally bear the large-size initials 'JP' painted in underglaze-blue, one version of this is reproduced below.

The desirability and value of the Jacob Petit porcelains largely rests on their decorative merits. Colourful vases and suchlike showy articles are in demand by interior decorators. Typical examples are illustrated in *Godden's Guide to European Porcelain*.

C. PILLIVUYT & CO.

Charles Pillivuyt & Co., of Mehun and Nevers in France are mainly renowned for fireproof china cooking vessels of traditional French type. These wares were widely exported and much advertised, and were available in Britain from the mid 19th century. Typical advertisements are featured in *Godden's Guide to European Porcelain* (Chapter 10).

Name-marks or initials 'CP & Co.' can occur, but the standard marks give only the place-name of the manufactory as here reproduced.

The cooking or kitchen wares are not valuable, nor do they seem yet to have attracted the attention of collectors, but many examples of these fireproof wares are still available, although not in high class antique shops!

PIPE BOWLS

One of the specialities of the German porcelain manufacturers was porcelain pipe bowls for smoking tobacco. These were often highly decorated and one imagines the young bloods seeking to show off their standing by the elaborate decoration on their smoking equipment. As Charles Dickens's weekly journal *All the Year Round* of 23 June 1860, noted:

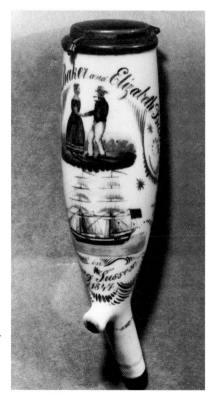

Plate 89. A German porcelain pipe-bowl inscribed and decorated for an English sailor and his lady-love. Dated 1847. 5½ ins high. (Private collection)

183

The Meershaum and the porcelain bowl find favour with the Germans, and the rivalry between their respective merits affords a constant topic of controversy among the burghers or youths of the universities. The possession and becoming use of the pipe, mark the transition from youth to manhood … It is to the Teuton what the fan is to the Chinese, ever present and in constant service.

These decorative pipes and their wood or other mountings were also popular with 19th-century tourists to Germany and were, on the evidence of the example shown in Plate 89, also available in Britain and on occasions were inscribed and decorated for the British market. It could be that sailors and the marine trade were instrumental in spreading the craze from the German states. If this was the case, these porcelain pipes would have found their way to most countries.

Whilst examples found today will probably date to the 1840–70 period and have been made for a middle class market, some are of an earlier date and were made for, or were used by, members of the royal family.

Messrs. Christie & Mason, the famous auctioneers, for example, in July 1843 sold 'The unrivalled collection of Pipes … the property of his Late Royal Highness The Duke of Sussex K.G. and removed from Kensington Palace'. This royal collection included:

A set of china bowls, for every day in the week.
A porcelain bowl, with view of Göttingen and ivory tube.
A porcelain bowl, with portrait of Mary Queen of Scots and tube.
A ditto with a Turk's head.
A large porcelain bowl, with wooden tube.
A smaller porcelain bowl and tube.
Two, with porcelain bowls and buck-horn tubes.
A Dresden bowl, painted with flowers.
A bowl of German porcelain with a dancer and horn tubes, silver mounted.
A pipe bowl, of Dresden porcelain, with a coronet of gold and chain and gold embroidered tube.

This royal collection included very ornately embellished Meissen porcelain pipes and the related fittings but other firms would have produced the cheaper standard types. Josef Hubner of Gablonz in Bohemia displayed 'porcelain pipe-bowls, painted' at the 1851 Exhibition in Hyde Park, as did Ziegler Brothers of Ruhla, who has as their London agent C. Holland of Finsbury Circus. The firm of Basse & Fischer of Ludenscheid (Westphalia) specialized in 'lids for tobacco pipes in German silver, pinchbeck and Britannia metal mountings, silvered'.

Although not common, these German 19th-century porcelain pipe bowls can be very decorative and should form an interesting, novel, collection without great outlay. However, three examples were sold by Phillips, in 1991 for just over £200 each. This price may be accounted for by the fact that they were well painted with attractive females!

PLAQUES

Porcelain plaques can represent the high-water mark of ceramic painting. Chapter 7 of *Godden's Guide to European Porcelain* is devoted to this class of porcelain picture.

Unblemished flat porcelain slabs or plaques are very difficult to produce, but they represent a superb 'canvas' to show off the

Plate 90. A well-painted Berlin porcelain plaque by C. Haag after a Murillo original. c.1850–70. 7½ x 10 ins. (Messrs. Sotheby's)

skill of the most talented ceramic artists. Once correctly fired (in several stages) the ceramic colours will remain permanent and will not fade or discolour as might a watercolour or oil painting.

Most of the leading Continental factories produced porcelain plaques, but the leaders were Sèvres, Meissen and the Berlin factories. These, and other manufacturers, employed leading talented and celebrated artists. Eighteenth-century plaques now very rarely come on the market but many Sèvres-styled later copies exist.

Most of the German plaques are of 19th-century date and some can be quite late. The Berlin ('KPM' marked) plaques are always of extremely high quality. Here the size and subject matter is more important than the period of the plaque – for they are valued largely for their decorative qualities, as pictures.

In recent years the more decorative plaques have commanded very large sums, often in thousands rather than in hundreds of pounds. However, the market is extremely particular and changeable!

It must be clearly understood that not all porcelain plaques are of superb quality or of popular subjects. Most would-be buyers prefer an attractive young female to a perhaps grim religious subject!

Neither must it be thought that a signature, necessarily proves that the subject was entirely hand-painted or by that artist. Many later plaques are based on a printed base or photographic process. The signature Kauffman (in various versions) indicates both a late date and a form of decorative forgery, for this much-favoured 18th-century artist probably never painted a single piece of porcelain.

PLATES

Plates are probably the most plentiful ceramic article. A dinner service would have large (9 or 10-inch diameter) meat course plates, soup plates (equally large in the 18th- and 19th-century sets) as well as smaller side plates, pudding or even cheese plates. A pre-1900 service sold to a reasonably wealthy family who would expect to entertain, could well have included over 100 plates.

Likewise the popular dessert services would have 12, 18, 24 or more dessert-size (approximately 8-inch) plates. Many families would have more than one dinner and dessert service, perhaps a best and a second best, apart, of course, from the plain wares used by the servants.

In addition there were, particularly from about 1860, a mass of plates made purely for decoration. These might be sold as a single plate or as pairs. Some would be destined for a display cabinet, or arranged around the room on the plate rail high up near the ceiling or merely hung around the walls as one might a picture or print.

Thousands, if not millions of plates were made with printed views of various towns and villages to be sold in local shops, markets or stalls. A typical low-priced example is shown in Plate 31. The ones with pierced edges, the so-called ribbon plates, were especially popular.

Obviously not all such plates were made on the Continent, many were of British manufacture. But the market for cheap, decorative plates, often as mementoes, was so large that the French and German manufacturers of inexpensive wares enjoyed a good part of this remunerative trade.

I am not suggesting in these general statements that all plates are plentiful and inexpensive. Obviously some will be of above average quality, or from an early, sought-after manufactory, but as a class plates are more plentiful than most other articles.

PLAUE (Thuringia)
C. G. Schierholz & Son of Plaue-on-Havel in Thuringia produced a wide range of decorative Dresden-style porcelains in the second half of the 19th-century. The firm's date of establishment, 1817, is included in some printed marks but this feature indicates a late, rather than an early date.

These, often floral-encrusted centrepieces, baskets and various novelties (see Plate 91) can be very ornamental, but they were produced in large quantities at relatively low cost and must be considered as decorative articles not as collectors' items. Various hand-painted, double, crossed-line marks occur as the sample shown below. Other, printed, marks incorporate three oak (?) leaves usually within a shield which was sometimes crowned:

The firm continued into the 1930s as Schierholz'sche Porzellan-Manufaktur Plaue.

PORCELAIN
The great Continental porcelain factories were set up to emulate the superb Chinese, and to a lesser degree the Japanese, porcelains which were being imported into Europe in increasing quantities in the 17th century. Great fortunes were being made from the popular Chinese imports and even greater riches and prestige was promised to those who could make similar wares in Europe. Kings, princes, the rich and noble were all attracted to the quest which seemed rather simpler than the old desire to turn base-metal into gold!

The successful production of a pure white vitrified porcelain, however, presents many real problems and many early efforts

Plate 91. An inexpensive but decorative Plaue porcelain floral-encrusted bowl, rather fun in its way. Crossed-lines mark in blue, with model number 303 impressed. c.1880–1900. 4 ins high. (E. H. Chandler)

proved unsuccessful. We have, for example, the Medici semi- or soft-paste porcelains made at Florence in the period c.1575–87, but such pieces are extremely rare and not now found outside the great museums. A long gap took place before we have the rise of some French soft-paste porcelain factories such as those at Rouen, St Cloud, Chantilly or Mennecy. The Royal factory at Vincennes and later at Sèvres also originally produced soft-paste porcelain or 'pâte-tendre' to use the French term.

The soft-paste, artificial porcelains were fired at a rather lower temperature than that needed to vitrify true or hard-paste porcelains, at about 1100 to 1150 degrees C as opposed to about 1300 degrees needed for most hard-pastes. It follows that the covering glaze is relatively soft on the low-fired wares and hard and glass-like on the hard-paste wares. The soft glaze seems, to the practised hand, rather warmer than the glittery hard glaze.

True, hard-paste porcelain was, however, made at several ceramic centres from the early to mid 18th century after deposits of the vital ingredients koalin and petuntse were discovered. Meissen porcelains can date from about 1710 but you are unlikely to happen on pieces made much before 1750. Vienna porcelain can date from 1718 and by the 1740 there were several factories in the German states producing true porcelains.

By about 1772 all Continental porcelains were of the hard-paste type, except for some Italian wares containing in the mix a proportion of soapstone. These types are classified by the French authorities as 'Hybrid Porcelains'.

It is often stated that porcelain is translucent, but this property can be very variable and much depends on the firing temperature; an underfired porcelain mix will be opaque. Translucency also depends on the thickness of the piece; a thick dish, or a solid arm will not permit any light to show through, whereas a correctly fired cup, saucer, plate or similar thinly-potted porcelain article will show the shadow of one's hand if held up to a strong light.

The French spelling of porcelain is porcelaine, while in German the term is porzellan.

PORCELAINE DE PARIS

The above description applies to a modern firm of Paris porcelain manufacturers, one with a long somewhat complicated history, detailed in Chapter 2.

Michel Bloit, President of the modern firm, has written an excellent book entitled *Trois Siècles de Porcelaine de Paris*. The splendid illustrations show the high quality of the porcelains which have real decorative merit. Much use was made of gilt metal mounts and the range of models was very wide. The author was able to draw on official records which show this firm to have produced really sumptuous articles. Apart from the marks on pp. 55–6, copies of the Sèvres, Capodimonte and Vienna marks and a mock-Oriental seal mark were also used.

One imposing colour plate in Michel Bloit's book illustrates a garniture of two ormolu-mounted Sèvres-style blue ground vases with a matching open centrepiece. The caption states that these were made by the Eugène Clauss firm and that the models were introduced around 1880 and produced until 1930, while the figure subject panels were copied from Boucher paintings from the Rothschild bequest at the Louvre.

The French porcelains produced over a long period by the various succeeding Porcelaine de Paris partnerships are of very high quality and the articles usually have great decorative merit. The firms obviously offered serious competition to the better-known Samson firm. Indeed many examples now attributed to Samson were probably made at the Porcelaine de Paris manufactory. The firm continues today but does not now specialize in reproductions of antique specimens. The modern products usually bear a copy of the early Locré or La Courtille crossed-arrows device.

POTTER, CHRISTOPHER

By 1788 Christopher Potter had left England for France. There he petitioned the Council of Commerce of the National Assembly for sole rights to manufacture earthenware after the British manner; that is, presumably, for the right to manufacture creamware in France. Other authorities state that the petition related to the painting and printing of porcelain, pottery and glass. The petition was reputedly initially granted, but M. Glot the Administrator of Paris holding power of attorney from the French porcelain manufacturers, vetoed the Englishman's ambitious plans to set up a factory employing 500 persons.

Nevertheless Christopher Potter seems to have set up a porcelain manufactory in the rue Crussol in about 1790. Certainly in April 1792 Joseph Lygo, the manager of the London showrooms of the Derby factory, was able to report to William Duesbury in Derby, presumably in answer to Duesbury's enquiry:

> Enclosed I send you the best account I can possibly get of Potter, he has always been a very great speculator but very unsuccessful here, he got involved so much in this Country that he was obliged to leave it, and went to France, and there he began making china buttons and from that he is got to have a china manufactory in Paris and I am informed he has now got many people at work.
>
> His ware is very fine some that I have seen here, I am informed he buys all his clay ready prepared to make his ware of – he is a man of great spirit and is allowed to have pretty good ability ... I should suppose him to be a man near fifty years old ...

Some of Potter's hard-paste Paris porcelain bears painted name marks, either in underglaze-blue, in overglaze enamel or in gold. These comprise the name 'Ch Potter' or 'Potter' usually followed with 'Paris' or 'à Paris'. The city name can appear with a lower-case 'p'. These Potter Paris marks should relate to a date within the period 1790–8 for he sold the 'Prince of Wales' manufactory to Étienne Blancheron in 1798.

*potter
à paris*

The Potter porcelains illustrated in *Godden's Guide to European Porcelain* show that in the shapes and usually in the decoration, he was following French fashions, not producing English forms in France. The potting and the decoration is neat and workmanlike. They are also quite rare.

RANDALL, JOHN

John Randall (1810–1910) was the nephew of Thomas Martin Randall, and may well have learnt the craft from his uncle and perhaps he assisted him in the Randall's London decorating studio. His later ceramic painting at the Rockingham Works and particularly at Coalport is very much in the Sèvres style, usually exotic birds in landscapes. John Randall worked at Coalport from about 1835 to about 1881 when his sight failed. Much of his painting on Coalport porcelain has a distinct French or Sèvres appearance; the shapes were often modelled on the French, ground colours were employed and rich tooled gilding surrounds the colourful bird-painted panels or the Sèvres-style flower-painting of William Cook. Worse still, some pieces bear a copy of the crossed 'L's mark of the Sèvres factory. Initials such as 'C' and an 'R' sometimes found on these Coalport pieces may indicate the Coalport origin, or Randall's painting.

The Randall decorated Coalport porcelains would not fool a modern specialist but in the past they have tricked many buyers. If you have such Coalport essays in the Sèvres style consider them as good 19th-century Coalport porcelain rather than as bad copies of 18th-century Sèvres.

RANDALL, THOMAS MARTIN

Thomas Martin Randall (1786–1859) was an English porcelain painter mainly associated with the decoration of Sèvres or other blanks in decorative and fashionable 18th-century styles. He was reputedly born near to the Caughley factory in Shropshire in about 1786. He was probably apprenticed at the Caughley or nearby Coalport porcelain factories before being employed at the Derby factory. Thomas Randall moved from there to London in about 1813.

Again, reputedly, he joined in partnership with Richard Robins (or Robbins) at Spa Fields, Islington c.1813–25. However, I have not been able to trace any records of such a partnership, only of one between Richard Robbins and William Stevens 'china enamellers and gilders' at Hatton Garden. This was dissolved in February 1815. Randall either independently or in partnership with Richard Robins is credited (!) with the decoration of white or sparsely decorated Sèvres porcelains with ground colours, floral and figure subject painting and rich gilding to make such dressed-up blanks more commercially desirable.

After leaving London, he set up at Madeley, near to the Coalport works in Shropshire. According to family tradition Thomas Randall only decorated French blanks in his first few years at Madeley but he seemingly succeeded in producing (largely unidentified) porcelain before he moved in about 1841 to Shelton in the Staffordshire Potteries.

According to his nephew, John Randall, his uncle continued to decorate old stock in the Sèvres manner whilst in Staffordshire. From 1853 he seemingly traded as Thomas Martin Randall & Son, before retiring in about 1856. Although no marks are recorded on any of his products, his output of Sèvres-inspired ceramic decoration must have been very considerable spread over forty years.

A very helpful, detailed Paper 'Thomas Martin Randall: China Decorator and Manufacturer' by Roger S. Edmundson, was published in the *Journal of the Northern Ceramic Society*, vol. 10, 1993.

REFERENCE BOOKS

Reference books are all but indispensable for the serious collector or student. A good up-to-date reference book contains a fund of knowledge and experience by an author who should be a specialist in that subject.

It should also contain a good selection of clear illustrations showing both rare and typical examples. These should show characteristic forms, styles of decoration, marks, etc. You will find it better to purchase a modern authoritative specialist work at say £60 to £100 rather than ten general chatty guides at £10 each, for these seldom contain new research, in-depth study or new helpful illustrations.

I am very well aware of the fact that a library of reference books is costly to purchase. My collection runs into hundreds of books costing several thousand pounds. But the average collector need have only half a dozen well-chosen books at hand. Others can be consulted, if not borrowed, at most of the larger Public (Reference) Libraries. Some specialist libraries have a very large comprehensive holding including rare works and a mass of source material. The National Art Library at the Victoria & Albert Museum in London is such a repository.

I have listed in the Bibliography the books relating to Continental ceramics which I find most helpful. Some are obviously more comprehensive than others, some are specialist works on one manufactory or on one type of ware. Few are helpful on the later decorative articles.

REGISTERED DESIGNS AND SHAPES

The diamond device shown below relates to shapes or designs that were registered at the Design Office in London. This mark, with changing numerals and letters depending on the date of entry in the files, normally denotes a British origin for the goods bearing this mark. However, some Continental objects were so registered usually after about 1870, so that this mark can occur on French or German wares intended for the British market.

This registration system came into being in 1842 with the year letter in the top inner angle, and continued to 1867. In 1868 an amended version had the year letter at the right, continuing to 1883, when a system of simple progressive numbering was introduced (see Registered Numbers). The Class Mark (IV) relates to ceramics; other areas of manufacture were covered in other classes.

TABLE OF REGISTRATION MARKS
1843 – 83

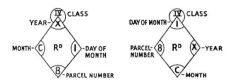

Above are the two patterns of Design Registration Marks that were in current use between the years 1842 and 1883. Keys to 'year' and 'month' code-letters are given below.

The left hand diamond was used during the years 1842 to 1867. A change was made in 1868, when the right-hand arrangement was adopted.

INDEX TO YEAR AND MONTH LETTERS
YEARS

1842–67 Year letter at top				1868–83 Year letter at right			
A	=	1845	N = 1864	A	=	1871	L = 1882
B	=	1858	O = 1862	C	=	1870	P = 1877
C	=	1844	P = 1851	D	=	1878	S = 1875
D	=	1852	Q = 1866	E	=	1881	U = 1874
E	=	1855	R = 1861	F	=	1873	V = 1876
F	=	1847	S = 1849	H	=	1869	W = (Mar.1-6) 1878
G	=	1863	T = 1867	I	=	1872	
H	=	1843	U = 1848	J	=	1880	X = 1868
I	=	1846	V = 1850	K	=	1883	Y = 1879
J	=	1854	W = 1865				
K	=	1857	X = 1842				
L	=	1856	Y = 1853				
M	=	1859	Z = 1860				

MONTHS (BOTH PERIODS)

A	=	December	H	=	April
B	=	October	I	=	July
C or O	=	January	K	=	November (and December 1860)
D	=	September	M	=	June
E	=	May	R	=	August (and September 1st–19th 1857
G	=	February	W	=	March

The code is shown above. From this the reader can ascertain the date when the object was entered in the official files and the mark issued. This date can only be regarded as the earliest possible date of manufacture; but as the protection was only for a three-year period, the date of manufacture should be within three years of the date of registration.

Plate 92. An elegant pair of Continental porcelain figures. The design registered at the British Design Registration office in London on 15 April, 1878, by the diamond registration mark. London firm of Nestle & Huntsman. 1878–80. 11½ ins high. (P. Underwood)

The registration mark will only show the date of the entry. To discover the name of the person or firm which registered the design, one has to consult the original files. These are housed at the Public Record Office, Ruskin Avenue, Kew. The basic references are BT 43 for the shapes and designs and BT 44 for the registers giving the date and names. Allow plenty of time to carry out any search and telephone first to see that the office is open. The number is 0181 876 3444.

Patent protection was given to a few items, , in which case a Patent number or the date of the Patent was added. In practise details of a Patent indicate a date after about 1880 and usually a 20th-century dating. Prior application to the Patent Office (Designs Registry), 25 Southampton Buildings, London WC2A 1AY is recommended (tel. 0171 405 8721).

Continental figures bearing these British registration numbers are shown in Plate 92. The French word 'Déposé' was very often used on Continental objects to protect the design or form from being pirated.

REGISTERED NUMBERS

In 1883 the British diamond design device was discontinued and from 1 January 1884 each new shape or design was given a number starting at 1. These numbers were normally prefixed 'RD. NO.'. This system again covered all types of material, but without group classes.

I give below the number reached by January of each year so that the reader can easily gauge the year and the approximate period within the year that the design was first registered. Again this exercise will show only the earliest possible date of manufacture.

Whilst most registered objects bearing these registration numbers will be of British manufacture, some were registered by agents here for Continental manufacturers when protection from copying was required in Britain. The files for numbers up to 548919 are at the Public Record Office at Kew, later entries are at present housed at the Design Registry, State House, High Holborn, London WC1.

1	=	1884	268392	=	1896
19754	=	1885	291241	=	1897
40480	=	1886	311658	=	1898
64520	=	1887	331707	=	1899
90483	=	1888	351202	=	1900
116648	=	1889	368154	=	1901
141273	=	1890	385180	=	1902
163767	=	1891	403200	=	1903
185713	=	1892	424400	=	1904
205240	=	1893	447800	=	1905
224720	=	1894	471860	=	1906
246975	=	1895	493900	=	1907

518640	=	1908	860854	=	1950
535170	=	1909	863970	=	1951
552000	=	1910	866280	=	1952
574817	=	1911	869300	=	1953
594195	=	1912	872531	=	1954
612431	=	1913	876067	=	1955
630190	=	1914	879282	=	1956
644935	=	1915	882949	=	1957
653521	=	1916	887079	=	1958
658988	=	1917	891665	=	1959
662872	=	1918	895000	=	1960
666128	=	1919	899914	=	1961
673750	=	1920	904638	=	1962
680147	=	1921	909364	=	1963
687144	=	1922	914536	=	1964
694999	=	1923	919607	=	1965
702671	=	1924	924510	=	1966
710165	=	1925	929335	=	1967
718057	=	1926	934515	=	1968
726330	=	1927	939875	=	1969
734370	=	1928	944932	=	1970
742725	=	1929	950046	=	1971
751160	=	1930	955342	=	1972
760583	=	1931	960708	=	1973
769670	=	1932	965185	=	1974
779292	=	1933	969249	=	1975
789019	=	1934	973838	=	1976
799097	=	1935	978426	=	1977
808794	=	1936	982815	=	1978
817292	=	1937	987910	=	1979
825231	=	1938	993012	=	1980
832610	=	1939	998302	=	1981
837520	=	1940	1004456	=	1982
838590	=	1941	1010583	=	1983
839230	=	1942	1017131	=	1984
839980	=	1943	1024174	=	1985
841040	=	1944	1031358	=	1986
842670	=	1945	1039055	=	1987
845550	=	1946	1047798	=	1988
849730	=	1947	1056076	=	1989
853260	=	1948	2003720	=	1990
856999	=	1949	2012047	=	1991

REPAIRS

Modern repairs to old pottery and porcelain can be extremely good, sometimes too good! Chips and cracks can be filled and the surface repainted, missing hands or other parts can be replaced to make a faulty piece look 'as good as new'.

This is fine if the owner or the new buyer is aware of the repaired nature of the damaged piece. Unfortunately, some extensively repaired specimens can be sold (not always by way of an auction sale) as perfect or at least a buyer is not warned of the deception. It must be deception, or worse, to sell a faulty, over-repaired, piece as a perfect specimen. For this reason the buyer should always insist on a full invoice or receipt and see that the description includes a statement to the effect that the piece has not been restored. No damage or subsequent restoration can enhance the value of a piece; the reverse is the case. Damage and repairs are acceptable if the buyer is aware of the position and is happy that the asking price has taken this into account.

The trouble with repairs is that they can hide the extent of the underlying damage, which can be great. Some dealers and collectors, like myself, are in the habit of removing often costly repairs with 'Nitromors' a strong (and dangerous) paint-remover, so that we can discover the extent of the damage. We are of the class that in most cases would rather see honest damage such as a chip or a crack, rather than look at an ocean of new paint and mock-glaze. We collect old china, not new paint! Others choose to repair their possessions. It is a matter of personal choice but remember that good professional repairs can be costly and they are likely to deteriorate with time.

If you wish to sell a damaged piece I would recommend that you do not have it repaired beforehand. Most dealers or auctioneers would rather handle an unrepaired piece than one that has obviously just been recreated by a repairer.

REPRODUCTIONS

My candid comments on reproductions present great difficulties. I have been brought up in the trade to despise all such later copies of earlier classics but I now feel, after some fifty years of such beliefs, that the case against reproductions has been over-emphasized.

Reproductions have always been made, because there is a good demand for less expensive copies, or because the supply of the original does not meet the potential demand. Most homes have reproduction antique furniture, because the graceful designs have proved so popular over a long period. Today some superb quality late Victorian or Edwardian copies of Chippendale or Sheraton style furniture are rightly valued in thousands of pounds. They are of a quality that can probably never be repeated.

Much the same case could be put forward for many reproduction pottery or porcelain objects, even if we were to resort to basic English and term such reissues 'fakes' or 'forgeries'. The difference between these terms revolves around their mode of sale. If a gold anchor marked French copy of a Chelsea figure is sold as a 19th-century French decorative figure, it can surely be classed correctly as a reproduction because no deception has been attempted.

Plate 93. A high-quality and very decorative hard-paste Continental group. Its main fault perhaps being that it bears a fake Chelsea gold anchor mark, a device better disregarded! Gold anchor mark and impressed number 93. c.1900–14. 9 ins high. (Messrs. Godden of Worthing Ltd)

The time has probably come to look with fresh eyes at many of the pieces that one has been taught to shun. I have in both this book and the larger *Godden's Guide to European Porcelain* been at great pains to explain how many fakes and reproductions there are of the popular collectable factories.

It is right that you should be forewarned of this, but I have repeatedly stressed that such copies can be of very good quality and that the pieces are often extremely decorative. The reproductions are also more plentiful than the rare pieces they seek to emulate, and they should be far less expensive than the scarce originals. In other words they fulfil a useful function and many of these pieces are 'antique' in their own right.

I purchased the two Toby jugs shown in Plates 20 and 21. These came from the same local house, I fancy the previous owners, perhaps over several generations, preferred the colourful porcelain example shown in Plate 21. It is certainly far superior in quality and decorative merit to the other which is a genuine, if rather late, Staffordshire earthenware example. The purist may well prefer the English jug to the French reproduction which has been made in the wrong (but superior) material – hard-paste porcelain. The foreign essay also bears on the reverse an improbable mock-Chelsea gold anchor mark. It is good decoration and nobody is going to take it for Chelsea as that factory did not produce this type of jug. These two jugs will most probably be purchased by different new owners, both will be happy with their own choice. For their own reasons both opinions will be correct, it is not a matter of right or wrong. There is (I trust) a market for both the genuine jug and the French copy – which happens to be nearly as old as the genuine article!

In much the same way I think we can give considerable credit to the decorative and fine quality Continental porcelain group shown in Plate 93. Its one fault is that it bears on the back an improbable gold anchor mark. Yet it is not a copy of any Chelsea group, it is a new creation, as are so many mock-Chippendale or Sheraton-styled pieces of furniture.

Many reproductions have great and real merit, as long as you understand their true origin and period. They may not be collectors' pieces but not everybody is a specialist collector of costly 18th-century originals.

RIBBON PLATES

This name has been applied to a class of display plate which has a moulded or rarely a hand-pierced edge. Coloured ribbon could then be intertwined through the pierced design and the surplus taken up to form a decorative bow from which the plate could be hung upon the wall. I would not, however, like to hang one of my favourite plates from such fragile material.

Although pierced-edged plates (as Plate 31) date back to quite an early period, the so-called ribbon plates are normally late Victorian or Edwardian. Like any plates, specimens are to be found in various qualities and price ranges. All ribbon plates are decorative and could be very good value for a modest outlay.

ROCOCO STYLE

Although the curving Rococo style of shape and decoration is to be found on British ceramics, its birthplace was in Continental Europe from around 1730. The wild, curvaceous scroll and counter scroll is found in so many art forms. In its original lively manifestation it is typically 18th-century and can be seen on the scroll-work bases of figures and groups, or in the ornate shape of vases.

However, the style has never really died, especially in the wares which to some degree emulate the old wares, see, for example, the rococo base of the group shown in Plate 93. You cannot therefore date a piece to the 18th century merely because it has rococo features. The term should merely be used as a description.

A good understanding of the meaning and scope of rococo can be obtained from the splendid Victoria & Albert Museum publication *Rococo. Art and Design in Hogarth's England*, which is the well-illustrated catalogue of a truly splendid exhibition held in 1984.

J. ROTH

The 'JR' monogram mark reproduced below appears in underglaze-blue on a class of late 19th-century ornamental porcelains which I believe to be of German origin:

However, this mark and these wares are sometimes attributed to Julius Richard of Milan. Joseph Roth, the London wholesaler, imported much decorative Continental porcelain into Britain from about the 1870s onwards. He registered at least eight Continental designs at the Patent Office in London between October 1879 and January 1882.

A 'JR' monogram mark appears in Joseph Roth's *Pottery Gazette* advertisement dated November 1880. These Roth imports are decorative novelties but not of the finest quality.

ROYAL DUX

The Bohemian figures, groups and centrepieces that bear the trade mark 'Royal Dux' are very decorative and fashionable although they were produced in large quantities after about 1880. Many examples within the period 1900–20 display an Art Nouveau style (see Plate 94) which has returned to fashion, but other examples can be earlier and display great care in the modelling and craftsmanship in the potting.

The Royal Dux wares, which were exported on a world-wide basis, were produced at Eduard Eichler's Dux Porzellanmanufaktur at Dux in Bohemia. The standard mark from about 1910 comprises a raised tinted triangle into which is impressed a central acorn device with the initial 'E' and the words (for British market wares) 'ROYAL DUX BOHEMIA'.

Plate 94. An elegant and large Royal Dux comport or centrepiece, decorated in mute colours and gold rather in the Royal Worcester style. Raised pad mark. c.1900–20. 20 ins high. (Messrs. Sotheby's, Sussex)

From the 1940s the initial 'D' replaced the former 'E'. The initial 'M' should occur on examples made from about 1954 onwards.

Today many of the old figure models and other wares are still produced, in more than 400 forms and over 800 styles of decoration. Old-style figures, centrepieces, vases and many animal models are still made and exported to many international markets.

Some early large and imposing Royal Dux models can command several hundred pounds, or £2,000 or so for a good pair of figures, but some of the later, more commercial, examples are much less costly. In general Royal Dux examples can be likened to Royal Worcester porcelains of the same period, but the Dux specimens have an obvious Continental appearance and often display an Art Nouveau feeling. The Royal Dux models are very popular because of their decorative merits.

ROYAL PRUSSIAN
A type of decorative late 19th- and 20th-century porcelain is sometimes termed 'Royal Prussian' or 'Royal Suhl'. Such wares were originally produced by Reinhold Schlegelmilch who, with his brother Erdmann started porcelain production at Tillowitz in Upper Silesia in 1869, having previously worked at Suhl in the 1861–9 period. From about the 1880s well into the 20th century the Schlegelmilch decorative and inexpensive hard-paste porcelains enjoyed a large export trade, particularly to North America. Great and good use was made of various colour-printing or photographic decorative processes.

Whilst those Schlegelmilch 'Royal Prussian' porcelains are not at present esteemed in Britain, they seem to be collected in the USA. A descendant, Clifford J. Schlegelmilch, has written a colour-printed booklet on these wares entitled *R S Prussia*.

Many printed marks were employed, most incorporating the initials 'RS', to which the place-names 'Suhl', 'Tillowitz' or 'Prussia' might be added. The country name 'Germany' can also occur replacing 'Prussia' and 'Poland' can also appear on account of changes in the border. I reproduce three typical marks. The Tillowitz factory continued to c.1917, the Suhl branch continued until at least the mid 1920s.

ROYAL VIENNA
This description was much used in the 19th century, after the original state factory had been sold in 1864. It therefore seldom or ever applies to what one might call old or genuine Vienna

porcelain but rather to examples decorated in the old style. For further information see Chapter 1.

SAINT CLOUD
This French manufactory of earthenware and soft-paste porcelain is of early foundation, dating back into the 17th century. The porcelains date from around 1700 but such early wares are all but unknown. Indeed all St Cloud porcelain is very rare although some typical blue lambrequin border designs were copied by British firms. St Cloud porcelains can be very attractive and are highly collectable, but they are not of the type featured in this handbook.

An early and rare mark comprises a hastily drawn sun face, while rather later marks of the 1730–66 period generally comprise the initials 'St C', with or without the initial 'T'. The factory closed in 1766.

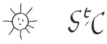

SAMSON OF PARIS
Further information on this major manufacturer of reproduction antique porcelains is given in Chapter 2 and in *Godden's Guide to European Porcelain*.

SAXE
The French term for Dresden or Meissen porcelain. It can be used as part of a mark. Such 'Saxe' marks are usually post-1880 and may be found on inexpensive Dresden-style porcelains.

SCHNEEBALLEN, see Snow-ball Decoration

SEVE
This is the spelling used in most 18th-century British sources such as catalogues, when referring to the French National factory at Sèvres.

SÈVRES
My main coverage of this famous French royal and later state porcelain manufactory is given in Chapter 1. I include this cross-reference to stress the important point that not all pieces bearing the well-known double 'L' mark will have been made at the Sèvres factory. The Sèvres style, shapes and marks have been very widely copied. Many of these copies will be antique in their own right and they may be of very good quality, as are the vases shown in Plate 95.

Decorative Sèvres-style porcelains of this popular type should be described in accurate auctioneers' catalogues as 'Sèvres'. The quotation marks are very important, indicating that the pieces

Plate 95. A superb quality turquoise-ground Sèvres-style vase (one of a pair) mounted on gilt metal plinth. The intricate gilding is enhanced with jewelling. c.1860–80. 21½ ins high. (Messrs. Phillips)

are 'in the school of' or 'in the style of' that manufactory but that they are not true original Sèvres productions.

SIGNATURES (SIGNED)

One should be very careful over signatures or when using the description 'signed'. So-called signatures are the easiest element of any item to forge. The 'signature' of well known famous painters has often been added to mass-produced later objects in order to make them appear earlier or more worthy than they are, or to give the impression that the piece is a unique, hand-painted object; this does not necessarily follow. Names such as 'Boucher' or 'Kauffman' very frequently occur and in all cases such 'signatures' are meaningless, or show the piece is late, probably mass-produced and of decorative merit only.

It would also be as well to bear in mind that 'signatures' on figures or groups usually relate to the modeller of the original master model and copies of such a signature on the many examples later produced from the working moulds does not really increase its value or indicate that the named person produced your example. If correct and genuine such a moulded copy of the signature merely identifies the originator of the model.

It is therefore misleading to describe such replicas as being signed, for this suggests that the piece is an individual creation made by a particular person.

The description 'signed by …' is also sometimes used when a design or mark bears a replica signature of the designer or artist. Again such a name relates only to the original composition and is really little different to a trade mark.

SILBER & FLEMING

This English firm of 'Manufacturers, Importers, Warehouse-men and Agents' of Wood Street, London, issued in the approximate period 1880–5 a colour-printed catalogue and price list featuring a mass of British, Continental and Oriental decorative and useful pottery and porcelain.

Chapter 3 gives good details of the types of Continental ceramics being sold by this firm in London in the approximate period 1870–90.

SITZENDORF

This place-name is now much used to describe a class of very many decorative Dresden-style porcelains; figures, groups, centrepieces, baskets and similar articles were all produced at Sitzendorf in Thuringia. The factory was established in the mid 1840s and in about 1850 was taken over by the Voigt brothers. The name of Alfred Voigt is generally associated with the Sitzendorf factory which was to become Alfred Voigt AG. Early in the 20th century the firm was retitled 'Sitzendorf Porzellanmanufaktur vormals [formerly] Alfred Voigt AG'.

The mark employed was two parallel lines in underglaze-blue intersected by a single line. This device being hand painted appears in various sizes, angles and other variations. It can be mistaken for similar marks such as the crossed double lines used by C. G. Schierholz & Sohn of Plaue, a firm that produced kindred Dresden-type porcelains at much the same period (see Plaue above).

Plate 96. A rather poor quality Sitzendorf porcelain Dresden-style figure, with some mock lace-work. Crossed, three-line mark in blue. c.1890–1910. 6½ ins high. (Mrs W. Southely)

Plate 97. A post-war Sitzendorf porcelain figure typically in the old Dresden style. Crowned 'S' mark with 'German DR' below. c.1960–80. 7¾ ins. (Mrs W. Southely)

It must be stated that such porcelains are merely in the accepted general style of the Dresden wares, they are not exact copies, nor is the cross-like mark very much like the crossed-swords device. Yet the fact remains that members of the public and most owners of such late 19th-century objects seem to regard them as real 'Dresden'.

Originally these Sitzendorf decorative pieces and similar pieces made by other firms, enjoyed a large sale for they were relatively cheap and cheerful. Being slip-cast rather than press-moulded they are relatively light in weight when compared to the heavy Dresden wares. The general colour range is also more subdued, more like a watercolour than an oil painting!

For all this, the better specimens have a real decorative merit and examples are more available and affordable than genuine Dresden porcelains. Although the Voigt firm has continued from the 1840s to recent times under various names, the bulk of the decorative Dresden-type floral-encrusted porcelains will have been produced in the approximate period 1870–1910.

It should be noted that several manufacturers used simple cross-type marks. It is after all the simplest of marks to draw and is traditionally used in lieu of a signature. Small cross devices were often used by workmen and painters as a personal tally mark to identify their work for quality checking purposes or for piece-rate counting.

The Sitzendorf factory survived two major wars and from about 1918 has used several marks comprising or incorporating a crowned 'S' device. A typical example is here reproduced:

From 1945 into the early 1990s the additional inscription 'GERMAN D R' has been added but the Democratic Republic initials were discontinued on the reunification of Germany. As can be seen from the post-war figure shown in Plate 97, the modern products tend to hark back to earlier (Meissen-style) times, but the quality can be very high and the productions very decorative.

SLIP WARE

British readers may believe that slip-decorated earthenwares – articles decorated with coloured or white slip (clays diluted to the consistency of cream) applied as one would ice a cake – are purely British in origin, but this is far from the case. This method of ceramic decoration is international and traditional. Continental examples will be found in most large European

Museum collections and many of these have a similarity to British country or Staffordshire slip-decorated wares.

It should be remembered, however, that the vast majority of pieces found in Britain will be of British origin, for Continental articles were, in the main, made for local sale not export. Some very fussy and decorative slip-decorated Swiss pottery was, however, exported in the late Victorian period. These and some other local products could also have been brought home by tourists visiting the popular holiday districts.

SNOW-BALL DECORATION (SCHNEEBALLEN)

This intricate form of ceramic decoration was introduced by Kaendler, the Meissen modeller, probably as early as the 1740s. The German term is Schneeballen.

It comprises balls of small blossoms, often applied to a blossom-encrusted ground. Various birds and branches were also often added. This form of (dust-trap) decoration became very popular in the 19th century and was widely copied, not only by German factories but also in France and Britain. The example shown in Plate 98 is almost certainly French although it bears a copy of the Meissen Marcolini period crossed-swords mark.

The Dresden examples are the best quality and are more desirable than the copies. Some damage can be expected on such fragile encrusted porcelains.

SPILL HOLDERS OR VASES

The cylindrical spill vases are usually of British manufacture and they can be very decorative and collectable. They were made by practically every 19th-century factory because spills were in such demand as a means of transferring a flame, to light a candle from a fireplace or to light a gentleman's cigar.

Some of these standard form spill vases can be of Continental origin, usually French but it is not often realized that some very decorative small vases or some figures and groups incorporating holders such as baskets were made for use as spill holders or as match holders. Contemporary trade catalogue descriptions make this clear – 'China figures, very richly decorated in colours and gilt, Dresden style; with brackets for spills … ' or 'Match stands, with figures in bisque china, decorated in colours and gilt … '

SPRINGER & CO.

Springer & Oppenheimer succeeded the Haidinger brothers at the Elbogen porcelain factory in Bohemia in about 1873. When Oppenheimer retired in 1885 the firm became Springer & Co. This firm, and presumably the previous partnership, produced and exported a vast amount of middle range porcelains and some earthenware.

The crowned shield mark was registered in 1891 but may have

Plate 98. A Continental porcelain close copy of a Meissen so-called 'snowball' or 'Schneeballen' vase of an extremely popular type. Copy of a Marcolini period Meissen crossed-swords mark. c.1870–90. 24¼ ins high. (Messrs. Bonhams)

been used since the 1870s. Various marks with the added 'OPIAG' or 'EPIAG' initials are of post-1918 date.

The general term 'Elbogen' is sometimes used, and refers to the Springer wares. The shield device can, however, be mistaken for the Conta & Boehme Possneck porcelains (see Conta & Boehme and Elbogen above).

STADTLENGSFELD
A wide range of low priced decorative porcelains, trinkets and novelty items were made at the Stadtlengsfeld porcelain manufactory in Thuringia in the last part of the 19th century and into the 20th century. The two most commonly found printed marks are reproduced below:

TEA SERVICES
It may be thought that tea services are confined to British manufactories, but this is far from the case. Although coffee may be the standard popular drink on the Continent tea wares and tea services have been produced in both porcelain and pottery since the early part of the 18th century.

As with the English wares the early Meissen and Sèvres porcelain teapots are small by modern standards, but they increased in capacity as the 18th century progressed. By 1800 Continental coffee wares tended to outnumber the tea wares but still tea services were produced for home as well as export markets.

As with the most classes of wares there was great interplay between the manufacturing nations. We in Britain tended to copy Continental forms and styles of decoration in the 18th century but by the 1820s several Continental manufacturers were adopting British forms such as London-shape tea wares.

The Continental porcelains by this period were all of the hard-paste variety covered with a shining hard glaze. The British wares by this time were all of the bone china body covered with a softer glaze resulting in rather more subdued effects.

One cannot in this concise guide give full information on all types of Continental porcelain tea wares but the products of the major firms will mostly bear an identifying mark and one can turn to specialist books to delve deeper into the subject (see Bibliography).

THIEME, CARL

This leading German manufacturer of decorative Dresden-type porcelain situated at Potschappel, near Dresden, produced a large quantity of very ornate porcelains, ranging from very large vases and centrepieces to small fancies, from the 1870s into at least the 1920s.

I have illustrated several good examples in *Godden's Guide to European Porcelain* but the firm also produced a large range of commercial copies of other types, especially Vienna, Sèvres and Capodimonte styled goods.

Apart from the relatively early (*c*.1875–90) cross and 'T' mark:

the following Carl Thieme printed marks are to be found on examples which I consider to date from the 1890s into the 20th century:

The Thieme porcelains can be regarded as mass-produced 19th-century decorative Meissen-style wares. There value largely depends on their decorative merit and condition.

TOURNAY (TOURNAI)

The Belgian porcelain factory at Tournay was a very important one in the middle of the 18th century, established in 1751. It produced a good range of middle-class blue and white designs which became exceedingly popular (Plate 99). The factory also produced fine quality decorative articles, figures and groups and well-painted useful wares.

There was seemingly an interchange of workpeople between Tournay and several English factories. Joseph Willems, the Chelsea figure modeller, reputedly trained and worked at Tournay. Henri Joseph and Fidelle Duvivier were talented Tournay artists who worked for periods in this country, the much-travelled Fidelle being especially popular when his work is found on English porcelains, including early New Hall.

Plate 99. OPPOSITE TOP *Representative pieces from a large French Tournai porcelain dinner service painted with a typical design in underglaze-blue. Crossed-swords and stars mark. c.1770–90. (Messrs. Christie's)*
Plate 100. OPPOSITE *A good quality moulded-edge Tournai porcelain plate, painted in the Continental style perhaps by Joseph Duvivier. Crossed-swords and star mark with initials 'I [J?] D' and 'R' incised. c.1763–71. Diameter 9 ins. (Victoria & Albert Museum (Crown Copyright))*

The less costly blue and white designs and several Tournay moulded service shapes were also copied by English factories, especially by Thomas Turner at Caughley. Production of porcelain reputedly ceased in 1800 but the production of earthenwares continued.

An early (now rare) mark comprises the design of a castle keep. This being hand painted varies considerably:

From the mid 1750s to the 1790s the standard hand painted or gilt mark comprised versions of the crossed-swords device with four crosses added. A typical version is shown here:

The Tournay porcelain and glaze is of the soft-paste type and as such can appear like early Sèvres or British porcelain.

As shown in Chapter 2, the Tournay factory in the second half of the 19th century, under the de Bettignies, was responsible for producing blanks of collectable 18th-century Sèvres and English porcelains which were decorated in Paris. It seems likely that they also produced copies of the more ornate types of early Tournay porcelain at this time. Certainly the existence of a Tournay mark should not be taken as conclusive evidence of its origin or period.

TRANSPARENCIES

This is an alternative name for Lithophanes (see above). While most of these moulded panels were of simple slab-type form, the light and shade technique was widely used for various novelties.

A range of Continental 'Bijou Transparencies' were illustrated in Messrs. Stenbridge's wholesale advertisement in *The Pottery Gazette* of 1889, and this interesting page is reproduced in *Godden's Guide to European Porcelain*.

VEILLEUSE

These decorative yet functional ceramic pots more than any other objects come in all shapes and sizes. Although examples were made in Britain they are very much a Continental fancy. We now use the French term, although other names were originally employed in different countries.

In essence they are a multi-part vessel for warming and storing liquid foods or beverages, for use at night or in a sick room. The base contained a simple heating device such as an oil container or night light candle. On top of the decorative main unit or pedestal sat a covered bowl or other receptacle (such as a tea or coffee container), the contents of which were kept hot by the flame.

Eighteenth-century examples were for liquid foods held in covered and often handled bowls, some of which were equipped with a pouring lip. Complete and perfect examples are now rarely found and are highly desirable collectors' items.

In the 19th century the potters substituted small covered kettle or teapot-like units for the earlier bowls. These now had a pouring spout and a handle. These tend to be called tea warmers or 'Veilleuses-théière', rather than the earlier food warmers, but other popular Continental beverages were also, no doubt, held within these heated pots. The small size of the pots suggest that they were made for the use of individuals rather than for a group.

As a single object these Veilleuses tended to be more ornately decorated than would have been a standard tea or coffee pot which was in most cases originally part of a complete service. From about the 1830s very fancy, novel forms were introduced but these never completely replaced the less expensive and more functional standard models.

Some of the novelty shapes were as human form – the 'personnages', or employed animal shapes. Several made decorative use of the light emitted from the heat source. Those incorporating lithophanic panels can be particularly attractive when lit from the outside.

A quite remarkable range of these objects are shown in Harold Newman's standard book *Veilleuses 1750–1860*, from practically every European country, with information on the whereabouts of the main collections. One good display is at the Musée des Arts Décoratifs in Paris. The Newman collection has been donated to the Wadsworth Atheneum, Hartford, Conn., USA.

Unfortunately few Veilleuses bear a maker's mark but this is to a large degree unimportant, as they are collected for their decorative merits, novelty or rarity of form. While not all examples are antique, or even old, and remembering that some are of average, commercial quality they still remain one of the most interesting ceramic objects to collect. However, 18th-century and fine quality, or rare, 19th-century examples will be costly.

VICTORIA (VIKTORIA)
This trade name was much used on porcelains exported by Schmidt & Co. of Altrohlau in Bohemia from the 1880s onwards. The firm was later retitled 'Viktoria Porzellanfabrik AG'. The English rendering Victoria was used in the marks found on wares exported to English-speaking countries. British wares can also bear this trade-name.

Plate 101. A yellow and blue ground showy but inexpensive trinket set. Printed Vienna shield-mark, with 'Victoria Czecho-Slovakia'. c.1920–30. Candlesticks 5½ ins high. (Present owner unknown)

The 'Victoria' porcelains are usually of a very inexpensive nature but the firm had a leading role in the mass-production market producing many printed copies of earlier popular designs.

The trade-name 'VICTORIA' over a crown was used for the standard mark. Country names 'Austria' or 'Czechoslovakia' were also often added, the latter signifying a date after 1919.

VIEW CHINA

Pottery and porcelain decorated with local views dates back well into the 18th century and such articles have always been popular. However, most examples found today are likely to be late Victorian or Edwardian, and many are quite inexpensive. They were extremely popular articles, perhaps purchased as a memento of a visit to the seaside.

Various German and French manufacturers catered for this great trade. I have quoted in Chapter 3 several trade advertisements. Here a few typical examples are quoted to show the extent of the trade in these goods – the views were usually associated with mottoes and inscribed articles such as plates or mugs inscribed 'A Present from Brighton' etc. 'Special attention given to orders with mottoes and seaside plates' (1885); 'Foreign China in Great variety … cups & saucers, mugs, jugs … also with mottoes, views' (1888); 'Mugs, cups and saucers &c., decorated to order, A Present from … or with views of any particular place or town' (1889); 'Novelties of every description for Seaside … view and motto china. Immense variety' (1895).

One could go on and on quoting such advertisements. One should also note that not all such articles were of Continental origin, some were British. In general the leading firms did not cater for this trade, because the wares were in general only saleable in the town depicted.

VION & BAURY

This partnership between August Vion and Charles Baury (formerly chief modeller to Jean Gille) took over and continued the celebrated Paris works of Jean Gille from c.1868. The new partnership continued Gille's speciality, the production of high-quality biscuit porcelains, chiefly attractive figure models or groups. It is certain that the most popular Gille models were continued in production by Vion & Baury, but this new partnership would also have introduced their own fresh designs.

The old Gille blue oval or circular pad mark was adopted to show the joined initial 'VB', as shown below. A large printed anchor device also seems to have been used by this firm:

Vion & Baury porcelains are not yet as highly regarded as the earlier Gille wares but the quality of the later (but still 'antique') Vion & Baury biscuit models can be equally high. Again they are valued mainly on the decorative merits of the individual pieces.

VOLKSTEDT

Volkstedt in Thuringia is a place-name much associated with Dresden-style German porcelains made in the second half of the 19th century and into the present century.

There are, or were, several porcelain manufactories in Volkstedt and in recent years several have claimed the title 'Aelteste Volkstedter Porzellanfabrik' or the oldest Volkstedt porcelain factory. The first seems to have been established by Georg Macheleid in about 1760, and this factory has continued under various owners with many changes of title up to the present time.

The 18th- and early 19th-century porcelains are unlikely to be met with by British readers. From c.1861 to 1877 the trade name was Macheleid Triebner & Co. Between c.1877 and 1894 the new partnership traded as Triebner, Ens & Eckert until Richard Eckert left to establish his own factory in Volkstedt. The remaining partners in the mid 1890s then continued under the long trade name 'Aelteste Volkstedter Porzellanfabrik Triebner, Ens & Co'. This was short-lived as Karl Ens left to found his own factory leaving Triebner & Co. to continue. In about 1900 Triebner formed a Limited Company, 'Aelteste Volkstedter Porzellanfabrik AG', which still continues today under an amended name.

Other Volkstedt porcelain manufacturers include Richard Eckert's own works founded in 1894 as 'Richard Eckert & Co. AG' which continued to c.1918. Eckert also had a decorating establishment in Dresden, the 'Dresden Art Publishers – Richard Eckert'. The Eckert porcelains were very much in the decorative Dresden style, and bore several close copies of the Dresden crossed-swords or the Volkstedt hay-fork device.

The basic mark of the Volkstedt factories was a hay-fork. This occurs both singly, as a pair, with one reversed and joined by two lines or a hay-fork with a sun-burst device dividing the handle. A single line divided by the sun-burst device also occurs. These underglaze-blue marks are reproduced below. One or other of these devices occur on a wide range of very decorative Dresden-style ornamental porcelains, made in the period c.1880–1910.

Originally these Volkstedt porcelains were quite reasonably priced as they were made for the mass market to undersell the Dresden originals. They are now considered to be quite respectable, and can be charming and certainly very decorative, in a florid manner.

WAHLISS, ERNST

Ernst Wahliss is a highly important figure in the history of ceramic manufacturing and retailing in the latter part of the 19th century. He had acquired the original moulds, etc., used by the Imperial Vienna porcelain factory and proceeded to reproduce, or rather reintroduce, these often superb decorative wares some twenty or so years after the original factory closed in the early 1860s. Seemingly he also employed some of the former decorators, or trained up new hands to work in the old styles.

His old Vienna-style porcelains are highly decorative and are usually of superb quality. He might even be said to have continued the old factory and retained its traditional styles.

Ernst Wahliss went further than the original management in that he also opened grand retail establishments to sell his own

Plate 102. A large Wahliss Royal Vienna figure decorated with typical muted colours. Applied pad mark 'Royal Vienna. Wahliss', model number 4700. c.1905–14. 23 ins high. (Messrs. Sotheby's, Sussex)

and other leading makes of ceramic art as well as glass wares. In London he opened in Oxford Street what he claimed was 'the largest Ceramic Art Galleries within the British Empire'. He advertised in such upmarket magazines as *The Connoisseur*, claiming the date of establishment of 1864 and listing the main British stock as comprising Royal Crown Derby, Minton, Crown Staffordshire and Wedgwood. His imports from the Continent included 'Royal Dresden, Imperial Vienna, Modern Vienna, Delft, Italian Fayence, Alexandra Ware, Art Terra Cotta'.

In *Godden's Guide to European Porcelain* various Wahliss products are illustrated with a contemporary photograph of his London showrooms. Wahliss surely is one of the most neglected 19th-century manufacturers, perhaps rather a showman, but his products and stock were made up to a quality not down to a price.

Apart from the reuse of the old Vienna shield-shape mark which he must have employed more legitimately than most manufacturers, Wahliss also used various printed marks of his own. These include several that incorporate the description 'Royal Vienna' but also his own surname Wahliss or the trade description 'Alexandra Porcelain Works' which were situated at Turn in Austria. The Wahliss Vienna wares and marks often bear the place name 'Vienna' or 'Wien'. A selection of typical printed marks of the post-1880 period are shown below:

I have seen present day dealers describing their Wahliss figures or groups as being made 'from original moulds made prior to 1864'. This may be true in some cases, but the date of the original conception does not effect the late, probably 1900s, date of the articles made from old moulds and it is probable that Wahliss commissioned some new fashionable models. Indeed some display a decided Art Nouveau flavour of the 1890–1910 period, and obviously have no connection with the old models.

Many Wahliss ornamental porcelains and various types of earthenware or stoneware have no connection with old Vienna at all but they are decorative middle-market articles in their own right. In many cases Wahliss established his own styles and was proud to use his own name or initial marks.

WALL PLAQUES

Wall plaques come in all shapes and sizes and were made at all periods. Tiles are a form of wall decoration but wall plaques are free-hanging decorations that can be taken down or moved.

The simplest form of wall plaque was the slab or porcelain

picture that was framed and hung on the wall as an oil painting would be. These are a subject in themselves and are discussed under the heading Plaques above.

Other wall plaques took the form of large circular dishes usually in earthenware, the entire centre of which was hand-painted. Some superb Italian faience dishes take this form and original (non-reproduction) examples are rare and costly. The footrim might be pierced so that the piece could be suspended.

Later porcelain plaques may have an ornate border design. The typical Vienna-style examples are of this type and such pieces are rightly expensive on account of their obvious decorative merit. Other, mainly late Victorian, specimens are broadly painted, often in slight relief. These too can be very decorative and unique specimens signed by leading ceramic painters or from collected factories, such as that of Theodore Deck of Paris, can be very desirable. However, the quality and decorative effect of these later plaques can be very variable.

Other wall plaques were mass-produced for sale at popular prices; in the main these will be of earthenware rather than porcelain and the decoration is likely to be printed rather than hand-painted. Such examples may well be decorative and perhaps have a period charm, but their modest original cost should be reflected in today's cost.

A further quite large class of wall plaque was embellished if not enhanced with relief ornamentation, such as inexpensive flowers and leafage applied to the surface. They are obviously dust traps and are difficult to clean so that it is perhaps understandable that they have now lost their popularity.

Other attractive French and German wall plaques of a modest size are embellished with modelled figures. These are often in bisque (unglazed) china and are decorated with pastel colours, often with slight gilding. Plaques of this type dating after about 1860 are quite popular and were made in pairs.

Other moulded wall plaques have figure or other subjects in slight relief in the Wedgwood style. The Danish terracotta examples which were advertised in 1882 are of this popular and tasteful class. Being devoid of added painted decoration or gilding they offered good value and are still not costly.

The subject of wall plaques is a vast one and is dealt with in more detail in *Godden's Guide to European Porcelain*.

WALL POCKETS

These were very popular mid to late 19th-century porcelain ornaments. They were made in matching pairs and often took the form of fancy shapes. They were both decorative and useful. Flowers, grasses, tapers, etc., could be placed within the hollowed centre. In general specimens do not bear a maker's mark. Their present-day value depends very much on the decorative merit of each model and on its condition!

WITTMANN & ROTH

I wish to mention this London wholesaling partnership as they were large-scale importers of Continental novelties into London and their goods were then distributed far and wide. They were one of the few such firms to have employed their own initial

Plate 103. A selection of Continental porcelain novelty oil lamp bases as stocked by the London wholesalers Wittmann & Roth. Reproduced from The Pottery Gazette of October 1886.

marks and in some cases their popular lines were registered in the British design registry office, giving them copyright protection. These registration marks (see pp. 192–5 above) can lead owners to believe that the articles are of British manufacture, but this is not the case.

The partnership specialized in novelty-form oil lamp bases. A page from their British trade advertisement as issued in October 1886 is shown in Plate 103. The reference or model numbers range from 525 to 1090 and can be found on the objects. All these lamp bases now seem to be very scarce. All pieces seem to be above average quality and many models are amusing and decorative.

The most popular Wittmann & Roth oil lamp base must have been the owl model which was registered in London on 29 July 1881. This comes in various sizes and in different treatments. These usually bear the relevant diamond shape British registration device and in some cases the 'WR' monogram mark in underglaze-blue, as shown below:

Little is known about the partner Roth, although he was probably Joseph Roth who had his own business and registered various Continental designs under his own name between 1879 and 1882. However, the original firm continued to trade under the old style Wittmann & Roth. In 1895 the partners in this concern were Sidney Adolphus and Richard Charles Wittmann who were presumably the sons of Philip Adolphus Wittmann who was trading in the 1850s. By 1897 the name Wittmann & Co. occurs but the firm seems to have been discontinued before 1900. The Wittmann & Roth Continental imports sometimes bear one of several painted, printed, impressed or incised initial marks:

W & R   WR   W & R
                                          L

WOLFSOHN, HELENA

The Wolfsohn decorating establishment in Dresden was established in the early 1840s, but while Mrs Helena Wolfsohn claimed 1841, another official claim cited 1843.

Initially at least this studio decorated Dresden and other types of white blanks for resale at a profit. Over the years the concern prospered until the late 1870s. Helena Wolfsohn decorative porcelains bearing a copy of the old Meissen Augustus Rex mark, the 'AR' monogram, became so popular that the state factory belatedly took legal action to prevent her from using this old Meissen mark. An example is shown below, but being hand-painted and used over a long period, many slight variations

Plate 104. Front view of a yellow ground vase (one of a pair) decorated at the Wolfsohn works in Dresden. These vases are of very good quality and are extremely decorative. Underglaze-blue 'AR' monogram mark. c.1870–80. 6¾ ins high. (Messrs. Godden of Worthing Ltd)

occur. The Meissen factory probably succeeded in taking action to prohibit the use of this mark in 1881. Consequently pieces bearing this 'AR' device should pre-date 1882:

One of several other versions has an arrow-like device incorporated:

The Wolfsohn porcelains, which were much cheaper than the true Meissen or Dresden contemporary productions, were extremely popular in all markets. They were decorative and inexpensive, with the added attraction of bearing an old form of Meissen mark which the reference books stated was reserved for Augustus the Strong's own use! As stated under 'Augustus Rex' these mid 19th-century porcelains bore little or no resemblance to the original restrained products of the early 18th century. The Victorian Wolfsohn pieces were, in their mass middle-market way, far more saleable, cleverly tailored to the Victorian taste. (See Plates 39 and 104 for typical examples.)

The Wolfsohn 'AR' marked decorative wares sold in quantity and were better quality than most imitations of Dresden porcelains. Colour grounded cups and saucers with Watteau-style figure decoration sold in huge numbers, as did a host of miniature cabinet pieces and the rarer large vases.

In July 1877 Helena Wolfsohn registered the 'AR' mark as her trade mark in Britain (stating that the mark had been used over the last thirty-four years) but this registration may only have been because the Saxon state factory was seeking to prohibit her use of this early Meissen mark. Its action was presumably all the more difficult if the mark was already legally registered in Wolfsohn's name! Nevertheless the state factory won their action and the Wolfsohn establishment employed a new form of mark from *c*.1882, a crown over the cursive letter 'D'. This mark was used well into the 20th century, indeed it was still listed in the mid 1930s.

Some authorities have stated that this firm also used the Crown Dresden mark of a crown over the word 'Dresden'. This does not seem to be the case. (See Crown Dresden above.)

Although Wolfsohn porcelains are universally associated with the Dresden-styled patterns, it is highly probable that other popular types were also emulated and exported far and wide. The firm apparently issued at least one illustrated catalogue of their productions but I have been unable to locate a copy in British libraries.

Helena Wolfsohn's daughter succeeded to the company on Helena's death in about 1882. In the 20th century new partners or proprietors were added, Leopold Elb (Helena's grandson) and then Walter Stephan, but the main Wolfsohn name remained in the trade style until after the 1939–45 war.

In the 1930s the firm advertised various decorative table and ornamental porcelains in the styles of old Dresden, Berlin and Vienna porcelains. The main export markets catered for were North America, Britain and her colonies, Scandinavia, Switzerland, Italy, the Balkans, France and Belgium. The firm also exhibited at various international exhibitions and won various awards, including Sidney in 1879 and Melbourne in 1880.

Further information on the Wolfsohn decorative porcelains and illustrations of typical examples are given in *Godden's Guide to European Porcelain*.

ZURICH

Good quality hard-paste porcelain was made at Schooren, near Zurich, in Switzerland from the early 1760s. Figures as well as decorative useful wares were made but the output was relatively small. Genuine specimens are rarely found in Britain, but they are certainly commercially desirable.

Different authorities cite various dates for the factory's closure between 1791 and 1897! The production of porcelains, however, probably ceased in or soon after the 1790s, but some later porcelains occur with the Zurich mark. This was a large capital 'Z' with a central horizontal bar, painted in underglaze-blue. Earthenwares were also produced, but specimens seem even rarer than the porcelains.

5

GENERAL GUIDES TO DATING,
MARKS AND VALUES

MARKS

Some general comments on trade or other types of identifying marks may well be of assistance to the layman for there are many complications. It is certainly not merely a question of looking up a mark – perhaps an anchor in a mark book and jumping to the conclusion that your electric light ornament must be 18th-century Chelsea!

Firstly, one should remember that the well-known factory marks of prestigious factories such as Meissen, Sèvres or Vienna have been copied by all and sundry over a very long period. Today the marks of these three collectable factories are more often found on forgeries or reproductions than on genuine specimens! Nevertheless in most other cases, a mark offers the only available evidence to enable one to identify the maker and to fix at least an approximate period of manufacture. The difficulty is that with Continental marks, there are thousands of different firms and tens of thousands of marks.

In many cases, particularly in the 1860–1920 period, these firms were quite small concerns and their products are not generally available in this country. Many of the 19th-century makes will be collectable although in most cases the decorative merit (or otherwise) of the piece will dictate its commercial value. A superb quality Paris porcelain vase can, for example, be more valuable than a sparsely decorated 18th-century plate or cup and saucer.

Ceramic factory marks fall into different classes: (1) clay marks; (2) underglaze marks; and (3) overglaze marks:

1. Clay marks are those that were formed or added before the piece was fired, that is they are added while the body was in a malleable condition. These clay marks cannot therefore be added at a later period, they are part of the piece from its birth. Most clay marks are incised or cut into the body, as you can scratch or draw into butter with a match or similar object. An incised mark is drawn or made by hand and different versions of the same device may occur. An impressed mark or model number was usually impressed with a metal (or other) die or stamp. The result will look mechanical and neat, although small details of the device may not be all that clear. Other clay marks were moulded and therefore form part of

the original shape, the details of the mark being part of the original moulds. Such moulded marks may occur on the finished piece in high relief or recessed. Moulded marks are not normally very clear.

Another type of clay mark comprise applied or sprigged seal-type marks appearing as raised pads. These applied marks are sometimes termed pad-marks.

2. Underglaze marks are also reliable as they were added before the article was glazed. Underglaze marks usually occur in cobalt blue and may be hand-painted or printed. I can only state that they were reasonably reliable because the manufacturer may have set out to add a misleading or fake mark to its products. A Dresden-style crossed-swords mark in underglaze-blue can be painted on anybody's porcelain if they so wish!

3. The overglaze marks are the most plentiful and can be the most dangerous to collectors, as they can be applied with little trouble at a later period with intent to deceive. Overglaze marks may be painted, stencilled or printed. They include very many different types and styles.

It should be noted that an overglaze mark may be ground off or more commonly hidden by another mark being placed over the original. Sometimes a gilt leaf or similar device was used to conceal a mark. If any of these three methods has been employed it indicates that the piece has been decorated outside the manufacturing factory. There were in Europe a surprisingly large number of decorating studios that enhanced white blanks. This is not necessarily a bad thing as they were specialists, but in general the decorating studios were usually endeavouring to undersell the products of the leading factories.

I have in previous books dealing with British ceramics and marks given various Godden rules that will save you from such silly errors – *The Encyclopaedia of British Pottery and Porcelain Marks*, and *Encyclopaedia of British Porcelain Manufacturers*. When we turn to Continental marks these rules need amending, but the list of helpful pointers is rather longer. Before discussing them, it is essential to remember that one must always date a mark to its latest feature, not its earliest. A printed mark might, for example, comprise a crown or shield with the trade name 'Royal Saxon' and the date 1765. There might also be the helpful note 'Hand Painted in W. Germany'. This mark includes four pointers to the correct dating of the mark and the object, but most owners will only pay attention to the date '1765', assuming that the piece was made in that year, rather than after 1945 when Germany was divided into the Western and Eastern sectors. The fact that the mark is printed in itself precludes the 1765 dating!

COUNTRY OF ORIGIN

With British marks it is now generally realized that the country name, usually 'England' (rather than Scotland, Wales, Britain or Great Britain), denotes a date after 1891 and that the longer version 'Made in England' was often used after the end of the First World War. These rules of thumb, based to some degree on the requirements of the American McKinley 1890 Tariff Act, do not necessarily hold true for Continental wares imported into England.

The country of origin can occur from the mid to late 1880s and the longer version 'Made in Germany' or 'Made in France' can appear on articles as early as the late 1890s. These differences are, however, not always a reliable guide, the post-1925 plate shown in Plate 31 bears only the one word 'Germany'. These country names certainly do not appear on all post-1880 Continental wares, for instance, 'Germany' or 'Made in Germany' never appears on Meissen porcelains.

The country name itself can give an approximate indication of date. For example, 'Czechoslovakia' and variations such as 'Tschechozlowakei' denote a post-1918 date for the country did not exist before then; conversely the old name 'Bohemia' should not occur on marks after 1918.

The division of Germany into different zones after 1945 is also reflected in marks. Some will have additional wording such as 'US Zone'. Rather later and more commonly we find the two main divisions being recorded as 'W. Germany' or 'Western Germany', and the Russian or Eastern zone as 'German D R'. These marks should have been discontinued from 1991 as Germany was then reunified.

FOREIGN

As an alternative to giving the country of origin in full some imports only bore the description 'Foreign'; this normally indicates a 20th-century date. A difficulty, however, arises from the fact that sometimes the 'Foreign' statement appeared on a stick-on paper label which has long since been removed.

It is important to remember that the non-appearance of a country of origin mark or of the word 'Foreign' does *not* prove a pre-1880 date.

DATES

A date incorporated in a mark is almost always the claimed date of establishment of the firm (or its predecessors) or of the pottery. For example, a common 'Royal Bonn 1755' mark will relate to the second half of the 19th century or later. As a general rule you can take it that full dates were not included in 18th-century porcelain marks.

ROYAL
It is a sound Godden rule that trade names such as 'Royal Bonn', 'Royal Saxon', and so on, denote a date after about 1850 and in most instances such wording signifies a 20th-century date. It can also be assumed that pieces bearing such marks were intended for English-language markets.

TRADE MARK, FABRIK-MARKE, SCHUTZ-MARKE
The wording 'Trade Mark' or foreign language equivalents added to a mark to signify that it has been officially registered, will show that the piece was produced after 1865. Usually one only finds such wording used after about 1900.

CO., CIE, AG
These English, French and German additions to a ceramic work will usually indicate a 19th- or 20th-century date. Each indicates that the concern was a company, or the owners included others in addition to the one or two named. If, for example, I had partners or backers named John Brown and Richard Smith, I might well trade as Geoffrey Godden & Co. rather than as Godden, Brown & Smith. Although the above abbreviations usually indicate the relevant country of origin, it can happen that German firms used the description '& Company', so that some German initial marks include '& Co.'.

LTD, GMBH
These English and German abbreviations for a Limited Liability Company added to a mark will indicate a late date, usually after 1900.

PATENT, DÉPOSÉ, DEP
Such claims relating to a process, shape or design suggest a post-1860 date. 'Déposé' or the abbreviation 'Dep' usually indicates a French patent.

REGISTRATION DEVICE OR NUMBER
The British system is explained in Chapter 4 under Registered Designs and Shapes, and Registered Numbers.

PATTERN NUMBERS
Pattern numbers were widely used by British porcelain manufacturers and a study of these has led to helpful short-cuts to attribution and dating. However, the Continental manufacturers seem to have largely managed without them, at least in the 18th and first part of the 19th century.

MODEL NUMBERS
While as stated above pattern numbers do not usually occur on Continental porcelain, one does find a wide use of model num-

bers appearing incised or impressed on ornamental objects, such as figures. The practice was perhaps started at the Meissen factory, but by the 1880s most Continental figures, groups and even cheap fancies bore a model number. These can reach quite high numbers when the factory was of long duration or had a large output of new novelties.

WORKMEN'S MARKS
Incised initials or ciphers widely occur on Continental porcelain even in the 18th century. One would even expect to find such faint marks in the body on some makes such as 18th-century Sèvres and would question the source of a Sèvres-marked example without a potter's personal identification mark. Some specialist books will give lists of such marks but they were solely used for internal factory reasons and they seldom will, on their own, lead to a definite factory attribution. They are, however, much more commonly found on Continental pieces than on British wares.

YEAR MARKS
Several Continental factories have employed year marks. These can be incorporated in painted marks, such as the year letters used from 1753 to 1793 on Sèvres porcelain. Other printed or impressed marks show the last two (or three) numerals of the year, for example, '99' for 1799 or '801' for 1801 to cite examples impressed into the Vienna porcelains. Other factories, such as Meissen in recent years, have used various private signs or different placing of a line or dash. These marks can be regarded as sound indications of at least the year of potting but in the case of underglaze marks they may have been decorated and sold at a later period.

ÖPIAG AND EPIAG
Several Austrian and Czechoslovakian marks incorporate these initials. They both relate to forms of co-operative mergers or federations under which several firms pooled their resources and publicity, taking for example a group advertisement in the *Pottery Gazette* trade paper.
    ÖPIAG or 'Österreichische Porzellan-Industrie AG' was formed in Vienna in March 1918. EPIAG or Erste Porzellan-Industrie AG was formed in June 1920.

RETAILERS' MARKS
Some Continental wares bear the names of British or other retailers, often leading London stores. You may safely assume that such articles were made after about 1880. This is especially true if the full address is given.

HAND PAINTED, HANDMALEREI, ETC.

Some printed or handpainted marks will include the claim 'Hand Painted' or foreign equivalents. Most will be on 20th-century products, probably post-1945 items.

FINE PORCELAIN

Such a claim incorporated in printed marks indicates a 20th-century date, usually after 1930.

PORCELAINE

It will be observed that the French add an 'e' to our English spelling of porcelain. When this occurs in marks it give a fair indication that the piece is French. However, there is at least one exception. A late 19th-century elaborate printed mark used by Sampson Bridgwood & Son of Longton in the Staffordshire Potteries, includes the description 'Porcelaine Opaque' for its durable ironstone-type wares.

SE

This abbreviation for 'Societas Europaea' may well be found incorporated in company names from 1992. This is the new Eurostyle designation for a Public Limited Company and it can be used by companies engaged in international trade or having branches or divisions in different European countries.

BAR CODES

It could also happen that some post-1990 ceramics will bear added labels or printed devices incorporating or comprising the bar code style of pricing or commodity identification.

HARD-PASTE

Almost without exception, the Continental porcelains produced in the 19th and 20th centuries have been of the hard-paste type. The unglazed bottom of the foot will feel hard and your nail will usually audibly grate against the body. The glaze too will be very hard and glass-like. The exceptions to the 19th-century Continental hard-paste rule are some Tournai and the de Bettignies St Amand porcelains, typified by their copies of old soft-paste Sèvres porcelains.

I conclude with a few remainders concerning some basic marks that can give rise to confusion. One must not take famous factory marks at their face value!

ANCHOR MARK

So many people know that the anchor mark denotes that the article was made at the famous 18th-century Chelsea porcelain works. It is true that the Chelsea factory used such a device to mark some of their products but so did several other factories. The mark, for example, reproduced here, when painted in red enamel, is more likely to be found on Italian porcelain from the Venice factory during the Cozzi period from the 1760s into the 19th century.

This Venice version and most non-Chelsea anchor marks are quite boldly painted, whereas the Chelsea anchors are under a quarter inch high and are sometimes almost hidden away.

While Chelsea, Venice and several other factories, producing either porcelain or earthenwares, used the anchor mark, the reader is more likely to find it on fakes or reproductions made on the Continent from about the 1860s onwards. The gold anchor especially should be taken as a warning rather than accepted with glee! I have in Chapter 2 attempted to warn the reader of such outright fakes and reproductions which bear a mock-Chelsea anchor mark. This chapter should be studied carefully. These illustrations show only the tip of the very great problem, and I must suggest once again, that if you are being sold a specimen as Chelsea you should obtain a written receipt that states clearly that the piece is genuine Chelsea porcelain of the correct date.

Many of these hard-paste gold anchor marked Continental figures or groups are very decorative and charming and there may well be a case for making a purchase – but not at a Chelsea price!

Several mainly 19th-century Continental porcelain manufacturers added their initials to an anchor device. Such marks as the Bohne example here should not be confused with the simple, unadulterated, Chelsea anchor.

Any printed anchor mark (as the Vion anchor on p. 217) or an anchor mark on earthenwares obviously will not relate to the Chelsea factory, which only made soft-paste porcelain.

A R MARK

As recorded in nearly every book on ceramics, this monogram mark was used on early Meissen porcelain, reputedly on pieces made expressly for King Augustus II or III. It follows that the high-quality, early and rare porcelains bearing this mark are seldom found outside museums. It also follows that very many 19th-century copies of such early porcelains occur and the 'AR' or so-called 'Augustus Rex' mark was widely used. These later essays can have decorative merit and are collectable in their own right but not as true early Meissen porcelains.

Most of the later 'AR' porcelains of the types shown in Plates 39 and 104 were produced or rather decorated at the Dresden studios of Helena Wolfsohn from about 1850. The Meissen management belatedly took action to stop the incorrect use of this mark in the early 1880s and this device should not have been used after 1882. Further information is given in Chapters 2 and 4 but it is now a safe bet that any colourful porcelain with coloured grounds and figure subject panels bearing this mark will have been made, or decorated, in the 1850–82 period in Dresden, but not at the state factory at Meissen.

CROSSED-SWORDS MARK

As noted several times in this book the crossed-swords mark, which seems to be universally acknowledged as the mark of the famous Dresden, or more correctly Meissen, factory was widely copied. It must not, therefore, be assumed that this mark necessarily indicates a Dresden or Meissen origin. Even if the mark is genuine it must not be assumed that the piece is 18th-century; the mark (with variations) has been used by Meissen to the present day. The reader is advised to read Chapter 2 very closely and to be on guard when purchasing crossed-swords marked porcelains for large sums. The piece may be decorative and attractive but it is not necessarily Meissen.

CROWN

Although it may be thought that a printed crown device signifies a British ceramic product (and reference books tend to confirm this belief), it is not necessarily correct, as several Continental firms used such a mark. A crown mark also does not guarantee a royal factory or any royal connection.

Middle-range hard-paste German or Bohemian porcelains of the period 1890–1930 often bear a printed crown mark. These porcelains, which may be decorated with lithographic-type transfers, were probably made by Bloch & Co. of Eichwald in Bohemia (now Dubi in Czechoslovakia). This firm was established in 1871. These porcelains may have a decorative value but they are not especially collected.

DRESDEN MARK

As I have explained in earlier chapters, this description is widely and erroneously used to describe porcelains made at the state factory at Meissen. True Meissen porcelain never used the word 'Dresden' as a mark, or as part of a mark. There were, however, in and around the city of Dresden several decorating establishments which from the 1840s onwards used various initials or other devices in association with the place name 'Dresden'. Almost without exception these 'Dresden' marks were employed to add value or interest to wares of only commercial quality. Decorative they may be but Dresden they are not in the normally accepted sense of a Meissen source.

VALUES

The question of values is a perplexing one, even to the professional. Certainly one cannot, or should not, value a piece without seeing and handling it. A reliable valuation cannot be made from a verbal or written description.

Nevertheless, it may be of some help if I indicate some of the points a specialist would take into account in valuing an item, perhaps a teapot. These points, which I have not listed in any particular order, would be weighed up against the specialist's own judgement and experience; no two persons would form precisely the same judgement. Always remember that the valuation of antiques is not an exact science!

The main points a specialist would consider are:

AGE

Many folk have the idea that the older the object, the more valuable it must be, but this is not necessarily so. An old, broken, stained earthenware teapot from an unknown factory may be all but valueless or at least difficult to sell. Whereas, a decorative, fine 20th-century example bearing the mark of a leading and collectable firm may well be highly prized. Age in itself is not a virtue.

CONDITION

This can be vital: any damage adversely effects the commercial value of a teapot or any other object. Certainly relatively minor damage to a rare and desirable example will be overlooked, the piece is still very saleable. However, if you have a standard, ordinary, example, even minor faults will be damning, for better examples are available and are preferable.

REPAIRS

Damage can, in most cases, be repaired but a bad repair will detract further from the appearance and value of a piece. A good repair will be costly and will not return the piece to a perfect, mint, state. The faults will merely be less obvious. If you are thinking of selling a damaged specimen, it is better to offer it in an unrestored state. It could well be that the repair will cost more than the consequent market value of the article!

MAKE
Obviously some makes, individual factories or ceramic artists, are more desirable than others. People collect some factories' products – usually those praised in books – and neglect others. A teapot or other object from a leading factory will obviously be more desirable than a pot made at an unknown back-street, third-division, pottery. Experience will suggest which makes are especially desirable and to whom.

MARK
In general terms, a marked specimen is more desirable than an unmarked one, as long as the mark is genuine! However, an unmarked piece that a specialist can confidently attribute to a commercially desirable manufactory is likely to be more valuable than a marked example from a less popular factory or period. All these separate points of consideration interplay with one another.

DESIRABILITY OF FORM
Some shapes or types of object are generally more popular than others. Teapots are popular as many people collect them and several books have been written on the subject. Yet this does not mean that any second-hand teapot is valuable.

In general terms small or miniature examples are more desirable to a collector than over-large objects that may be difficult to display in an average home or display case. On the other hand a very large decorative figure group or vase may be desirable to some or in the decorator's market. Rare or novelty forms are obviously more desirable than standard, common examples. All teapots are, of course, rarer than cups and saucers as the original tea or coffee service will have only one teapot but twelve cups and saucers.

DESIRABILITY OF DECORATION
As with shapes, some decorations are generally more popular than others. Yellow grounds (or bands) are rarer than blue and are consequently more desirable and costly. Finely painted shell or feather decoration is more saleable than dead birds or animals. Flower subjects and landscapes were standard forms of ceramic decoration and consequently they occur in varying standards of painting and finish. Some can be superb, others rendered in a slapdash style. Named botanical specimens or named views are more desirable than simple purely decorative unnamed floral sprays or mock views.

In general terms hand-painted subjects are preferable than cheap printed designs. A painted piece could be unique, a printed subject will be repetitive and mass-produced (I am writing mainly of post-1800 Continental porcelain, not of 18th-century English wares). However, it can be that a good quality printed design from a major firm is superior to a run-of-the-mill hand-painted piece from a minor factory.

GENUINE, REISSUE OR COPY?

Obviously a genuine piece from say the Meissen or Sèvres factory will be much more valuable than a later copy. The valuer, therefore, has to decide if the piece is genuine and of the correct period.

A genuine Meissen figure of the 1760s may be worth £1,000, a later example of the 1860s made from the same moulds may be worth £400 pounds whilst a good copy made by another factory may not be worth £100. Yet these examples will look much the same in a photograph or to an inexperienced eye. Expertise is vital and normally is acquired from long experience. It must be stated that there is a market for later reissues, copies or even fakes but the value is small in comparison with the genuine originals. The later examples are normally of a purely decorative value, they are desirable at lower prices because we cannot all afford to purchase (or insure!) genuine Meissen figures, groups, vases, etc., costing thousands of pounds.

POPULARITY

This can be very important, for popularity and fashion vary greatly and changes in collectors' taste can occur at short notice. A type or make of object commanding high prices today may be a dead duck in five years' time. The collectors who started a fashion may have died or moved on to collect a new fashionable line, dumping on an already small market their now-unwanted 'treasures'. Conversely, once-neglected lines may come into fashion and command unheard of prices. I can quote a non-ceramic fad – teddy bears – as a typical example. I cannot predict if demand for such toys will continue to grow or if grown collectors will forsake the collecting of other peoples' cast-off cuddlies. In real terms some once highly collected ceramics have fallen in price over the past hundred years but others have come into prominence. The valuer needs to have a knowledge of the current popularity or otherwise of an object.

COST

It is often thought that the cost of a piece relates to its value; this is not necessarily so! You may have purchased a bad unsaleable object from an expensive source. You might have been the first person in ten years to have fallen for this example, you may have overlooked the damage or clever repair. You might have been the unfortunate winner of an auction sale battle, perhaps bidding against an unrealistically high reserve! Believe me such things happen, the cost of an antique does not dictate its value or resale value!

ASSOCIATION

As with cost, one's personal association with a piece, does not effect the commercial value. Because the cracked, lidless teapot belonged to your grandmother, does not turn an unsaleable crock into a highly desirable museum specimen. It may well be priceless in your own family but it is valueless to anyone else!

On the other hand if a piece does have a strong family or other association do take the trouble to note the facts so that the knowledge or tradition does not pass away with you. It takes only a few moments to affix and write a label, which may be of interest to future generations.

SIZE

I have already mentioned that over-large articles can be difficult to house or display to advantage. Conversely miniature articles although useless can be very decorative. They can be charmingly well arranged in a small display case, on wall brackets or shelves. The value of ceramics can be in inverse ratio to the size but again many other considerations come into play and it would be nonsense to suggest that a poor, late, miniature Dresden-style cup and saucer is worth more than a two-foot high 1750 Meissen vase just because it is a miniature.

PEDIGREE

This can be quite important if the piece has previously been in well-known collections and bears the label relating to such ownership. Similarly former exhibition labels can add to the interest of a piece and consequently its value. It follows that such labels should never be removed.

QUALITY

This attribute is highly important. High-quality potting and decoration normally denotes a leading manufactory and, of course, discriminating collectors will also appreciate quality of workmanship. The difficulty can be that less experienced folk may have difficulty in distinguishing between quality and mere show. Masses of cheap gilding (that may be printed) does not equate with quality, a printed Kauffman-like figure subject (see Plate 72) is mass-produced commercial decoration – attractive maybe, but not quality decoration.

Likewise a signature does not necessarily denote quality or even that the piece was hand painted. Signatures of well-known decorators or artists can occur on cheap, mass-produced, printed wares made long after the named person had died!

These very basic considerations must be taken into account when determining the commercial value of ceramics – old and not so old. This commercial value may be valid for insurance purposes, for Probate valuations or for the possible sale value.

Such valuations for these three purposes will differ, even if made by one person. Firstly, the valuation, for insurance purposes, should reflect the replacement value of a object and you may have to make the new purchase from an expensive source – not a car-boot sale! Valuations for Probate are normally based on the assumption that they may be sold at an inopportune time in perhaps not ideal conditions. In other words Probate values will be less than an insurance valuation and, of course, a Probate value reflects a selling price, the insurance value relates to retail purchase.

A valuation for sale purposes gives rise to more difficulties – it is best described as a 'guesstimate'. Are you selling to a dealer, by auction, by private treaty or by some other system? A dealer may make a firm, expenses-free offer that will be higher than the payment you will receive from an auctioneer, after the deduction of various charges. All depends, however, on the dealer – is he a specialist in this line, does he have good customers waiting to purchase similar wares, is he (or she) a 'merchant', happy to take a reasonable profit for a quick sale? Likewise auctioneers vary greatly and you are committed to the sale at one place, at one time. The same piece offered by even one auctioneer at different sales can be expected to 'fetch' varying prices – different people will be present. Just because piece 'A' is recorded as being sold for £10,000 in January 1996 does not mean that an identical specimen will command the same price in March. The original buyer will hardly want a second example, so the main buyer is now out of the market. Many other considerations; personal, commercial, political or even the weather can effect the price. It is also as well to remember that a published auction price does not reflect the sum received by the seller! The auctioneer will charge both the seller and the buyer and will also normally deduct insurance cover while the object is in his care – and charge the owner for any catalogue illustration! Likewise it would be naïve to suppose that a dealer will offer a would-be seller the marked retail asking price of a similar piece on show in his expensive showroom or stand at a Fair.

In essence the old view that an object is only worth what you can get for it, is based on wide experience and truth. It is no good believing that your teapot is the finest in the world, a unique specimen, worth £10,000, if nobody agrees with you. The old adage that all values depend on supply and demand is also true and I would place the emphasis on 'demand'. As I write, there are hundreds of houses 'for sale' in my home town, seven in my road alone; few buyers are available even for such a basic commodity, and consequently prices are on the decline. You or your professional agent or adviser can fix a price or value but no sale is made until you have found a willing and able buyer who is in agreement.

It is much the same with old pottery and porcelain or indeed with any commodity. Nothing has a sure fixed, guaranteed value; the market – the buyer (if you can find one) – has the last word.

Due to the complexities of the subject and the fact that so many later reproductions and forgeries exist I do not feel it right and proper to offer opinions on pieces where the owner is only able to give a written description or send a drawing or photograph. A true judgement or valuation can, in my opinion, only be made when the specialist is able to see and handle an object and size up all the many pointers.

Readers should note that whilst many illustrations are credited to Messrs. Godden of Worthing, Geoffrey Godden retired (after more than fifty years in the trade) early in 1996 and he no longer has a shop or stock in Worthing.

Select Bibliography

There are many good books available on Continental porcelains. These fall into two basic groups; general works which endeavour to cover the whole field and specialist books which are concerned with one factory, period or type. I here list a selection of both types of reference book which I have found most useful. The listing is arranged in order of publication. In the case of translations, the name of the publisher and the date of publication relate to the English edition.

Few worthwhile ceramic reference books will be stocked by general bookshops. There are, however, several dealers who specialize in collectors' books. Several of these, such as Reference Works of 12 Commercial Road, Swanage, Dorset, BH19 1DF, issue catalogues which give general information on each work. Some attend antiques fairs with a selection of their stock and most advertise from time to time in collectors' magazines. Most specialist book dealers also stock, when available, old (out of print) books. These works can be very costly (but not necessarily expensive!) as they were published in relatively small numbers. The best can be over £100.

You do not have to buy all your reference books. Some can probably be loaned from or consulted at your local library. If a book is not available you might wish to suggest that it should be stocked or you can request that it be obtained on loan from the British Library.

MARK BOOKS

The detailed history of the major factories will obviously appeal to many collectors but most owners of a few pieces of pottery or porcelain will really only wish to know where and when it was made. They therefore need a reliable book on ceramic marks. There are various mark books on the market but these are not always as reliable as one would hope and they can even be misleading. The basic faults are that the stated date of introduction of a mark is generally too early, or the mark is not given at all. Very often, not enough warning is given that the fashionable marks have been widely copied or faked at later periods.

Most general books reproduce the basic marks of the main factories. Also, the best and most up-to-date specialist books on the major factories will give far more detailed information on a larger range of marks than can be found in a general book of marks. However, such specialist books published in relatively small numbers do tend to be costly!

I include here a number of older works, as it can happen that some of these once-standard books contain information that is lacking in more modern works. A rare early book is Felix Joseph's *Table of Monograms and Marks placed on various potteries of known origins* (privately published, 1857). This Bond Street dealer (1840–92) presented 'a larger collection of marks than is found in any single work'. Perhaps its interest today is in showing what marks and types of ceramics were known and collected in the mid 1850s. Obviously, too, all marks listed were in use at or before this period, but several errors occur in this pioneer slim list.

A standard book that is in many old libraries, both private and public, is William Chaffers's *Marks and Monograms on European and Oriental Pottery and Porcelain* (modern editions published by William Reeves Booksellers Ltd, London). This London dealer first published a poster-like leaflet of ceramic marks in the middle of the 19th century, which gave rise to various handbooks and the large work just mentioned. Over the years this book has been updated by various authorities, notably Frederick Litchfield from the 8th edition published in 1897. However, while I updated the British section for the latest two-volume edition in 1965, I believe that the Continental and Oriental sections have not been updated since the 1930s. The information is in most instances sound but it is by no means comprehensive as it does not give details of some marks and factories that are now collectable.

A 19th-century American paperback is quite helpful, particularly for Continental and American marks. This is *A Book of Pottery Marks* by W. Percival Jervis (Wright, Tyndale & van Roden, Philadelphia, 1897).

W. Burton and R. L. Hobson's *Handbook of Marks on Pottery and Porcelain* (Macmillan, undated, *c*.1929) is today rather unhelpful and in some respects out of date, but it was in its day a popular standard book covering a very large range of marks. It and other pre-war books have been superseded by the following more modern reference books:

Handbook of Pottery and Porcelain Marks. John P. Cushion. This standard British mark book has been published by Faber & Faber since 1956; the 4th revised and enlarged edition was in 1980.

Pocket Book of German Ceramic Marks. John P. Cushion (Faber & Faber, London, 1961).

Pocket Book of French and Italian Ceramic Marks. John P. Cushion (Faber & Faber, London, 1965).

Porcelain Marks of the World. E. Poche (Hamlyn, London, 1974).

Directory of European Porcelain. Ludwig Danckert (N.A.G. Press, London, 1981). Although the title does not make it clear, this is really a book of marks with a larger text than most such works.

Marks on German, Bohemian and Austrian Porcelain, 1710 to the Present. Robert E. Röntgen (Schiffer Publishing, Exton, USA, 1981). The text is in both German and English.

Kovels' New Dictionary of Marks, Pottery and Porcelain 1850 to the Present. R. and T. Kovel (Crown Publishers, New York, 1986).

A Dictionary of Marks. Edited by M. Macdonald-Taylor (Barrie & Jenkins, London, 1992, 5th edition revised by Lucilla Watson).

Godden's Guide to European Porcelain. Geoffrey A. Godden (Barrie & Jenkins, London, 1993). While not a specialist mark book this does correct many of the errors and omissions found in some mark books and draws attention to the many fakes and reproductions that abound.

Continental authorities are greatly helped by the various Trade Directories published over the last hundred years, which usually include tables of current ceramic marks with basic details of the manufacturer. These trade directories and address books, such as the *Adressbuch der Keram-Industrie* published in various editions by Müller & Schmidt of Coburg, are only available in very specialist libraries, but the marks and relevant details also appear in the following Continental publications and in some English-language books:

Les Poteries – Faiences Porcelaines – Européennes (France excepted). Tardy (Chez l'auteur, Paris, n.d.).

Les Poteries – Faiences Porcelaines – Européennes. Tardy (Chez l'auteur, Paris, n.d.).

Les Porcelaines Françaises. Tardy and others (Tardy, Paris, 1950).

Marken Lexikon, Porzellan und Keramik Report 1885–1935. Dieter Zühlsdorff (Arnoldsche, Stuttgart, c.1989). A very detailed work on German marks.

GENERAL EUROPEAN PORCELAIN

Collections towards a History of Pottery & Porcelain. Joseph Marryat (J. Murray, London, 1850).

Official Descriptive and Illustrated Catalogue of the Great Exhibition, vol. III, *Foreign States. The Reports of the Juries*. (Spicer Brothers, London, 1851 and 1852).

History and Description of the Crystal Palace and the Exhibition of the World's Industry in 1851. John Tallis (John Tallis & Co., London and New York, c.1851).

A Guide to the Knowledge of Pottery, Porcelain and other objects of vertue (based on the Bernal Collection sale). Henry G. Bohn (G. Bell & Sons, London, 1857 and later editions).

The Keramic Gallery. W. Chaffers (Chapman & Hall, London, 1872). Later editions entitled *The New Keramic Gallery*.

The Bric-a-Brac Hunter. Major H. Byng Hall (Chatto & Windus, London, 1868).

Pottery and Porcelain of All Times and Nations. William C. Prime (Harper Bros, New York, 1878).

Pottery and Porcelain, A Guide to Collectors. Frederick Litchfield (Bickers & Son, London, 1879 and Truslove & Hanson, London, 1901, 1905, 1912 and 1925).

How to Collect Continental China. C. H. Wylde (G. Bell & Sons, London, 1907).

Pottery and Porcelain. Emil Hannover, 3 vols (E. Benn, London, 1925). This book has the advantage of having been edited for the British edition by Bernard Rackham of the Victoria & Albert Museum. Volume III, which relates to European Porcelain, is still in the 1990s a most useful general guide and is well illustrated. Good information is given on fakes and later copies.

Porcelain as an Art and as a Mirror of Fashion. R. Schmidt (London, 1932).

The preceding titles contain interesting information and give some idea of collectors' tastes in the pre-First World War period. However, the following later books will be found to be more reliable and to contain a better range of illustrations.

Porcelain Figures of the 18th Century in Europe. David Rosenfeld (The Studio Publications, London, 1949).

European Ceramic Art. W. B. Honey, 2 vols (Faber & Faber, London, 1949 and 1952).

Early European Porcelain as Collected by Otto Blohm. Robert Schmidt (F. B. Ruckmann, Munich, 1953).

The Concise Encyclopaedia of Continental Pottery and Porcelain. Reginald G. Haggar (André Deutsch, London, 1960).

Modern Porcelain. Alberta C. Trimble (Harper & Brothers, New York, 1962).

Continental Porcelain of the Eighteenth Century. Rollo Charles (E. Benn, London, 1964).

Continental China Collecting for Amateurs. John Cushion (Frederick Muller, London, 1970).

The Book of Porcelain. G. Weiss (Barrie & Jenkins, London, 1971).

The Colour Treasury of Eighteenth Century Porcelain. Siegfried Ducret (Elsevier-Phaidon, London, 1976).

History of Porcelain. Edited by Paul Atterbury (Orbis Publishing, London, 1982).

Ceramics of the Twentieth Century. T. Préaud and S. Gauthier (Phaidon-Christie's, Oxford, 1982).

European Porcelain of the 18th Century. P. W. Meister and H. Reber (English edition, Phaidon, Oxford, 1983).

Nineteenth-Century European Porcelain. A. Faÿ-Hallé and B. Mundt (English edition, Trefoil Books, London, 1983).

Porcelain from Europe. S. MacDonald (Manchester City Council, 1986). Catalogue of Manchester City Art Gallery's collection.

Encyclopaedia of Pottery and Porcelain, the Nineteenth and Twentieth Centuries. Elisabeth Cameron (Faber & Faber, London, 1986).

Sotheby's Concise Encyclopaedia of Porcelain. Edited by David Battie (Conran Octopus, London, 1990).

Decorative Arts 1850–1950. Judy Rudoe (British Museum, London, 1991). Catalogue of the British Museum collection.

European Ceramics at Burghley House. Gordon Lang (Burghley House Preservation Trust, 1991).

Godden's Guide to European Porcelain. Geoffrey A. Godden (Barrie & Jenkins, London, 1993).

MEISSEN (DRESDEN)

The Dresden Gallery Marks and Monograms on Old China. S. Litchfield (privately published, London, c.1884).

Festive Publication . . . of the Oldest European China Factory, Meissen. K. Berling (Meissen, 1910).

Dresden China – An Introduction to the Study of Meissen Porcelain. W. B. Honey (Faber & Faber, London, 1934 and later editions).

Meissen. Hugo Morley-Fletcher (Barrie & Jenkins, London, 1971).

Meissen Porcelain. Otto Walcha (Studio Vista/Christie's Cassell, London, 1981).

The Book of Meissen. Robert E. Röntgen (Schiffer Publishing, Exton, USA, 1984).

Meissen Porcelain of the Art Nouveau Period. J. Just (Orbis Publishing, London, 1985).

Meissen Portrait Figures. L. and Y. Adams (Barrie & Jenkins, London, 1987).

Marcolini Meissen Figures, Engraved by Friedrich Elsassen 1785–1792. T. H. Clarke (T. Heneage Art Books, London, 1988).

Early Meissen Porcelain in Dresden. I. Menzhausen (Thames & Hudson, London, 1990).

Meissen Domestic Porcelain. Günther Sterba (Barrie & Jenkins, London, 1991).

GERMAN, AUSTRIAN AND BOHEMIAN PORCELAIN

Hill-Ouston Co. Ltd. Catalogue (privately published, Birmingham, various dates in 1920s and 1930s, undated).

German Porcelain. W. B. Honey (Faber & Faber, London, 1947).

Viennese Porcelain of the Du Paquier Period. J. F. Hayward (Rockliff, London, 1952).

18th Century German Porcelain. George Savage (Spring Books, London, 1958).

Victorian China Fairings. W. S. Bristowe (Adam & Charles Black, London, 1964).

Victorian Fairings and their Values. M. Anderson (Lyle Publications, Scotland, 1975).

Bohemian Porcelain. Emanuel Poche (Artia, Czechoslovakia and Spring Books, London, *c*.1965).

R. S. Prussia. C. J. Schlegelmilch (privately published, Flint, USA, 1970 and later editions).

German Porcelain of the 18th Century. E. Pauls-Eisenbeiss (Barrie & Jenkins, London, 1972, vols I and II).

Vienna in the Age of Schubert – the Biedermeier interior 1815–1847. (Victoria & Albert Museum, London, 1979). Exhibition catalogue.

Berlin Porcelain of the 20th Century. Margarete Jarchow (Dietrich Reimer, Berlin, 1988).

German Porcelain of the Eighteenth Century. Clare Le Corbeiller (Metropolitan Museum of Art, New York, 1990).

SÈVRES

The Soft Paste Porcelain of Sèvres. E. Garnier (Minoo, Paris, 1889 and 1892. Reprint by Best Sellers, London, 1988).

Sèvres Porcelain of Buckingham Palace and Windsor Castle. G. F. Laking (Bradbury & Agnew, 1907).

Sèvres Porcelain – The James A. de Rothschild Collection at Waddesdon Manor. S. Eriksen (Office de Livre, Fribourg, 1968).

Sèvres. Porcelain from the Royal Collection. Sir Geoffrey de Bellaigue (Lund Humphries, London, 1979).

Sèvres Porcelain, Vincennes and Sèvres 1740–1800. S. Eriksen and Sir Geoffrey de Bellaigue (Faber & Faber, London, 1987).

The Wallace Collection, Catalogue of Sèvres Porcelain. Rosalind Savill, 3 vols (Trustees of the Wallace Collection, London, 1988).

The last two are particularly helpful modern works, containing good bibliographies including learned papers, articles, etc. However, most general books on French or Continental porcelain will give at least a résumé of the history of Vincennes and Sèvres porcelains and illustrate some of the richer 18th-century examples.

FRENCH PORCELAIN

A History and Description of French Porcelain. E. S. Auscher, translated and edited by William Burton (Cassell, London, 1905).

Porcelaine de Paris. Porcelaine de Paris trade catalogue, 1950s.

Seventeenth and Eighteenth Century French Porcelain. George Savage (Barrie & Rockliff, London, 1960).

Paris Porcelain 1770–1850. Régine de Plinval de Guillebon (Barrie & Jenkins, London, 1972).

French Exhibition Pieces, 1844–1878. Elizabeth Aslin (Victoria & Albert Museum, London, 1972). Exhibition catalogue.

French Faience. Arthur Lane (Faber & Faber, London, 1948).

The Collector's Encyclopaedia of Limoges Porcelain. Mary Frank Gaston (Collectors Books, Paducah, USA, 1980, revised 2nd edition, 1992).

Trois Siècles de Porcelaine de Paris. Michel Bloit (Editions Hervas, Paris, 1988).

Celebrating 150 years of Haviland China. Exhibition catalogue (Haviland Collectors International Foundation, New York, 1992).

DANISH PORCELAIN

The Arts and the Artistic Manufacturers of Denmark. Charles Boutell (J. Mitchell, London, 1874).

Royal Copenhagen Porcelain. A. Hayden (Fisher Unwin, London, 1911).

Chats on Royal Copenhagen. A. Hayden (Fisher Unwin, London, 1918 and 1928).

The Royal Copenhagen Porcelain Manufactory and the Faience Manufactory Aluminia past and present. Xenius Rostock (privately published, Copenhagen, 1939).

Applied Arts in Denmark. Agner Christoffersen (Det Danske Selskab, Copenhagen, 1948).

Royal Copenhagen. H. V. F. Winstone (Stacey International, London, 1984).

ITALIAN PORCELAIN

Vinovo and its Porcelain. L. De Mauri (Batsford, London, 1925).

Capodimonte and Buen Retiro Porcelains. Alice Wilson Frothingham (The Hispanic Society of America, New York, 1955).

Italian Porcelain. Arthur Lane (Faber & Faber, London, 1964).

Italian Porcelain. Francesco Stazzi (Weidenfeld & Nicolson, London, 1967).

OTHER BOOKS

Pottery and Porcelain in 1876, an Art Student's Ramble through some of the China Shops of London. Anon. (R. Mawley) (Field & Tuer, London, 1877).

Ceramic Literature, an Analytical Index. M. L. Solon (C. Griffin & Co., London, 1910).

Nineteenth Century Pottery and Porcelain in Canada. Elizabeth Collard (McGill University Press, Montreal, 1967).

Oriental Export Market Porcelain and its Influence on European Wares. Geoffrey Godden (Granada Publishing, London, 1979).

Lowestoft Porcelain. Geoffrey Godden (Antique Collector's Club, Woodbridge, 1985).

Fakes and Forgeries. David Battie (Sotheby's, London, *c*.1991). Adapted and abridged version of a chapter in *Sotheby's Concise Encyclopaedia of Porcelain*, 1990.

The Victorian Catalogue of Household Goods. Messrs. A. M. Silber's Catalogue of the 1880s. Introduction by D. Bosomworth. (Studio Editions, London, 1991).

Pâte-sur-Pâte. The Art of Ceramic Relief Decoration 1849–1989. B. Bumpus (Barrie & Jenkins, London, 1992).

The Pottery Gazette Diary (from 1882). Smith, Greenwood & Co, Ludgate Hill, London.

The Pottery Gazette. Monthly trade journal 1877–1970.

Index